Please return/renew this item by the last date shown
Thank you for using your library

Wolverhampton Libraries

LS 1636a 6.11

About the Author

Group Captain Johnny Kent received a string of awards, the DFC, AFC and the highest Polish military award, the *Virtuti Militari*. He died in 1985 at the age of 71.

JOHNNY KENT

ONE OF THE FEW

A Triumphant Story of Combat in the Battle of Britain

This edition first published 2008

The History Press Ltd
The Mill, Brimscombe Port
Stroud, Gloucestershire, GL5 2QG
www.thehistorypress.co.uk

British Library Cataloguing in Publication Data.
A catalogue record for this book is available from the British Library.

ISBN 978 0 7524 4603 5

Typesetting and origination by The History Press Ltd.
Printed in Great Britain by Ashford Colour Press Ltd, Gosport, Hampshire

Contents

Foreword

by Air Chief Marshal Sir Keith Park GCB KBE MC DFC

This book could have been dedicated to Lord Dowding who laid the foundations for the RAF Fighter Command during three years immediately prior to the outbreak of the Second World War. By his foresight and dedication to his job and his moral courage he prevented the British fighter forces being frittered away on a lost cause; the Battle of France which had already been lost in May 1940.

In July 1940 England was under serious threat of invasion as openly intended by Hitler. England had not been invaded for 800 years and the last threat was when Napoleon's Army was assembled along the French shores facing the English Channel. To invade England, Germany had firstly to destroy the Royal Air Force Fighter Command to permit her Army to cross the English Channel and land; and this was when the British Army had barely recovered from being driven off at Dunkirk.

Paying tribute to the part played by the Author obliges me to make special mention of the Polish pilots of No. 303 Fighter Squadron. Their fighting spirit became legendary even among so brave a band of men as the British fighter pilots. The Poles fought with reckless abandon because their cause was to revenge the brutal destruction of their homeland by the armoured divisions and Stuka dive-bombers of Germany.

During the Battle of Britain I kept my Hurricane at Northolt Aerodrome from which No. 303 Polish Squadron operated daily and on several occasions I witnessed the fiery spirit of the Poles when ordered up to intercept the enemy. On other occasions I saw the Polish pilots landing back from combat and enthusiastically recounting the action. I was told by my RAF ground crew that on many occasions the Polish Fighters were spattered with the blood of the enemy so close had they engaged the Germans.

It should never be forgotten that this historic battle could not have been won without the dedication and bravery of the ground crew (including WAAFs) who serviced the Spitfires and Hurricanes in spite of heavy bombing of their aerodromes by day and often by night.

As will appear in reading this excellent account of the Battle of Britain, the Fighter Squadrons were frequently and desperately short of replacement pilots in August and September 1940 due to bad planning at Air Ministry. Thanks to the wonderful job done by Lord Beaverbrook as Minister of Production, my fighter squadrons were never dangerously short of Hurricanes or Spitfires.

Johnny Kent has written a very realistic and not flamboyant account of his life in the Royal Air Force and especially of the exciting times when he led the famous No. 303 Polish Squadron into action against very heavy odds in 1940.

I can thoroughly recommend the book for the young and the mature of age.

Keith Park, Air Chief Marshal

1

Early Experiences

I circled the column of oily black smoke that rose from the petrol which still burned on the surface of the water where the Messerschmitt had struck and exploded. The excitement and tension of the sudden violent combat culminating, as it had, in the final screaming dive and destruction of the Messerschmitt began to die down. I became acutely aware that I was alone and that enemy activity was at its height and I – if not on constant lookout – could also be sent crashing to join the enemy who had just hurtled to such violent destruction below.

The strange and exciting tang of burnt cordite was still in my nostrils as I searched for signs of others of the enemy, but not an aircraft was to be seen so I climbed away and headed for home there to refuel, re-arm and be ready to fight again.

It was 15 September 1940, the day that the Battle of Britain reached its zenith and the day, more than any other, that decided Hitler to abandon his plans to invade Britain.

But how had I, a native of Canada's prairie land some 5,000 miles away, become involved in this titanic struggle that has since been recognised as ranking with the greatest battles in history? Perhaps it would be as well if I went back to the beginning!

I was born and lived for the first twenty years of my life on the outskirts of the city of Winnipeg and my earliest recollections of aeroplanes are of one with which a young American was experimenting about two miles from my home. I must admit that I do not remember many details as I cannot have been much more than four years of age at the time. I do, however, recall that it made a noise like a threshing machine, and to my childish eyes, looked like one too. It was not until I had reached the mature age of about five and a half years that I was to see a real aeroplane. At that time a favourite place to take children for a day's outing was River Park on the banks of the Red River where there were many things to delight the child, a giant Ferris wheel, ponies to ride, a large roundabout with a steam calliope and a zoo. Then, one day, there was in addition a real aeroplane that took people for flights over the city. I was enthralled and can still remember shedding bitter tears when my mother not only would not let me go up in it, but flatly refused to let me get anywhere near it!

In the early twenties there was very little aviation activity in Western Canada and what there was was carried out chiefly by the Royal Canadian Air Force Forestry Patrol – but their aircraft spent most of their time in the North and there was only limited activity at their base in Winnipeg. As soon as I was old enough to ride a bicycle, I used to ride down to the seaplane base on the river and spend hours admiring the graceful Vedette and Varuna flying boats with which the RCAF was equipped at that time.

As the twenties progressed and the wave of post-war prosperity soared towards its peak a considerable amount of interest began to be taken in aviation by the men who had profited from this great period of expansion; aircraft belonging to wealthy mine owners and grain dealers began to make their appearance in the West. At about the same time there occurred an event which, more than any other single achievement, focused attention upon the aeroplane and put aviation on the map and that was Lindbergh's solo flight from New York to Paris.

Interest increased at an almost unbelievable rate and companies operating a wide variety of aircraft came into being and commenced, amongst a host of other things, to open up the North. At about the same time the flying club became popular; they sprang up all over the West and it became the thing to belong to one and to fly. More and more record breaking flights were carried out and the Schneider Trophy races received increasing publicity, all of which surrounded aviation with a romantic aura that I doubt has ever been enjoyed by any other profession. The result was a great rush to get into aviation and schools of varying standards made their appearance through-out the United States and the East of Canada but Western Canada lagged behind and most of the flying training then took place in the Government subsidised clubs.

I was one whom the flying bug had bitten badly, long before Lindbergh's flight, and I was determined to learn to fly. I read everything I could find about my heroes of aviation, such men as Barker, Bishop, McLeod, Mannock and McCudden. I suppose, like many others, I was most thrilled by the tales of the great fighter aces but I never supposed that there would ever be a convenient war which would allow me to take part in similar battles.

As a treat on my fifteenth birthday my father took me out to the Flying Club and allowed me to have my first flight. The pilot kindly showed me over the Gypsy Moth which the club had only recently obtained and then, thrill of all thrills, I was put into the front cockpit, told what not to touch and away we went for a most glorious half hour over the city. I can still recall the terrific exhilaration that I felt and my surprise when I had no sensation of height. When we returned and landed my father saw from the expression on my face as I waved to him that there was no doubt about it – I had to fly!

The next twelve months were a torment of waiting for the next birthday flight, but during this time I finally succeeded in convincing, not only my father, but my mother as well, that I was really serious about making aviation my career. Having accepted the situation, my parents and I set about investigating the various means by which one could start on such a career and to select the most suitable.

Naturally I was terribly keen to fly with the RCAF but when I found that this entailed undergoing a six year university course I decided, reluctantly, that such a career was not for me. There was, it turned out, only one possible way and that was for my long-suffering father to dig into his not too well lined pocket and pay up. This he finally agreed to on condition that I waited until I was seventeen and passed my Senior Matriculation examinations. Naturally I agreed most readily to these terms, but as time went on I found it increasingly difficult to concentrate upon my studies.

Finally arrangements were made for me to start my flying lessons at the Winnipeg Flying Club under the tuition of Konrad, or 'Konnie' as he was always called, Johannesson, a Canadian of Icelandic parentage who had served in the Royal Flying Corps and Royal Air Force in the First World War.

Early in June 1931, a couple of weeks or so before my seventeenth birthday, I had my first flying lesson from Konnie in the club's

Cirrus Moth, a trusty old aircraft on which many pilots qualified. I was absolutely thrilled with the experience of actually handling the controls and I managed to cope with most manoeuvres including an approach although, naturally, I was not allowed to try an actual landing – still, at the end of this first lesson, I knew I could fly.

The summer in Western Canada gets terribly hot and the air becomes very bumpy and the wind gusty so that the only really suitable times for flying instruction in the light aircraft we used were early morning and evening. The latter period was, of course, the most popular and both the aircraft and the instructor were kept busy every evening that was suitable. In order to maintain some reasonable continuity in my instruction it became necessary for me to concentrate on the early morning periods. Unfortunately, the weather reports were extremely unreliable and on numerous occasions I made my rather tedious way to the airfield only to find that the wind was too high, the cloud base too low or the aeroplane was unserviceable. I could then only sit around and hope that the situation would improve – sometimes it did and sometimes it didn't.

There was no such thing as a Ground School where one could have made good use of the hours waiting so, to pass the time, I used to visit the other organizations on the airfield, these being the North-West Aero Marine Company which ran a charter service and gave flying instruction, and Western Canada Airways, a really huge concern for those days.

It was during these visits that I met many of the personalities that made up the flying fraternity of those days and laid the foundations for the opening up of Canada with the aeroplane. Amongst these people were many who had distinguished themselves in the First World War – such men as Roy Brown, who shot down the great Richthofen, and 'Wop' May, who had been Richthofen's target on this fateful occasion. Others were Donald MacLaren, who was credited with forty-eight victories, and Freddie McCall, who had forty enemy aircraft to his credit. In addition there was the other Roy Brown, a noted First World War pilot and perhaps the most experienced 'bush pilot' in the country.

Compared to such organizations as Western Canada Airways, the Winnipeg Flying Club was very small indeed and, in fact, possessed only three aircraft at this time. This lack of aircraft coupled with the other difficulties made the task of learning to fly both a lengthy and exasperating affair.

My own instruction dragged on and on while I impatiently awaited the return of the Moth which had been damaged, as it was the only aircraft we had in which spinning and recovery could be taught; one was not permitted to fly solo until such instruction had been given. Eventually the Moth came back into service and I was introduced to stalling and spinning. It was a great thrill to throttle back, pull the nose of the aeroplane high above the horizon and wait for the spine-tickling sensation as, with a slight shudder, the nose dropped – at this instant full rudder was applied and the aeroplane commenced spinning rapidly downwards. Then – full opposite rudder, until the spinning stopped, rapidly centralise the rudder and simultaneously ease the stick forward as the nose came back on to the horizon, the engine opened up and normal flight was regained.

Although to many people it is a nausea-inducing manoeuvre I personally loved it and took every opportunity of practising it. At any rate my progress seemed to please my instructor for, on 29 September, some three and a half months after I started taking instruction and after spending some six and a half hours in the air, the great day came!

Konnie and I took off in the normal way in the Moth and climbed to 3,500 feet where he told me to do a spin to the left, which I did, and he then told me to climb back up again and do a spin to the right, which I did. He didn't say very much but merely grunted something about being 'safe; anyway'. He then told me to do a 'spot' landing as close to the circle in the centre of the airfield as I could. After I had complied he asked me to do three more; he seemed bored with the whole proceeding. When we had rolled to a stop after the fourth landing, he suddenly climbed out of the front cockpit, did up the lap-strap and then climbed off the wing: 'You will find her a lot lighter on your own,' he said, 'and she will climb more rapidly, but on the whole you will find that she has a better response than with two up. Now, off you go and land as close as you can to me – I don't want to have to walk all the way to the hangar.'

Although I had been looking forward to this moment for an age, it seemed it still came as quite a surprise that the time had, in fact, arrived. It was with an indescribable feeling of exultation that

I opened the throttle, rapidly took to the air and climbed away, circling to the left around the airfield, always keeping Konnie's tiny figure in sight. I kept repeating my instructions to myself; I had to be careful not to let her climb too high and also I must remember to widen the circuit a bit to allow for the shallower gliding angle, but now we were in position, throttle back, watch the speed, glide gently towards a spot a little short and to one side of Konnie, now here we are at twenty feet, start checking, now ten feet, level out and start holding off, gently back on the stick – a little bump – and I was down. I had done it; I had flown by myself with no one to take over, it was a thrill the like of which I was not to experience for another nine years!

The next morning I narrowly escaped disaster – it appears that the great legislative machine in Ottawa was beginning to pay more attention to aviation and someone had decided that practising flying instructors who had not been through the RCAF School must requalify at this establishment as early as possible. Konnie Johannesson had qualified before there was an RCAF School but, nonetheless, he was one of a number who had to requalify. He was due to go to the school early in October and he was anxious to get two of us, in particular, safely solo so that we could build up our flying time while he was away. The other person had soloed a few days before me and Konnie was anxious that I should catch him up so that he could leave the pair of us with a fairly peaceful mind. Such a set of circumstances can nearly always be relied upon to produce an accident and they very nearly did so in this case.

After my successful solo flight Konnie had told me to be ready at the airfield as early as possible the next morning. I got there while it was still dark and waited for him to arrive. The weather did not look too good to me, being cold, blustery and with rather low cloud, but as far as I was concerned Konnie knew best and if he said go, I'd go! Finally he appeared and it was not long before we took off and climbed away. It was extremely rough, but with Konnie's weight in the machine I was able to handle it reasonably well, he got out and told me to have a crack at it. I don't think he would have done so had time not been so pressing. At any rate I opened the throttle and almost immediately found myself in the air being tossed about like a cork and struggling to keep the machine under control. I managed to fight it round the circuit and made an attempt to land – but my 'switch-back' approach made it well nigh impossible to judge just where I would make contact with the ground; I did not even hope to make a reasonable landing. Finally, I did make contact with a resounding bump and shot straight back into the air again then back down again and up again. I cannot remember now just how many times I bounced as I went across the airfield but I realised that it was time to have another try so I climbed away and made another circuit and approach. On this attempt I made a very much better job of the approach which, in turn, made the landing somewhat less hazardous. All the same I managed to bounce at least four times on this second attempt but, fortunately, came to rest close to where a very worried Konnie was standing. He quickly climbed into the machine and taxied it back to the hangar.

He told me a little later that my series of 'landings' were the most Gawd-awful he'd ever seen and it was a mystery to him how in hell the undercarriage had taken it! Then he added: 'Still, I guess as you only had ten minutes solo time you did all right!' Which cheered me up a lot.

For the next month I applied myself diligently to practising for the flight tests for a Private Pilot's Licence and to learning the Air Regulations upon which the written examination for the licence was based. These regulations were certainly all-embracing and I remember still that an aircraft in fog was to 'proceed with caution making a loud noise such as ringing a bell' – apparently life in certain quarters had not quite caught up with events.

Early in November I passed the flight tests for my licence and I was also successful in the written test; there remained the Medical Examination. I had learned all I could about the various tests, and I practised hard to ensure that I would be able to tackle them in the right spirit and not lose confidence, which I felt was one of the main issues. I had only a few days to wait before I reported to the Medical Examiner and again I was fortunate and I was passed as 'fit'.

The final hurdle over I was awarded my Private Pilot's Licence No. 919, and became the youngest licenced pilot in Canada at the age of seventeen, in fact the great Billy Bishop received his licence after I did! I need hardly say that I was extremely proud of the fact and pleased also with my having made the grade; even my mother relaxed her attitude towards flying and was, if anything, even more proud of me than I was myself – which is saying a lot!

The winter of 1931 was late in coming and it was not until well into November that the aircraft were fitted with skis in place of the normal wheels. Konnie was still away at the Instructors' School and the supervision was carried out in his absence by the Manager and Chief Instructor of the North-West Aero Marine Company. Naturally he did not know quite how far we various Flying Club students had progressed and, in a fit of mental aberration, he told me to go off one day and re-familiarise myself with the problems of flying off snow; away I went on my first flight with a ski under-carriage – I could not re-familiarise myself as I had never done it before, but I found no real difficulty whatever and was thrilled with the incredibly smooth landing. Taxiing was a little strange at first but I soon became used to it and thoroughly enjoyed it.

All through the winter I continued to build up my experience and learned many tricks of the trade.

I also qualified on another of the club's aircraft, a small cabin aircraft called a Desoutter Coupe, and was permitted to carry passengers – my first being my father. Later he maintained that he had tossed a coin with a friend of his to see who would be the first – and he lost!

The worst feature of the flying was the cold which ranged from -20 to -40°F, and an open cockpit aeroplane was very breezy, making it impossible to stay up for any great length of time. On landing the oil was drained out of the engine immediately it had stopped and then placed in a large tin and put on the stove to keep it from solidifying. When the aircraft was required again the hot oil was poured back into the engine.

I soon began to realise what an incredibly hard life the bush-pilots led as, for the most part, they had to service their own aircraft without shelter and many miles away from civilisation in temperatures that sometimes went as low as -60°F.

In the following summer and just before my eighteenth birthday I was successful, much to my surprise, in persuading my mother to let me take her for a flight. Knowing now just how much she loathed everything to do with aviation, I hate to think what it cost her in nervous strain, but she bravely climbed into the Desoutter beside my father and never let go of his hand the whole time. I took them round the city and pointed out various landmarks and her interest began to overcome her nervousness. After we had landed she declared that, on the whole, she had really rather enjoyed it, but she wasn't at all sure about going again. I was very pleased that she had flown with me and took it as a great compliment; also I think it helped to lessen her fear of my flying which was a very good thing for both of us.

About the middle of the summer another young chap arrived at the club to commence flying instruction; his name was Al Bocking and it was with him that I later joined the Royal Air Force. When he started flying he was barely sixteen years old and on his first solo he celebrated by looping the aeroplane or, to be more precise, he pulled the nose of the aeroplane skywards until the machine fell over on its back and then somehow regained level flight. None of us had ever been given any instruction in aerobatics, nor had we been told anything about them, so his knowledge came straight out of a book and, as he said, 'I must have missed out a couple of pages!' As I gained experience I developed a more critical attitude and became aware of the fact that there was a sort of Country Club atmosphere about the Flying Club and the aeroplane was considered by many as purely incidental and, in a way, a damned nuisance! At the Aero Marine, however, I noticed that everyone was much more professional in outlook and they were all genuinely interested in aeroplanes and flying. Another aspect that appealed to me was that the company did nearly all its own repair work, whereas the Flying Club did only minor work. In view of this I resigned from the club and joined forces with the Aero Marine Company as a sort of unpaid apprentice; in this way, I was able to learn quite a lot about the technical side of aviation which has stood me in very good stead.

Whilst with the Northwest Aero Marine Company I worked steadily towards obtaining my Commercial Licence although I was still below the minimum age. It was an expensive business building up the required number of flying hours and, like others, I was always on the lookout for some means of getting cheap flying. The sad fact was that the great economic 'boom' was over and we were now floundering in the awful 'Depression' of the thirties; things were really tough.

One method we adopted to obtain cheap flying was to persuade a friend that he really ought to have a flight to see if he liked it and then offer to take him up if he paid for the hire of the aeroplane. You led him to believe that this was the cheapest way to do it as there would be no fee to pay the pilot. This arrangement worked quite well but I have sometimes wondered how many of our victims found out later on that there was no fee to be paid to the pilot anyway!

Another way was to get the company to 'employ' you temporarily to help with work on the aircraft, on condition that you drew your pay in flying time. This was not too easy to arrange, however, as there were too many of us with the same idea. However, by these various means, I did manage to supplement to some small degree the efforts of my father to pay for my flying and eventually I managed to top the number of flying hours that were required before a commercial licence could be obtained. I began to make my preparations to take the examinations and flying tests as soon as I reached my nineteenth birthday.

On a balmy day the following spring, 1933, I suddenly got the idea of seeing just how high I could coax a Gypsy Moth. Although warm enough on the ground, I expected it would get very cold up high so I took the precaution of dressing warmly. I took off and started a steady climb in a wide circle around the city. After a number of circuits and about an hour and three quarters in the air I got to a height where I just could not persuade the little aeroplane to climb any further. The altimeter was then reading 17,000 feet and it was extremely cold, but the view was magnificent. To the south I could see right down into Minnesota and to the north I had a lovely view of a large part of Lake Winnipeg, while to the west and north-west I could see most of Lake Manitoba and just make out Lake Winnipegosis.

Having reached this altitude, I then found myself faced with another problem. I was getting short of fuel and it was going to take a long time to get down; there was the double danger of either running out of fuel or losing my engine through its getting too cold on the long glide down. The resultant forced-landing from either cause might not be successful so I decided that the best thing to do was to spin down.

I kicked the little thing into a spin to the left and, after a number of turns, pulled out and went into a spin to the right and then pulled out and spun to the left again, and so on, alternating the direction until I had completed forty-five turns of a spin and reached 2,500 feet!

On landing I found that I had caused some consternation as my aircraft had been sighted coming down but, at first, the observers could not make out what it was – all they could see was the flash of the silver wings as they glinted in the sun until eventually the 'thing' resolved itself into a spinning aeroplane!

The flying tests for a commercial licence consisted of a triangular cross-country flight, a series of specified manoeuvres followed by four spot landings from 1,500 feet without using engine, the procedure being to fly over the airfield and, when the examiner on the ground fired a Very pistol, you cut your engine and glided down and landed as close as possible to a flag that the examiner had placed on the airfield. This practice of using a Very pistol had interesting results and during the hot dry summer I have seen the grass on the airfield well and truly alight, thus adding interest to the proceedings.

After completing the four landings from 1,500 feet, one took off and climbed to 5,000 feet, closed the throttle, spun the aircraft once in each direction and then, still without engine, landed as close to the aforementioned flag as one could, although one was allowed a greater margin of error than on the first landings.

As one had to spin on these tests there was a requirement to wear a parachute – I had never had one on before and it took some little time to find out how the harness was fastened, but eventually I managed with the help of several others. Then I got into the aeroplane and started to taxi out. Suddenly I saw the Chief Instructor rushing after me, so I stopped and waited to see what he wanted. He rushed up and yelled in my ear: 'If you get into trouble, stick with the ship – don't jump, that thing hasn't been packed in years!'

With these parting words of comfort I took off and was successful in passing the tests first time and thus became the youngest commercial pilot in Canada.

Shortly after getting my commercial I managed to persuade my mother to fly again and this time she willingly flew in the open cockpit Moth. To my surprise and delight she thoroughly enjoyed it and she described her sensations as like being suspended in the centre of a huge bubble – a very good description too, I thought!

As time went on it became more and more apparent that to have a licence was one thing but to get a flying job was quite another. The cutback in aviation activity as a result of the depression was bad enough but the Canadian Premier, R.B. Bennett, not only cut the air-mail contracts that subsidised a number of companies but 'fired' a large number of RCAF officers virtually overnight. They, of course, had vastly more experience than the likes of me and, naturally, they were preferred for such jobs as were going. The hard slog of building up flying time remained, making it imperative to keep a constant eye open for ways and means of increasing one's experience.

One day I met a corporal in the RCAF by the name of Dave Burley who, although terribly keen on aeroplanes and flying, was debarred from ever getting an aircrew category because of a very bad accident he had suffered. He had succeeded in making a recovery from the accident and had managed to enlist in the RCAF where, although he was not allowed to train as a pilot, he had become a member of one of the first parachute demonstration teams. Despite the ban on flying he never lost interest in aircraft and when I met him he had nearly finished constructing a little single-seater aeroplane that he had designed himself. I offered to help him complete it and he accepted. In a few days the funny little machine was delivered to the airfield and it took up residence in the Aero-Marine hangar. The 'power plant' was a Heath-converted Henderson motorcycle engine which developed some twenty-seven horsepower.

The finishing touches to the little machine took about two weeks, but I was disappointed in not being the first to fly it; this honour went to another pilot also on the lookout for extra flying. There were one or two minor adjustments necessary that were revealed in this first flight and, after these were made, it was my turn to take it up.

Although it was rather under-powered the little machine flew very well – despite the fact that the engine stopped and my first landing was 'dead stick'. After this I managed to do quite a fair amount of flying on the aircraft but, as the engine was so unreliable, I seldom took it outside the airfield circuit. On one occasion the engine stopped just after take-off and I had no choice but to land straight ahead, ending up in a local resident's back garden, fortunately without doing any damage to either the garden or the aeroplane. The surprised citizen came out of his back door and asked if I'd had a forced landing – well, ask a silly question!

The next bit of bother we had was when the engine caught fire and, at the same time, the oil pressure line burst covering me with hot oil. Fortunately I was only at 500 feet and managed to side-slip the aircraft and blow out the flames before landing; I was out of the machine like a shot almost before it had completed its landing roll.

After this experience we decided that the aeroplane really needed another engine; luckily, Dave managed to find a two-cylinder Lawrance and, as this seemed to be just what we needed, it was acquired. Although it had only two cylinders to the Henderson's four, it produced slightly more horsepower – but was somewhat heavier.

This engine had an interesting history. Originally it had been designed to power the clipped-wing 'Penguin' aeroplanes used by both the French and American Air Services for initial training during the First World War. These machines could not fly, but ran along the ground while the pupil endeavoured to get some idea of how to control the aeroplane by experiencing the 'feel' of the controls before being actually launched on his own in an aircraft that would fly! Aircraft engines being both expensive and scarce made it imperative to find some cheap power-plant with which to equip these Penguins and the Lawrance engine was produced to satisfy this need.

The cylinders were horizontally opposed and the crankshaft had only a single throw. The result of this was that it set up a fierce vibration which, although it made little difference to the Penguin aeroplanes, was much too much for the light planes in which the engine was tried in the years following the First World War; consequently the Lawrance engine fell from favour. Eventually, however, some enterprising enthusiast managed to find the solution, crude though it was, and produced a two-throw crankshaft. This meant that the connecting rods had to be bent in order to meet the off-set cranks, which, of course, had the further effect of altering the compression ratio; so the connecting rods had to be cut and then welded up to restore the compression ratio, any slight discrepancy being taken care of by using shims under the cylinder barrels. It was rough, but it worked remarkably well and quite a large number of these surplus engines were so modified and used to power the many home-made light aircraft that put in an appearance in the late twenties and early thirties.

The engine Dave had found had already been converted, so were faced with the relatively simple task of designing and building a new engine bay and motor mount, which we did. It was only a few weeks before the aircraft was ready for its test flight and this time I was to make the first flight. As I had already done quite a bit of flying in the machine with the old engine, I did not anticipate any trouble and happily took off. I was really taken aback, however to find that the new engine had altered the trim of the aircraft far more than we had anticipated and I had to keep the stick pulled back in order to maintain level flight. At the time I only weighed 126 pounds and when one of the other pilots, who weighed about 180 pounds, flew it his weight just about balanced that of the new engine and the little aeroplane flew very nicely. After this I only flew it a few times and then only with ballast which was difficult as the machine was so small.

As time went on I began to get occasional charter trips from, and acted as an assistant instructor for, the Aero Marine Company, all of which added considerably to my overall experience. In addition I managed to qualify on seaplanes which again added to my 'market-ability', but it still proved impossible to get a full-time flying job.

Many were the wild schemes that I turned over in my mind, but none ever came to fruition. At one stage in this long drawn out struggle to get started I became very excited over a tentative offer from the Chinese to fly for them against the Japanese in Manchuria. I was quite ready to become a soldier of fortune and didn't mind whom I fought as long as I flew and got paid for it. The pay mentioned was in the region of one million dollars a month – which seemed to me to be adequate!

On making further enquiries, however, my enthusiasm waned rapidly as it appeared that the aircraft that one would be expected to fly were Sopwith Camels of the First World War – they had only recently been taken out of their original crates and assembled by semi-skilled Chinese mechanics. It seemed unlikely that, under these circumstances, I would be around long enough to collect even one month's pay. As it happened the problem was resolved by Premier Bennett who issued an edict to the effect that any Canadian who volunteered to fight for China would automatically forfeit his Canadian citizenship.

It still seemed to me that the best way of getting in the tours was to team up with one or two others and build a small, cheap-to-run aircraft. I was lucky enough to find three others who had actually started on such a project. This was the building of a little single-seater biplane designed by an American aircraft firm who supplied blueprints for the amateur construction of the machine. It was a pretty little thing and quite a few had been built and flown success-fully. The engines recommended were the 35hp Anzani or the 45hp Szekeley, both three-cylinder radials. Unfortunately both of these engines were virtually unobtainable in Canada and the import duty was much too high for our very limited resources; we were left with no alternative but to find an engine and somehow to get it into Canada without paying duty.

Eventually, an engine was located in the States and bought, the vendor agreeing to ship it to a certain small town just south of the Canadian border, and three of us set off to collect the precious engine.

On our arrival in the small American town, which closely resem-bled Dodge City as portrayed on television, we reported to the US Customs and Immigration authorities and, after passing the time of day with them in true Western style, we sauntered around by a circuitous route to the railroad station. To our dismay, although the engine was there we could not collect it without the Bill of Sale which, for some unknown reason, had been sent to another small town some forty miles further south.

We were in a quandary – if we went back to the US authori-ties and said that we now wanted to go further south they would undoubtedly smell a rat and so we decided to take a chance and go without telling them.

We drove fast so as to make the return trip as quickly as possible and thus reduce the chances of our absence being noticed – it is amazing what ideas a guilty conscience will cook up! On the way we met three other cars also being driven at top speed, a small Ford and, some little distance behind, two larger black saloons. We didn't think anything of it except that they seemed to be driving rather dangerously.

Having collected the all-important piece of paper we set off at speed to collect the engine. We had gone about halfway back when we came across the small Ford we had seen earlier, in the ditch on the wrong side of the road, so we stopped and went back to see if we could help. What we saw scared the wits out of us – the car looked like a pepper-pot: it was shot full of holes and all three men in the front seat were obviously very dead indeed. What it was all about we never discovered but, presumably, it was some little side show of the gang warfare that was rife in the United States at that time. In any case, we decided that it was none of our business, especially as we shouldn't have been there anyway. So we shot off, collected our engine and said good-bye to our Customs and Immigration friends – who didn't even bother to come out of their office where they were consuming the 'two per cent' beer that had only just become legal with the recent repeal of the Prohibition Laws; it was a hot day so they needed it.

The Canadian Customs Office was in another small town some few miles from the American town and so we had no difficulty in finding a farm boy to look after our engine, for which we paid him a dollar, while we went on, cleared Customs and then came back for the engine after which we drove thankfully back to Winnipeg, not entirely devoid of a sense of guilt.

We were all very anxious to get the aeroplane flying and this – and the fact that we did, perhaps, work too hard – resulted in a few mistakes being made, one of which nearly proved disastrous on the first flight. As I had by now more experience than the others on what would today be called ultra-light aircraft, it fell to me to make this first test flight. The aircraft handled well on the ground and after a bit of taxiing I took off. There was no immediate trouble; but as I held it down to get a comfortable climbing speed the aircraft began to 'hunt' for no apparent reason – I decided to land immediately as I still had a lot of airfield ahead of me. I was startled to find that nothing happened when I pulled back the throttle. I glanced down and saw that the throttle rod was disconnected from the throttle level and the end of it was resting on the floor.

With my right hand I managed to retain control of the aeroplane, whose pitching was getting worse as speed increased, and we were only about twenty feet from the ground while I groped for the throttle rod with my left. After what seemed an age I managed to get hold of it and then put the aircraft down stopping only a few yards from the boundary fence. I found upon inspection that one of us had neglected the safety pin securing the rod to the throttle lever – a small thing but a damnably important one.

We were to be dogged by misfortune, however, and after re-setting the tail-plane which, having been incorrectly set initially, had caused the hunting, one of the others made the second flight but landed heavily and bent the axle badly. This resulted in quite a major modification to allow the use of a Moth axle which was considerably tougher than the original mild steel tube.

Once again I was to fly the little machine and on this, the third flight, all went well and she handled beautifully. The speed rapidly built up and we were soon indicating 110mph which, for a 45hp biplane, was very good indeed. Altogether I found it a most delightful aircraft and on landing she just 'greased in' – as the saying goes.

We were very elated with the success of this flight and after making a thorough check of the aircraft I was ready for another flight to take advantage of the cool still air of the early morning, the first flight having been made shortly after dawn. Away I went again, full of confidence, and ran straight into trouble!

The take-off was straightforward and I climbed away to the south-west over the golf course until I had reached about 800 feet over a mass of trees. At this point the engine just faded away and I was faced with putting the machine in the only open space available – the driving range of the golf course. The actual touch-down was very smooth, in fact I was just congratulating myself on this fact, but I did not know that there were two sunken roads, with ditches running at right angles across my path. I was still rolling fairly fast when I hit them – all four ditches! The aircraft bounced and bucketed and eventually came to rest on its nose and one wing tip.

The others were not long in reaching me and between us managed to get the aircraft back to the airfield. Again it was a case of too much haste; we had never really carried out a proper inspection of the engine or I am sure we would have found the faults that caused the accident. After this accident, we found several maladjustments that had resulted in fuel-starvation and engine failure.

In my constant lookout for a flying job I had, towards the end of 1933, come across an advertisement in the British publication *The Aeroplane* offering Short Service Commissions of six years duration in the Royal Air Force. I had made, along with several others, an application to be considered for such a Commission and in January of 1934 I received a letter telling me to report to Fort Osborne, just outside Winnipeg, for a medical examination and an interview with the Brigadier Commanding. I duly attended and was both medically examined and interviewed, but nothing happened for a month or so, when I was again instructed to report for another medical examination. This happened four times and I got so fed up I wrote and asked for my papers to be returned and advised the authorities that I wished to withdraw my application.

Back came a letter advising me that I had been selected as a candidate for a Short Service Commission and that I was to make my own way to London and report to the Air Ministry not later than the beginning of March 1935, for interview and a further medical examination. It was to be so understood, of course, that this journey was to be entirely my own responsibility and that I was to realise that, if I was not accepted, then I must make my own way back to Canada – His Majesty's Government accepted no responsibility whatsoever!

Later I heard from Al Bocking, who hadn't waited to hear officially but made his way to London around October 1934, that when he was undergoing his medical he asked if there was any news of my coming over. According to Al the Medical Officer was interested to hear that he knew me and asked what I looked like. Al described me as being somewhat 'long and skinny', the MO said: 'Yes, he must be – all his medical reports say his legs are six feet long!'

It seems incredible that the medical examiners could consistently make the same mistake time after time and fail to note that the form asked for *Height Sitting* and *Length of Leg* – not *Height Standing*.

When I received the notification to proceed to London it caused a frightful amount of soul-searching as, at long last, I had been promised a job as a flying instructor and arrangements had already been made for me to go to Camp Borden to undergo the qualification course. Here, however, was something that was anything but firm and, if I failed to be accepted, my instructor's job would have gone too. On the other hand the RAF held greater rewards if one was successful and so my long suffering mother and father agreed to sell the family jewels and give me a chance to see what I could do in a strange environment. In February I said my sad farewells and set off for England and, I hoped, a career in the Royal Air Force.

Looking back I realise more and more just how great were the sacrifices made by my parents to give me this chance. My father had gone off to the First World War when I was only six months old and

I did not see him again until I was five; during those ghastly four and a half years I was all that my mother had and, naturally, I assumed an importance to her out of all proportion. She was making a far greater sacrifice than I realised when she let me go.

When my father returned from the war he had changed so much as a result of wounds he had received that my mother actually went up to him and asked him if he was on the train! He seemed to realise what she had been through and, for some reason or other, seemed to feel he had let us down by going to war. I could never understand this as we were both very proud of him but he literally bent over backwards in an attempt to make it up to us. I can only say that I shall be eternally grateful to them both for all they gave and did for me.

2

Flying Training

On arriving in London I met up with Al Bocking who, although he had been in England for five months, had not yet had his interview at the Air Ministry. We teamed up, found digs for ourselves and a few days later were informed that we were to report to the Ministry at once. Upon doing so we were given our interview and medical examination both of which we passed. Another few days went by and then we received instructions to report to the RAF Depot at Uxbridge where we met up with the rest of the intake among whom were two other Canadians, one from Ontario and the other, John (Moose) Fulton, from Kamloo.

After two weeks of square-bashing, lectures and indoctrination, during which time was found to fit us out with our uniforms, we were divided into two groups, one, which included both Al Bocking and John Fulton, was assigned to No. 3 Flying Training School at Grantham in Lincolnshire while the other, in which I found myself, was destined for No. 5 Flying Training School at Sealand near Chester.

This unit, I discovered on arrival, was divided into four training flights, two *ab initio* equipped with Avro Tutor aircraft and two advanced training flights, wherein the Senior Term pupils carried out their flying exercises in operational aircraft, in this case the Armstrong Whitworth Atlas and the Bristol Bulldog.

Initially the instructors and staff pilots flew us around the country in the Atlas and Dual Bulldogs so that we could get used to the various landmarks, but after two weeks we started our proper training programme which pleased me very much as I found the Tutor such a delightful and easy aircraft to fly. After the official minimum of three hours dual, I was sent solo. After a month of practising the various exercises in the syllabus there came the great day when we commenced aerobatics. This was what I had been looking forward to;

it was not long before I had mastered stalled turns, loops and rolls off the top of a loop. I thoroughly enjoyed throwing the aircraft about the sky, but one day my instructor announced that we were to practise slow rolls and promptly inverted the aircraft.

It was a most extraordinary feeling and I just could not bring myself to trust the harness – I couldn't believe that there was any weight on it, I was hanging on to the bottom of the seat far too tightly; in fact, I shouldn't be surprised if my fingerprints were permanently imprinted there.

Fortunately my instructor appreciated the situation, righted the aircraft and told me to undo my harness and do it up again as tightly as I possibly could. I followed his instructions and he again inverted the machine and I gradually slackened my grip until I felt the reassuring pressure of the straps on my shoulders. Before long I became quite confident although it was some little time before I could invert an aircraft without getting a slight 'ulp' in my stomach.

Towards the end of the term various competitions were held and I was fortunate to win the forced landing silver cup – the only cup I have ever won. At the end of the term I was gratified to find that I was the only pupil assessed as 'Exceptional' as a pilot.

About this time the upsurge of militarism in Germany following the seizure of power by the Nazi Party brought to the Prime Minister the truth of his own words that our frontier was indeed on the Rhine. This and the knowledge that Germany was rapidly building up a modern air force convinced him of the need for a great increase in Britain's air power; the machinery was set in motion to implement the planned expansion of the Royal Air Force.

One feature of this programme was the utilisation of the training facilities offered by civilian flying schools which made it possible to increase greatly the number of trainee pilots and to provide a much cheaper 'weeding out' system. The course to which I belonged at Sealand was the last wherein the pupils were taught to fly from the beginning. From this time on pupils arriving would have completed their ab initio training at the civil school and were ready to go straight on to operational types.

Between terms we had one month's leave and while we were away the school at Sealand was completely re-equipped and re-organized to fit in with the new training scheme. Both 6 and 7 Flights, previously *ab initio,* now had Hawket Hart trainers, while 8 and 9 Flights had Hawker Audax and Fury aircraft and a new Instrument Flight had been formed and equipped with Tutors.

We were all thrilled to see these gleaming new machines and could hardly wait to get them into the air. I was lucky in getting away quickly and had managed to get in about ten hours in the Hart by the time the end of the month rolled round. But the machine that really intrigued me was the Fury, an aircraft I had heard so much about and which, in its day, was even more glamorous than its descendants are today. It was a lovely little biplane with a long pointed and highly polished nose – I was to learn just how long when, every Friday, we set to washing and polishing the machines. It was tiny by today's standards but could do over 200mph and climb to 20,000 feet in under 10 minutes.

After some instruction in formation flying and low flying in a Hart, I was let loose in a Fury and it was the thrill of a lifetime to find myself at last at the controls of a real front-line fighter. The handling was superb and I looked forward to flying it at every opportunity. It was not long before I became aware that I was being allowed to spend more and more time on the Fury which pleased me immensely although it did not seem to be the sort of training that was likely to condition me for airline work.

I always experienced a terrific exhilaration when flying the Fury and I loved to climb it as rapidly as possible to 20,000 feet where, from its open cockpit, you had the most wonderful view – far and away better than one gets from a modern airliner. To get down I just rolled the aircraft on to its back and pulled it through into a dive, keeping the nose just beyond the vertical. The tough little Fury would scream for the ground, rapidly reaching its terminal velocity of about 400mph, a terrific speed in those days.

As time went on I became more and more familiar with the Fury and I got to a stage where I felt that I could do anything with it. As usual this is the time when something happens which shakes you badly and you get rid of some of your conceit. The experience which dispelled a large portion of mine followed upon a lecture on the theory of flight during which the instructor had mentioned the effect of ailerons upon the speed of rotation of a spinning aircraft. I decided to investigate the matter myself and prove or disprove the validity of his statements – as I did not believe that there would be any noticeable effect on an aircraft such as the Fury with its small span and relatively small ailerons.

I climbed the Fury to 18,000 feet and then put it into a spin to the left; after about two or three turns, I pushed the control column into the spin and was surprised that the spin did, in fact, slow up and another interesting effect was that the nose came up on to the horizon and the aircraft developed a strange 'whipping' action as the spin progressed. At about 10,000 feet, I decided to recover. I took normal recovery action but found that the controls were slack and did not seem to be connected to anything; the aircraft continued in its strange flat spin. I tried everything I knew, opening up the engine, rocking the controls and alternating the movement of the control column with the movement of the–throttle, but all to no avail.

The rate of descent was very slow, but when I saw the altimeter go through the 5,000 foot mark I decided that it was time I got out. I undid my harness, reached up and caught hold of the hand–holds in the centre section and pulled myself up, preparatory to rolling over the side of the cockpit. This action seemed to upset the stability of the spin and the aircraft immediately stopped spinning and dropped its nose sharply, throwing me on to the centre section. I was still hanging on to the handholds and my feet caught under the instrument panel, and for a very long moment I stared straight down into the River Mersey! As the machine gained speed it pulled itself out of the dive quite sharply and I was thrown back into the seat. It then took about twenty minutes for me to settle down before I ventured to land the machine. This flight taught me a very sharp lesson although I never did discover just why the flat spin developed nor was I ever able to repeat the performance.

Eventually, early in 1936, we reached the end of our course and the Air Officer Commanding conducted his regular inspection, during which the various aspects of our training were subjected to a close scrutiny. Fortunately all went well and I was told that the AOC had been particularly pleased with the display of synchronised aerobatics in Furies carried out by myself and Lac Boore, one of our airman pilots, which was very pleasing to hear.

A few days after the AOC's Inspection we were all paraded and sent in one by one to be interviewed by the Commanding Officer, Group Captain Norton. I was gratified to learn from him that I had passed out top in flying, getting 490 marks out of a possible 500. My ground subjects had also improved and overall I came fifth in order of passing out, only a few marks separating the first half dozen. Next came our postings, and I found that I was to go to No. 19 Squadron at Duxford not far from Cambridge. I was highly delighted as this was the only Squadron so far equipped with the latest Fighter, the Gloster Gauntlet, at that time the fastest fighter in the world and I looked forward eagerly to flying it.

Two of us at Sealand were posted to 19 Squadron, the other being Guy Corder, and when I arrived at Duxford I found that R.L. Smith, who had been with us at Uxbridge but had gone on to Grantham, was also a new boy in the squadron. Other newly arrived officers were two university entrants with Permanent Commissions, Arthur Fane de Salis and 'Blondie' Walker. There was also an Australian who had been trained at Point Cook, John Pascoe-Webbe who continued to wear his dark blue Australian uniform.

The squadron was commanded by Squadron-Leader J.W. Turton-Jones and Flight Lieutenant Broadhurst was the Flight Commander of 'A' Flight. Broadhurst was away running an Air Firing Instructors' course at Sutton Bridge near the Wash, while the Flight Commander of 'B' Flight, Flying Officer Jimmy MacLachlan, from Ottawa, was on the course – which left the Flight Commander of 'C' Flight to train the new boys. He sent me straight off in a Tutor to familiarise myself with the local countryside and immediately after I had returned he sent me off in a Gauntlet. I found the latter even more delightful than the Fury and its handling qualities were the nicest of any aircraft I have flown with the possible exception of its descendant, the Gloster F.S/34.

A few days later our mentor took Smith, Corder and myself on a tour of the Fighter Stations in the immediate vicinity of London and we practised formation flying on the way. The first leader was Corder, but as we approached North Weald he waved us away – sticking his arm out too far in the process; he dislocated his shoulder so we had to leave him there. On our return to Duxford I was flying on the flight commander's right with Smith on his left when to my surprise I suddenly realised that our leader was bringing us in for a formation landing which we had not done before. Our approach led us over the boundary fence at an angle which put me closest to it and, while keeping one eye on my leader, I kept the other on the fence which seemed to be getting too close for comfort. To be on the safe side, I eased on a little engine and pulled up slightly but, by so doing, I lost position – so I opened up and went round again.

I landed separately, taxied in and climbed out of the aeroplane to be subjected to a veritable broadside of invective and abuse which was repeated when I tried to explain why I had acted as I had. The flight commander, in his tirade, made it quite clear that it was not for me to watch the fence, but for him; all I had to do was to watch and follow him – he would see that all was well.

I slunk away to lick my wounds and escape from the derisive laughter of the others – one in particular! Our friend had not finished for the day, however, and he detailed this officer and another to get ready for formation practise. In a few minutes they were off, the officer who had laughed loudest at my discomfiture flying number two – the position in which I had been.

About half an hour later I saw the three of them approaching for a formation landing. As I watched they came lower and lower until, as they reached the fence, the axle of number two's aircraft struck one of the steel fence posts. The aircraft somersaulted on to its back and collapsed in a heap of wreckage.

The other two continued on, landed and taxied in; the flight commander switched off, climbed out, gave a casual glance at the wreckage and muttered something that sounded like: 'Stupid bastard!' He went on into the hangar while I remained with the impression that, in this man's Air Force, you just couldn't win! Actually the pilot scrambled out from under the wreckage none the worse for his experience, aside from one or two minor bruises.

Flight Lieutenant 'Harry' Broadhurst returned from Sutton Bridge about two weeks after my arrival; I was transferred to 'A' Flight under him and we began to get down to a proper training programme. Being, without doubt, the best front gun shot in the Air Force at this time, he was very keen indeed on air-to-air camera gun exercises and these were carried out day after day against single aircraft and formations.

One of the annual competitions in which the Squadron participated was the Flight Attack Trophy and the Squadron Team was led by 'Broadie' with Jimmy MacLachlan and Brenus Morris, the Squadron Adjutant, as his wingmen. We newly arrived officers often acted as target for the team and it was thrilling to watch them diving away after an attack and then pulling up vertically in line-astern to position themselves for a second attack. With the sun glinting on the silver fabric and the bright red spinners and tail of the leader's machine they presented a lovely sight.

This same team made up the formation Aerobatics Team and they were a treat to watch. The three aircraft had their wings tied together with cord to which streamers were attached so that the spectators could see that they were tied together. They taxied out, took off, went through their routine and landed with the cord unbroken – it was most impressive and a really masterly piece of flying, as the manoeuvres were more difficult to carry out in these aircraft with their relatively low-powered engines than in a present-day jet.

So far we had done no night flying, something I was rather looking forward to, and so I was pleased to learn that we had reached that part of the training programme where we were required to qualify at night. The training leading up to our first night flight consisted of being flown round the circuit in a Moth and shown what the flare-path looked like. This flight took about twenty minutes and was all the night experience I had, aside from a little in Canada, before being sent off in a Gauntlet.

The night was very clear and by climbing to 20,000 feet I had a most magnificent view of the countryside dotted with lights and, away to the south, the lights of London lighting up the sky. The beacons of other airfields could clearly be distinguished and identified. These beacons were made up of neon light tubes and they flashed a letter in code that identified the airfield, that at Duxford flashing the letter 'X'.

I found landing a little tricky as, although a left-hand circuit of the airfield was standard practice in daylight, at night we were required to make right-hand circuits. The reason for this was rather comic – the standard night bomber at this time was the Vickers Virginia wherein the pilot sat in the right-hand seat – and it was easier for him to see the flare path from a right-hand turn so, at night, every other aircraft was required to make a right-hand circuit.

Although I found this a bit awkward I duly completed my six hours night flying in a Gauntlet and so was considered as qualified in night flying – not a lot of experience judged by today's standards. The whole approach to night flying was, I think, wrong as it tended to make one feel that one had accomplished something very unusual and rather hazardous, instead of teaching one to accept it as a perfectly normal part of one's flying. The lack of aids, of course, made things more difficult, but even so I think there was too much mumbo-jumbo about night flying during this period.

In addition to 19 Squadron, the Meteorological Flight and the Cambridge University Air Squadron were both based at Duxford, the former being equipped with Bulldog and Siskin aircraft. The Siskin was a product of the Armstrong-Whitworth Company and a number of squadrons had been equipped with them but the Met Flight had the last two remaining in service. Being very keen on flying different types of aircraft I tried hard to persuade the flight commander to allow me to fly both types, but he would only agree to my flying the Bulldog.

When I took off in the Bulldog, everything seemed normal but, for some reason I don't know, I started my turn at a lower altitude than normal. It is just as well that I did. As I flew along the line of hangars at about 500 feet there was a sudden bang and smoke poured back from the engine, oil spattered over my goggles and the engine stopped dead. I did a wild diving turn to port, at the same time side-slipping to blow the smoke away so that I could see something – by which time I was almost on the ground – and managed to round out and make quite a good landing. It was found later that a connecting rod had broken and a piston in one of the cylinders had been smashed to pieces – the pity of it all was that I never again had a chance to fly one of these aircraft as the Met Flight was moved away to Mildenhall.

The Squadron was due to go to Sutton Bridge for its Annual Practice Camp in September and so most of August was spent preparing for the detachment. This mainly consisted of countless exercises in which we practised the various attacks against a drogue which was towed by one of our aircraft. Initially we were all given dual instruction in these attacks by my Flight Commander and then we went on to practise, using a camera gun to show how accurately one was carrying out the attacks. Unfortunately these guns were all of the single shot variety and did not give a true record of one's shooting ability. Cine-guns were the real answer, but they were very much in their infancy and there were none available for the squadron – which, of course, was where they were really needed.

The Practice Camp of Sutton Bridge was situated beside the River Nene, about three miles from the shores of The Wash – near the spot where, it's said, King John lost his jewels. The station itself had a very strong resemblance to an airfield of the 'Kaiser's War' with its canvas Bessoneau hangars and hutted accommodation. Perhaps it was this operational atmosphere that had some effect upon us as we all tended to let off steam in a sort of holiday spirit. These high spirits did not always meet with the approval of either the Station Commander or the Staff pilots who flew the aircraft that towed the drogues at which we shot; unlike us, they were required to spend a complete tour there and it was a pretty dreary and out of the way spot.

Before being allowed to fire at the towed targets in the air we had first to qualify on a ground target; I qualified on my first attempt which helped to increase my conceit and belief that there was nothing to this air-firing – my camera gun results completely convinced me of this. It came as a nasty shock, therefore, when, on my first air-to-air shoot, I failed to hit the target at all! I was certain that the wrong drogue had been examined, although finally I had to admit that the 'virgin' drogue was, in fact, mine.

This shook my confidence completely and, try as I would, I could not get a higher score than 44, the score being made up of three marks for every hit on the front half of the drogue and one for every hit on the rear. It became very clear that there was something radically wrong and I approached 'Broadie' for help. He took me up in the Hart and we made a number of dummy attacks on a drogue and after this he sent me off to the ranges for another shoot.

On my return I did not even bother to go into the small office where the scores were recorded until someone congratulated me on my shooting. I thought at first that they were trying to take the Mickey out of me, but I did go and check my score. I was amazed to find that it was 287 – which was a good bit better than average. The short spell I had had with Broadie made all the difference and I never looked back.

After the three-week detachment at Sutton Bridge we returned to Duxford and settled down to the normal training routine, although there were changes taking place that upset this routine to a greater or lesser degree.

At about this time it was officially announced that the number of fighter squadrons in the Royal Air Force had been doubled. No doubt it was necessary politically to make such a statement, but it made us wonder: as far as we could see, all that had happened was that the squadrons were reorganized on a two-flight basis instead of three. The redundant 'C' Flight of an existing squadron broke away and was given another number, so becoming another Squadron – in our case 'C' Flight became No. 66 Squadron.

Admittedly these under-strength squadrons did provide a framework upon which to build a full-strength squadron so perhaps the misleading statements of the Government spokesman of the day can be forgiven – obviously it would not have been politic to tell the public the whole truth.

In fact, the output of the Flying Training Schools, increased in number as they had been, was noticeably higher and new pilots were arriving every few weeks. At the same time, however, others were being posted away to these new squadrons and so the general level of experience within a squadron dropped considerably.

I was one who was posted away just as I was reaching the stage of being a fully trained fighter pilot and, therefore, useful to the squadron as a whole. In their wisdom the powers-that-be had decided that with my training and experience I would do well in a bomber squadron on the North West Frontier of India. This annoyed me considerably and I said so. On hearing my views, Pascoe-Webbe chimed in to say that he wished he had got a posting like that, as he would be so much closer to his home in Australia. I jumped at this and dragged him off to the Commanding Officer who arranged a swap and so we were both satisfied. It was most unfortunate that less than a year later John Pascoe-Webbe crashed on take-off on his way to bomb some tribal village, caught fire and was blown to pieces when the bombs exploded.

In the reorganization of the squadron, Fane de Salis was given command of 'B' Flight to which I was transferred from 'A' Flight; Broadie himself had departed for Egypt. One day de Salis announced that I was to be detached along with an aeroplane to carry out some work for one of the departments in the Royal Aircraft Establishment; Farnborough. I was to proceed the next day to Catterick where I would meet the Farnborough representatives which would explain what they wanted done.

On arrival at Catterick I found Mr Vic Harrison, an ex-RAF pilot, now with the Radio Department of the RAE. He was in charge of the special assignment which turned out to be for the calibration of a number of key Direction Finding stations that were destined to play such an important part in the coming struggle and would help to defeat the *Luftwaffe*.

Vic Harrison and I got on very well together and he told me that the head of his department had merely requested the Air Ministry to supply a pilot and an aircraft from one of the fighter squadrons; it was pure chance that I had been put on to the job. In future, he assured me, they would make a point of asking for me personally, an arrangement very much to my liking as I had free use of the aircraft and was virtually my own boss on these detachments. I was to enjoy quite a number during the next twelve months.

I had been in the squadron for nearly a year when I had one of the most unpleasant experiences of my life. I had been detailed to carry out a night cross-country flight at 12,000 feet, my route being North Weald, Hornchurch, Hatfield, Henlow and then east to Duxford. So I worked out my courses and took off on my detail.

It was a beautiful night, very dark with no moon but perfectly clear, and when I got to Hornchurch, London looked so fascinating that I could not resist flying over it to have a closer look. When I reluctantly dragged myself away and headed for Hatfield I was thoroughly enjoying the flight and so was not as alert as I should have been. Consequently when I arrived over Hatfield right on schedule it should have been evident that something was wrong considering the time I spent over London. The point did not occur to me, however, and I cheerfully set course for Henlow. This airfield also came up right on time and I duly turned east for the short flight to Duxford and so to complete my detail.

The lights on the ground appeared to be fewer than I expected and I could not make out Cambridge at all. I called the ground station, but could not get a reply although I could hear them calling the flare path crew and other aircraft. Then I heard them calling me. I answered them time and again but could get no reply, which I could not understand being, as I thought, so very close.

I began to get a bit worried as I flew on and on, still without a sign of the station; the lights I could see were getting fewer and fewer and also taking on that orange tinge that denotes ground mist. As I flew on, wondering what to do, I suddenly saw the beacon and, very relieved, I lost height rapidly and prepared to land. As I got closer I was puzzled by the fact that there was no flare-path; then I noticed that the beacon was flashing the letter 'B' and not 'X' as it should have been. I looked hastily at my maps but could find no letter 'B' listed so I decided to fly south towards London so that I could re-orientate myself and find my way back to Duxford. I turned south and climbed back to 12,000 feet.

I had been flying south for perhaps ten minutes when my engine began to splutter and I realised that I was out of fuel. I turned on the reserve tank and, looking back, was surprised to find that I could still see the mysterious beacon, and it was still comparatively close, so I turned back and let down towards it.

At this time almost every service airfield in the country was so laid out that the hangars were on the north side of the airfield and I had noticed when I had circled the beacon that it was situated on the top of a hangar and so I positioned myself to land to the south of it.

As I lost height and judged that I must be near the boundary, I set off one of my wing-tip flares which glared blindingly against the ground mist; I doubt if I could have maintained control, but for the fact that I was lower than had realised and could see that there was a ploughed field immediately below me and a row of trees right in front of me. Expecting to hit the trees, I threw up my left arm to protect my face and pulled back the stick to 'mush' the aircraft into the trees.

I must have been going faster than I realised. Instead of an ugly crash, the aircraft soared over the trees and landed gently in a field. I just sat there wondering just how lucky could one get when a man with a flashlight appeared beside the aeroplane and demanded: 'Where in hell have you come from?'

'Who cares?' I replied. 'Where the devil am I?'

'You're at Bircham Newton,' he yelled. This was an airfield not far from Kings Lynn and close to the coast of Norfolk. I must have looked a little bewildered as he continued: 'You're not on the airfield, you know – you're in my back garden and I am the Station Commander!' – Bircham Newton of course, was one of these few airfields that had its hangars on the south side…

In no time quite a crowd gathered despite the lateness of the hour and everybody seemed to be giving advice as to how to get the aircraft out of the field and on to the aerodrome. It soon became clear that the aircraft would have to be dismantled as there was no access to the field big enough to allow the aeroplane to be manoeuvred through it. This would mean a team of men from Duxford, which would take some time. To complicate the issue even further, the Orderly Officer appeared on the scene with a gale warning, which meant that the aircraft could easily be damaged if it was left in the field unprotected against the high winds that were expected. Suddenly, the CO turned to me and said:

'Do you think you could fly it out?' 'I don't quite know, sir,' I replied. 'When?'

'Tonight!' he answered.

This really put me on the spot and I was not altogether happy about it, but I walked over the field, pacing it out and, despite its rough surface and long grass, I decided that I could probably make it. I asked for and was given enough petrol to fill the reserve tank and three flares on which to line up. I then had the aeroplane pushed back as far as possible so that its tail was practically in the hedge and I got six men to hang on to the wing tips.

I started up, applied the brakes fully, pulled back the boost override, opened the throttle wide and, when I was satisfied that I was getting full power, waved away the men and released the brakes. The aircraft shot forward, lurching and bouncing, and finally got into the air – I think only a Gauntlet could have done it. I had to turn slightly to avoid a wireless mast that was almost directly in line with my take-off path, I then circled the airfield and came in to land where a proper flare path had been laid out for me. The ridiculous thing was that, having landed with scarcely a jar with my eyes shut, I now proceeded to bounce beautifully.

What had happened, I found later, was that during my flight a 100mph gale had sprung up at altitude and I had overshot Henlow; the airfield I mistook for it was further north, probably Peterborough.

The next day I flew back to Duxford, but before leaving Bircham Newton I had a look at the field in which I had landed – it was minute! Had I realised just how small it was I would never have attempted to fly out of it in daylight, let alone at night. Also I was even luckier than I had realised at first as, by pure chance, I had landed, with thirty feet to spare on either side, right between an old concrete gun emplacement and a stone quarry that was twenty feet deep! Altogether it was an experience I have no wish to repeat, despite the happy outcome.

In February of the new year, 1937, I was selected to attend an Air Firing Instructors' Course at Sutton Bridge. Or arrival I found that all those selected were roughly of the same vintage and the majority were Short Service officers very representative of the types who flocked to join the RAF in the four or five years immediately preceding the outbreak of war. They came from all over the world and amongst them were such outstanding men as 'Sailor' Malan, Caesar Hull, Harry Peck, Johnny Loudon, George Feeney, 'Blondie' Walker and others of similar stamp. We all got on extremely well and shared a delight in flying and shooting – as a result a highly operational atmosphere was engendered which led to various escapades that were not entirely appreciated by the staff. It was really, I think, nothing more than an outlet for the spirit that was to play such a large part in the survival of Britain and, for that matter, the world as we know it.

By the middle of 1937, the expansion of the Royal Air Force was becoming noticeable and the skeleton squadrons were getting flesh on their bones in the form pilots and aircraft. One new squadron, No. 73, was formed at Mildenhall and suddenly there arrived posting notifices for four of us, ordering us to report to this new squadron.

Three of the four selected had become the most experienced pilots in the Squadron and the Commanding Officer, quite understandably, protested at this bleeding of his unit. Reason prevailed and he was permitted to substitute the newly arrived pilots for three of us while he let the fourth pilot go without attempting to stop his posting. This was Pilot Officer Neville Heath, a strange and rather unpleasant young man who had arrived from Wittering about six months before.

He was a moody sort of character whom nobody liked and he seemed quite incapable of taking the 'ribbing' that was handed out to all junior officers at one time or another. On one occasion he lost his temper completely and flew at the nearest person to him – it happened to be me. I realised that he had lost all control so I hit him first – hard! He stopped dead, glared at me as though he could have killed me, turned on his heel and walked out. We didn't see him for two days. Where he went or what he did I don't think any of us ever found out, although the CO probably knew as two days' unauthorised absence is not the sort of thing that is overlooked.

I have often wondered if the fact that he was let go so readily while the other three of us were kept in the Squadron was such a blow to his pride – he was decidedly conceited although no more than average as a pilot – that it pushed him over the brink and perhaps started him on the life of crime and deception that would ultimately come to an inglorious end on the gallows.

Although the re-equipment of the RAF was coming on apace it was the bomber squadrons that were receiving the new equipment rather than the fighter squadrons. There had always been a school of thought that the bomber was the primary weapon of the Air Force and, of course, this is quite correct. But, it did not seem to be realised that before such a striking force could be utilised effectively and economically, the fighter force must establish the necessary air superiority. More emphasis should, therefore, have been laid on the re-equipment of the fighter squadrons, however, they were destined to lag behind and an extremely dangerous situation was allowed to develop.

It was infuriating during the summer Exercises to find that our fighters were quite incapable of catching the new bombers whose performance closely approximated to that of their German counterparts, the Heinkels and Dorniers. On one occasion, although I had made an ideal quarter head-on interception on a formation of Blenheims and was 2,000 feet above them, I could not stay with them, let alone catch them, despite the fact that I had half-rolled and started downhill when still ahead of the formation. I did manage to get off one or two snap shots but the target was drawing away the whole time.

It was during these 1937 exercises that I first made the acquaintance of the Sector Operations Room which, in this instance, was stuck away in a corner and was very primitive indeed. I could make very little sense out of it all as nobody explained, probably because they didn't know either, how the position of the enemy aircraft, or for that matter of our own, was known. I had never heard of RDF – or Radar – and I don't think many other people had either. For the purposes of the exercise, of course, the 'enemy' flew on predetermined tracks and these were known to the defenders, but I didn't really believe that the *Luftwaffe* would be so obliging should the worsening inter-national situation result in war.

In addition to these large scale exercises we carried on with the usual battle climbs in which a flight of three aircraft would make a rapid take-off and climb to 25,000 feet before descending and attempting to intercept another of our aircraft flying a predetermined track. This of course, was our introduction to the 'Scramble' technique that was used so effectively during the war.

On one such sortie I was flying number two to the new Flight Commander of 'A' Flight, to which I had been re-transferred. This was Pete Gordon, a laconic Canadian from Alberta. I followed him up through a layer of clouds, the base of which was at about 1,500 feet, and continued climbing with him to about 15,000 feet. At this point my engine started banging and coughing and then stopped. I had no option but to descend so I called Pete on the radio, told him what had happened and asked him if he knew where the airfield was. All he said was, 'Nope! It's down there somewhere; hope you find it and mind you don't break the aeroplane!'

With this cheerful and helpful little message ringing in my ears I resigned myself to having to make a quick decision on breaking cloud as to where to put the thing down. I was not too worried as the whole of Cambridgeshire is pretty flat. After quite a long time I reached the top of the cloud, straightened out and waited to break cloud. As I did so I could scarcely believe my eyes for there, on my left, was my own airfield and I was on the down-wind leg. All I had to do was to turn in, put the machine down – which I did – and roll to a stop right outside the hangar. What the odds were against this happening I have no idea but they must be quite fantastic – anyway, it most certainly solved my immediate problem.

Although, on the whole, I had enjoyed myself since I had been in England, I certainly missed Canada and at times I had an awful urge to return. One reason for this was, I think, that my image of England had been built up by my mother who, in her exile, considered Britain to be the greatest place on earth. When I found that this Utopia was, in fact, far behind Canada in quite a number of ways I began to form a disproportionate picture of my home, just as my mother had done with hers.

The first British train I saw was a goods train and it looked so quaint that I honestly thought it belonged to a circus – it looked ridiculous after the monsters of the Canadian Pacific and Canadian National Railways. Then there were the trams that reminded me of the contraptions in the popular American strip-cartoon, the Toonerville Trolley.

There were other oddities, too; I remember being defeated by the logic of an LCC vehicle solemnly spraying the streets of London while the rain was coming down in torrents. As for the weather it seemed unbelievably foul and unpredictable, especially to someone used to the regular weather of the prairies. The English attitude to such things as central heating was another surprise to me and I got the impression that the country was full of reactionaries. I had been brought up with the idea that 'any bloody fool can be uncomfortable' yet here were apparently intelligent people quite convinced that central heating was downright unhealthy!

I came to the conclusion that I did not really belong in England and the only thing that made life worthwhile was the flying. I felt, however, that I now had sufficient experience to get settled in commercial aviation back in Canada and so, at the end of the summer, I took two months' leave and went back to Winnipeg.

On arrival at the Railway Station I was welcomed by my family and whisked away home, where I was able to spend a full six weeks and see all my old friends. I was rather surprised, however, to note that Portage Avenue was not quite two miles wide, nor were the street cars and automobiles quite as big as I had thought they were. In other words, my sense of proportion was being readjusted.

It dawned on me that perhaps there was more to be said for Britain than I had realised and I began to have some serious second thoughts. Despite this, however, I finally decided that my place really was in Canada and I applied to the newly formed Trans-Canada Airlines for an appointment as an airline pilot, my commercial licence still being valid. I was interviewed by that great veteran of Bush Flying, 'Punch' Dickens, from whom I gathered there would be a place for me in about a year's time. I resolved to concentrate on getting as much flying in as possible when I returned to the squadron, and I planned to tell the CO of my decision immediately on my return to duty.

I thoroughly enjoyed my holiday and was sorry to have to say goodbye, but it was only to be for a short while and then I would be back for good – or so I thought.

3

Farnborough

The news that greeted me on my return from Canada altered my plans drastically and put paid to all ideas of becoming an airline pilot. I found that I had been posted to the Experimental Section of the Royal Aircraft Establishment at Farnborough for Test Pilot duties. To say that I was overjoyed would be a decided understatement. At this time, although the expansion of the RAF had got under way, the service was still small and selective, and to have been chosen as a test pilot was a very great honour indeed, indicating that my skills were held in high regard in the right quarters.

Although I was sorry to leave the squadron, I must admit that I looked forward eagerly to taking up my new appointment. I had only been to Farnborough once and had no idea how the place was organized or how I would be received by the vastly more experienced and senior pilots already there. As I was only twenty-three years of age and had been in the country but two and a half years perhaps some sympathy may be felt for the slight trepidation I felt despite my enthusiasm.

When I finally arrived at the RAE I found it even more extraordinary than I had expected. In the first place, I was surprised to find that it was almost entirely a civilian organization and that the pilots lived in the civilian Senior Staff Mess, despite the fact that there was an RAF Station with its own Officers' Mess on the same airfield. I soon realised that this was one of the perks of being a test pilot – no station duties, no parades, no dining-in nights. In short, one became a civilian who wore uniform only during the day while on duty. All the ground staff were civilians as were the flight observers who, in the normal course, worked in the laboratories.

The Officer Commanding the Experimental Section was Wing Commander B. McEntagart, a very quiet but extremely nice person.

He was pleasant to me when I reported to him and he explained the organization briefly so that l would have at least some idea of who was what. The section, it appeared, was divided into four flights – 'Aero-dynamic', 'Engine', 'Wireless' and 'Instrument, Armament and Defence' Flights – it was to this last that I was assigned. I next reported to my new Flight Commander who turned out to be Flight Lieutenant R.I.G. Macdougal whom I had met once or twice at Tangmere when he was with No. 43 Squadron, so I began to feel less strange. The other members of the flights were Pilot Officer Rooms, recently commissioned, who had been awarded an Air Force Medal as a Sergeant Pilot, and Flying Officer A.E. Clouston an ex-Short Service Officer now employed as a civilian test pilot. In fact there were four civilian test pilots in all, Charles (Tiger) Hawkins, H.J. (Willie) Wilson (who, years later established a new world speed record), and 'Spinner' White – the last having qualified as a test pilot when I was only a year old.

The other Flight Commanders were Flight Lieutenant Adam of the Wireless Flight, who had recently broken the world's altitude record in the Bristol 138, Squadron Leader Pat Fraser who commanded Aerodynamic Flight, and Squadron Leader 'Bruin' Purvis of the Engine Flight. The other test pilots were Flight Lieutenants Harry Burke, 'Cas' Cazalet, Reggie Monks and 'Peb' Pebody – not a great number to cope with all the flight test work.

I had only been at Farnborough for two days when I was called upon by Vic Harrison. I was very pleased to see him and he explained that, when we had completed the D/F site calibrations, he had suggested to his Chief that it might be a good idea to arrange for me to be posted to the RAE. His Chief took it up and had my name put forward to the Air Ministry where it was agreed and I was duly posted. So it was a job that had originally been looked upon as an onerous chore which had proved instrumental in changing my whole plan for the future and, in fact, my whole life.

Unfortunately I had not been assigned to the Wireless Flight, but despite this I found that the organization was such that the pilots flew with all four flights from time to time although nominally belonging to one. I flew the Wireless aircraft quite a lot and got to know many of the Radio Department people such as Bill Williams, who had put my name forward, Frank Bradshaw and Ben Bond to mention but a few. They were all very friendly and helped me enormously in my endeavours to understand the workings of the RAE which took some doing for someone as new as I was. I started my flying at Farnborough in a very modest way by doing a reconnaissance of the local area in a Tiger Moth. My Flight Commander then informed me that I would have to qualify on all the aircraft and that I had better get started. During the next week I flew five new types including the Vickers Vespa in which C.S. Unwins had set up a world altitude record a few years earlier; another was my first twin-engined aircraft, a Bolton and Paul Overstrand. My flight in this machine illustrated the attitude adopted at Farnborough as regards test pilots. Although I had been a little surprised at being let loose in several single-engined types that were unfamiliar to me, I did not think too much of it as they were all roughly in the same class as those I had flown previously. When it came to flying the twin-engined Overstrand I was quite unprepared for my briefing. After being shown the 'taps', as the various controls were called, I was told to get going. I then asked where he, my Flight Commander sat; 'Right there!' he said. 'But,' I exclaimed. 'I'm sitting there – where do you sit to give me dual?' He looked rather taken aback and then said: 'Look, boy while you are at Farnborough you don't get any dual, you just climb in and bog off. Now beat it!' So I did.

Actually I was surprised to find the aircraft one of the best I have ever flown. Since that time, of course, I have long recognised the common line-shoot of the chaps flying certain types, generally just after their squadron has been re-equipped: 'Oh, it really is a lovely aeroplane and has a fantastic performance, but you've got to watch it – the stall is really vicious and it lands really hot. As for spinning, you've got to be right on your toes or she'll go flat on you and then all you can do is get out!' What they are really saying is: 'This is a very difficult and dangerous aeroplane. Of course *I* have no trouble with it but you would have a hell of a time!' Of course, the aeroplane next makes its appearance as a trainer…

My experience with the Overstrand was the beginning of my realisation that all aeroplanes are basically the same and if you can fly one you can fly any other; I add hastily that in this statement I do not include Helicopters or such things as the X-15. At any rate this philosophy was accepted at the RAE and henceforth I always approached a new aeroplane with the thought that there was no mystery, just learn the drill and treat it with respect and one would be all right. I can honestly say that, apart from one or two shocks, I have always found this to be true.

Perhaps at this juncture I should say something about the airfield itself as the mass of concrete that exists today is a far cry from the tiny grass airfield that I found in 1937. The maximum landing or take-off run was barely a thousand yards and, when landing over the South Gate towards the south-west, the available run was about 800 yards. Taking off to the north-east, one had to clear rising ground, trees and the town itself. Just to add to the humour of the situation, whenever the wind went round to the west it would 'burble' around the buildings and produce a gremlin over the South Gate in the form of a strong down-draught – I don't call it an air-pocket as these were all sewn up years ago. Many a pilot has been horrified to find that, just as he is rounding out his approach, his aeroplane suddenly and without warning stops flying and falls to the ground with an ugly crunch. Some of the resulting accidents have proved fatal, but fortunately very few.

I personally encountered it with a two-seater fighter made by Hawkers and called a Hotspur. My approach had been just right and I was all set for the landing when the bottom dropped out and we hit the ground with an awful thump. The aircraft bounced and bunny-hopped practically the full length of the airfield before coming to rest, fortunately undamaged, it being a very strong aeroplane.

After I had been at Farnborough for about three months and having flown some sixteen different types of aircraft, the blow fell. The Adjutant of the Experimental Section was posted to Staff College at Andover and I was chosen as his successor – much to my disgust. I knew practically nothing about administration or office work and the only way I knew of getting rid of the files that came in to me was to take them out of the tray marked 'IN' and put them in the tray marked 'CO'. He never complained so I assumed that I was probably doing the right thing, although I did have some lingering doubts at times. I think I was saved by the good nature of the CO and the quite invaluable help of his secretary, Miss Betty Grinsted, who was the mainstay of the organization for many a year.

The outgoing Adjutant, 'Skid' Fyffe, put me on to the fact that, as the Adjutant, I was also the Flight Commander of the flight into which all aircraft came after they had been in for inspection or modification prior to being returned to the flight where they were used for experimental work. All these aircraft were meant to be test flown by the Flight Commander and passed as satisfactory before they were handed over. In recent times the Adjutant had not bothered too much about this and the machines were generally test flown by pilots from the flight for which they were destined. I resolved to claim my rights and, in one month, I managed to do some thirty hours flying on twenty-two different types, ten of them new to me.

By and large, I was not a howling success as an adjutant and I do not know how much longer I would have lasted without getting sacked if I had not obtained my release in another way. I had noticed that certain pilots were charged with particular experiments for which they did all, or nearly all, the flying and I resolved to try and get some special assignment with a view to making a bit of a name for myself. I rather hoped that this would help me to obtain a Permanent Commission. At this time Short Service officers who had been specially recommended were permitted to sit a competitive Specialisation Examination. It was only possible to sit this once and, if you failed or were not high enough up in the list, there was no second chance. Of course the number of vacancies varied each year so there was terrific competition to be in the top few who would be selected for training as Specialist Officers. There being no Technical Branch in the RAF at the time, all specialist duties were carried out by General Duties (Flying) Officers who had specialised in, for example, engineering or signals. Normally an officer did two years on a technical job and then two years on flying before returning to his technical role and so on.

Short Service officers who managed to come in the top ten to twenty places, depending upon the number of vacancies, were, upon the successful completion of their specialist training, appointed to Permanent Commissions. The wisdom of Lord Trenchard still influenced the Air Force, however, and it was appreciated that there were other officers who were excellent material for Permanent Commissions and higher appointments who were not particularly good at examinations or detailed technical matters. So, in order to ensure that such material should not be lost to the service, officers who had been particularly outstanding and had received an extra special recommendation from their Air Officer Commanding could be selected from anywhere in the list providing they had passed the examination.

It was with this in mind that I decided to try and persuade the CO to make me responsible for some particular project that might enable me to obtain the Air Officer Commanding's recommendation for what was called a Non-Specialist Permanent Commission. I was particularly anxious to obtain this type of PC as officers so appointed remained in flying appointments. Also I did not fancy my chances in the examination.

It so happened that Flying Officer Clouston was very anxious to make an attempt to break the England – Australia and return record and also to establish an England – New Zealand record using the original de Havilland Comet. He was, however, responsible for certain civilian defence experiments that were just about due to be carried out full scale for the first time; both the CO and the Defence Department of the RAE were far more interested in these experiments than they were in the prestige and money that would be Clouston's if he was successful in his record-breaking attempts. He, no doubt, thought otherwise and after some discussion it was agreed that he could go ahead with his attempt on the record provided that there was someone standing by to carry out the flight tests that were required should conditions be favourable whilst he was away.

The officer selected wanted no part of this arrangement and said so to the CO who, in view of the nature of the experiments, understandingly agreed that he need not take it on but asked if he happened to know anyone else who might be interested. This chap remembered that I had congratulated him on getting this job and had said that I thought he was very lucky – consequently he told the CO that I would be just the chap! I was duly sent for and asked if I would be agreeable to taking it on. Having expressed the opinion that I thought the other chap had been lucky, I could hardly turn it down, and so I lost my job as Adjutant and began to prepare for the experiments that I might possibly be called on to carry out.

During the First World War both we and the Germans employed a form of balloon barrage as a defence against raiding aircraft and it followed that before long people were busy trying to find some form of defence against the defence. The Officer Commanding the Experimental Section at Farnborough in those days was Major Roderic Hill, later to become Air Chief Marshal Sir Roderic Hill, and he elected to try out one of the defensive schemes that had been devised to protect our bomber aircraft from the German balloon cables. The aircraft used in the tests was a FE 2b, a pusher machine that normally carried a pilot and gunner; this particular aircraft was fitted with a long bowsprit with wires running from the tip of it to each wing tip, where a crude form of cutter was fitted. The wires were expected to act rather like a snow plough in that when the aircraft hit a balloon cable, the cable would slide out along the wires and into the cutters.

Initially the device was tried out on the ground and gave indications that it could prove effective. The first tests were carried out at Orfordness, a station which was commanded by Major Oliver Stewart, and he with a number of others watched Major Hill take off, gain height and then fly straight at the cable. It was an anxious moment. Despite the promising results of the ground experiments one never quite knew what different circumstances would arise in flight. Even at this distance in time one cannot but feel a tremendous admiration for Major Hill's courage in carrying out this extremely cold-blooded test, particularly when one reflects that the Major had no parachute.

Major Stewart has described to me how agonising it was to watch the lumbering old FE getting closer and closer to the cable. When it actually struck the cable the aircraft seemed to come to a halt and then it swung wildly and spun towards the ground a few hundred feet below, part of the wing tip breaking away at the same time. By a superlative piece of flying, Major Hill managed to regain control of his damaged machine and recovered from the spin which at that time was quite a feat in itself. He brought the FE in to a perfect landing and calmly began to help the technicians in an attempt to find the cause of the failure of the experiment.

I believe this deliberate collision was the only one ever carried out during the First World War by a test pilot in any of the Air Forces involved in the war. Between the wars nearly all the knowledge gained through experiments and experience of balloon barrages was, like so many other useful and important lessons, lost amongst the archives or destroyed. In the mid-thirties the RAF was charged with the task of investigating various forms of static defence against the bomber which was recognised as the greatest threat to Britain. A special Defence Department was formed under Dr Harold Roxbee Cox with Mr Ben Lockspieser as his deputy.

One of the schemes considered was a balloon barrage similar to that which had been strung across the Thames to the east of London barring the route generally taken by the raiding German Gothas during the First World War. As in that war, the initial series of experiments was conducted on the ground to determine the kind of damage that could be inflicted upon an aircraft by a balloon cable. It was realised that this could only provide part of the story and the only way to find out what the actual behaviour of the cable and its effects would be, was to carry out a series of full scale collision experiments in the air.

One of the first difficulties to be encountered was that there was no balloon to be had and no suitable aeroplane. As an interim measure it was decided to simulate the full scale experiments by using meteorological balloons to support lengths of strong cord – this being flown into by a small Miles Hawk trainer, which incidentally was entirely constructed of wood. Initially Squadron Leader Pat Fraser carried out these collisions and a considerable amount of valuable information was obtained. Later Flying Officer Clouston assisted in the tests.

Although one might not consider that cord would prove much of a danger to an aircraft the amount of damage sustained from time to time was remarkable. This was particularly so when some of the 'variations' were tried. One of these was to hang a number of 'bombs' along the length of cord – these bombs were, in fact, saucepan scourers, but despite their humble origin they inflicted a lot of damage on the Hawk. The low altitude at which the tests had to be carried out added to the dangers. The next phase of the experiments began when an up to date aeroplane was obtained – this was one of the two Fairey P.4/34 aircraft that were produced by Fairey's as a private venture; in general appearance it resembled the Battle but was smaller, faster and very much nicer to fly. As no balloon was yet available the second phase of the experiments concentrated upon investigating the impact damage sustained from a collision with a 'free' cable in flight. The information thus obtained proved not to have much value; as there was no tension in the cable it did not behave in the same way as an actual balloon cable.

The method of carrying out these trials was for one of the observers from the Defence Department to ride in the rear cockpit of the test aircraft and, when the pilot indicated he was ready, he would throw out a length of cable on one end of which was a small parachute. The pilot would then turn the machine rapidly, dive after the cable and endeavour to strike it with the wing. As can be imagined this was extremely difficult to do with any degree of accuracy and several nasty incidents occurred in which quite severe damage was sustained by the aeroplane and the occupants only narrowly escaped serious injury.

After this the aeroplane was armoured by covering the top of the canopy with a piece of sheet steel and the sides and windscreen with tough expanded metal mesh. A quick-release was fitted so that the canopy could be jettisoned in an emergency. A further safety measure was a spin recovery parachute. As a sort of afterthought, a small shield was fitted just forward of the rear cockpit where the unfortunate observers sat. I have always felt that they never received the recognition they deserved.

To begin with, Pat Fraser and Clouston shared the flying, but, gradually Pat, with his greater responsibilities as a flight commander, let Clouston take over and eventually it became his sole responsibility. At last a balloon was obtained and preparations were made for the full scale experiments. In addition a Fairey Battle was modified to carry a high speed cine camera so that the collisions could be filmed in slow motion thus enabling the behaviour of both cable and aeroplane to be analysed.

As had been feared the possibility of carrying out full scale tests coincided with Clouston's departure on his record breaking flight to Australia and New Zealand, so I found myself faced with the prospect of flying into a cable 8,000 feet in the air to find out whether or not the theories based on all the previous experiments were correct – the results could be quite conclusive.

I had done some familiarisation flying in the P.4 and found it a delightful aeroplane through all manoeuvres except for the spin which was really vicious; I had to fight to make the machine recover and this took both hands and knees to hold the control column. Eventually it did come out, but I had two large bruises on my thighs as a memento. I reported all this to my flight commander and he nearly had a fit when I told him about the spin; apparently it was widely believed that the machine could not recover from a spin.

Originally it was planned to carry out the trials at Rolleston Camp on Salisbury Plain, but this site was not suitable for a variety of reasons and so arrangements were made to send the balloon up from Lakenheath near Mildenhall in Suffolk while the research aircraft used the bomber base at Mildenhall RAF Station nearby. I should explain at this point that the collision was made against a cable suspended from the balloon behind the main anchoring cable. A weight was attached to its lower end to produce the same tension in this test cable as existed in the main cable so, in effect, it was the same as hitting the main cable.

To enable the pilot to hit the test cable and aim the aircraft so that it would strike the cable at a point about halfway along the wing, there was a number of marker flags attached to the experimental cable. Although these markers made it possible to hit the cable with great accuracy, one had to become used to allowing for drift; the balloon automatically turned into wind and the markers streamed out down-wind – one could only see them properly when approaching them cross-wind, thus making it necessary to aim off.

The day came when everything was just right for the first test and I flew up to Mildenhall, accompanied by the photographic aeroplane, and waited for the final adjustments to be made to the balloon and its cable. Some trouble was experienced and I began to get a little irritable – no doubt I was tensed up a bit as this was my first collision and, I believe, the first full scale trial to be carried out since Major Hill's effort twenty years before. Finally the go ahead came through from the site and I could see the balloon quite clearly from Mildenhall; we took off and climbed to height, the photographic aircraft keeping station on my starboard side. I first checked the height of the balloon and then descended and had a look at the aiming marks to make sure they were not wrapped around the cable, once lined up I gave the photographic pilot the 'thumbs up' signal and he widened the gap between us to a point where the photographer could get a good picture but be far enough away to be in no danger of collision should my aircraft get out of control. As he slid away I closed the armoured hood and the heavy thud of its closing sounded most ominous. I took a deep breath and watched the cable come rushing towards me at 200mph. Just what my thoughts were I have no clear recollection, but I have no hesitation in admitting that I was really frightened. I just did not have any idea at all what to expect when I hit the cable.

The difficulties in aiming rapidly became apparent and just as I thought 'This is it!' the whole mass of cables and flags went sailing by, well clear of my port wingtip. The anticlimax was awful, as I had to build myself up for another try. I missed again, and again, and again! In all I tried seven times to hit the cable and, on one try, actually passed between the anchoring cable and the experimental cable which put the wind up Frank Gomersall who was flying the photographic machine, as he suddenly found the cable nearly on his wing. On the seventh attempt I managed to hit it and there was an even greater anticlimax as the cable snapped without damaging the aircraft at all!

The relief at having got over this initial hurdle was enormous, although I was by no means convinced that it would always be as easy as that. In fact, if it was, there would be no point in doing it. We were very lucky with the weather and I managed to make no less than seven collisions before Clouston returned from his successful record-breaking flight. By then I had completely conquered my fear and had no further difficulty in hitting the cable on the first attempt each time. I decided, therefore, to ask the Wing Commander if he would leave me on this work and I explained that I thought it might help me to get a Permanent Commission. About a week later he informed me that he had talked it over with the Department and it had been agreed that I should continue with the work in place of Clouston.

At this point it is perhaps as well to mention several other safety measures, in addition to those described, that were taken to reduce the hazard to the pilot as much as possible. All the control surfaces of the aircraft were constructed of a wooden framework covered with fabric so that they would smash cleanly and not produce any 'tab effect' such as was likely to happen if they had been made of metal which will tear and bend; this can produce the same effect as a trimming tab, but without the pilot's selective control, and can make an aeroplane quite unmanageable. It was realised that the aircraft could still suffer serious alterations in trim, particularly laterally, and on each side of the cockpit there was provided three lengths of different sized 'bungee' each with a hook at the end that could be hooked on to the spade grip of the control column and so relieve the strain on the pilot's arm. Then, to prevent the cable getting tangled in the tail of the machine, small steel rod deflectors were fitted on the fin and tailplane. In the initial stages the leading edges of the wings had no protection, the object being to see how much they could withstand.

It was realised that the planned series of experiments would need more than one aircraft and it was not long before proof of this was forthcoming. On one of my collisions the cable cut through the leading edge of the port mainplane and cut the wires from the undercarriage to the position indicator in the cockpit. I did not know whether the port wheel was up or down and, having no radio, nobody could tell me. Mildenhall was a very much bigger airfield than Farnborough and the approaches were infinitely better so I decided to land there to check whether or not more serious damage had been done than was evident from the cockpit. I lowered the undercarriage and got a green light from the starboard wheel but nothing for the port. By flying low over the airfield I could see from the shadow that both wheels were down but I could not tell from this whether the port wheel was locked down. I then brought the machine in with plenty of speed in hand and gently touched the wheel on the ground, I did this two or three times and it seemed solid enough so I landed without incident. The damage was such, however that I had to leave the aircraft at Mildenhall and return to Farnborough in the camera aeroplane.

This incident held up experiments for about three weeks, by which time the second collision aircraft was ready. This was a modified Fairey Battle completely fitted out for our needs, but although it was a pleasant, sturdy and steady aeroplane it could not compare with the P.4. However, I soon got used to it and eventually became quite fond of it. Out of the first five collisions with the Battle the port wing and aileron were damaged four times; fortunately, being a production aircraft, spares could be obtained quickly and damage was rapidly repaired.

As we progressed with the experiments various weapons schemes were introduced for trial. One of these was a development of the pot-scourer idea but the 'bombs' were much larger and weighed about half a pound. When the cable was struck these bombs would whip round the wing on the end of the cable and smash into the upper or lower surface of the wing itself, often doing quite extensive damage. Other similar ideas were short 100-foot lengths of cable with a bomb on one end and a small parachute on the other; these were known as Short Aerial Mines and were meant to be used by bombers as a defence against fighters. The cable was intended to wrap around the attacker's wing and the drag of the parachute was expected to draw the bomb up to the wing which it should hit and blow off.

Another scheme was the Long Aerial Mine; this was intended for use against massed enemy bombers, the mines being sown across their path in the form of a curtain of 2,000-foot lengths of piano wire with a bomb on the end slowly sinking towards the ground supported by a parachute. In operation it was intended to act against the bomber in the same way as did the short aerial mine against the fighter. During the war these gadgets were used operationally, but proved impractical owing to the difficulty in getting the mine-sowing aircraft to the right height and position in time.

One of the most astonishing things about the collisions was the speed at which things happened. This was brought home to me very early on when colliding with one of the long aerial mines; my speed was about 300 miles per hour and I quite clearly saw the cable approach the wing; then, as I looked out along the port wing, I saw the aileron shatter and, at the same time, felt a jerk on the control column, but at no time did I see any sign of the cable actually on the wing or any sign of the bomb attached to it. On return to Farnborough, however, the film was run through and I was amazed to see that the cable and bomb had gone right round the wing two and a half times, the bomb striking the underside of the wing before the cable unwound itself. This all happened at terrific speed of course – it looked fast even on the film which reduced the actual speed to very slow motion.

It was also quite remarkable how, contrary to expectation, one tended to underestimate the effect of a collision on the aircraft as regards the alteration of its flight path. This was brought home to me after an experiment with the third collision aircraft, a Wellesley, against a 5,000 foot length of 3 Qr ton cable. Once having started the run I set the directional gyro to zero to get a rough check on how much the aircraft swung on hitting the cable. In this particular experiment I expected a fairly violent yaw so I was more than a little surprised when it turned out to be relatively mild and the gyro seemed to indicate a swing through only about twenty degrees.

On running the film through on return to Farnborough we were all amazed to see that the aeroplane had, in fact, swung through ninety degrees. At one point the camera showed a dead astern view of the Wellesley.

In the spring of 1939, I was pleasantly surprised to run into Moose Fulton again – he had been posted from the Middle East to one of the squadrons at Mildenhall. He was very interested in the work at Farnborough and so I had a word with my CO about him and it was not long before he joined me there and took over the job of flying the photographic aeroplane from Frank Gomersall.

The damage sustained in the experiments had become increasingly severe and the leading edges of both the Battle and the P.4 were armoured with sixteen-gauge sheet steel. The Wellesley, which originally had been intended for tests on a crude form of cutter that didn't work, already had an armoured leading edge.

By mid-1939, it was evident that war was not far off and it was obvious that when it did come we could not continue our work in Suffolk. After considering several alternatives Exeter was decided upon, the Defence Department itself to be accommodated in Exeter University while the Flight moved into Exeter Airport which it was to share with BOAC. The Flight thus became a separate entity, divorced from the Instrument Flight, and I became the Flight Commander. The move was commenced during the first week of the war but no collision experiments could be carried out until the last few days of the month.

The airfield was not really suitable for our purposes as it was too small, had a large hollow at one corner and a hill at another. For normal operations it was acceptable, but it would mean taking any damaged aircraft back to Farnborough. One day Professor Hill, Roderic Hill's brother who had taken over the Department, arrived at the airport with a number of officials to whom I was introduced.

The Professor then asked me to tell them exactly what improvements and extensions I considered necessary to make the airfield suitable for our operations. From this I assumed that they were all Air Ministry officials and I told them I wanted certain hedges removed so that two more fields could be taken in, the hill should be levelled and used to fill in the hollow, and finally the farm next to the hollow must go.

In no time things started to happen, which surprised me, but I put it down to wartime keenness to get on with the job. However, I could not quite rid myself of a feeling that all was not as it should be – and I was right. It turned out that the gentlemen whom I had met and who had now become so co-operative were contractors and nothing to do with the Air Ministry at all. Now, however, the Ministry had heard about the activity and it was not long before I had a visit from some very irate gentlemen who were practically beside themselves with fury at the temerity of this junior flight lieutenant who had taken it upon himself to order and authorise the work to be done. I thought that at least twenty years in the Tower would be my lot, but eventually I managed to persuade them that it was not me to whom they should talk but to Professor Hill, and this they did.

In his usual charming way, the Professor managed to soothe them down and persuade them that he had merely anticipated their good judgement as, he felt sure, they would have agreed wholeheartedly with the need for this work had there been time to place the scheme before them; they knew as well as he that the demands of war were such that on occasion, as on this one, one had perforce to take rapid action in order to ensure the continuance of work that was of vital importance to the nation. Somewhat mollified, and in any case stuck with a *fait accompli*, they retired from the field with as much good grace as they could muster.

The experimental work was increasing in intensity and the flight had grown in size, so when Moose expressed his wish to take part in the collision experiments instead of just flying the camera machine I welcomed the idea and so he became the second person to fly into the full scale experimental wire barrage weapons. He had just the right temperament, was an excellent pilot and did some magnificent work in the ensuing months.

The new balloon site was at Pawlett Hams near Bridgwater and I carried out the first collision there on 26 September 1939, against a

3 Qr ton cable at a speed of 180 miles per hour. The cable cut into
the wing and jammed; consequently, on arriving back at Exeter, I
made a high glide approach to avoid catching the 500 feet of cable
in trees, fences or other obstacles. Just as I crossed the boundary I
felt a terrific jerk. The aeroplane swung violently to port and the
port wing went down. I was just able, by applying full power and full
opposite rudder, to straighten the aircraft and land. When I got to the
hangar I was met by several pale-faced people who informed me that
I had, in fact, pulled down the high tension wires. Apparently when
I hit them there was an enormous blue flash which, being behind
me, I could not see; fortunately I had pulled clear before touching
down otherwise it is probable that the blue flash would have been
followed by a big red one!

The sequel to this episode came two days later when a representative of the local Electricity Authority called on me and was very rude
about the irresponsibility of the Air Force in general, and myself in
particular. I could not explain to him what we were doing or how
the accident had occurred as the experiments were secret. I did
suggest to him that I did not normally fly into high tension wires
just for the fun of it, but he was quite adamant that, in his opinion,
I was a menace to the peace and civilisation of South Devon and he
threatened me with prosecution and probable imprisonment. This
was too much, so I pointed out to him that he was on Air Ministry
property without permission and that, if he did not leave immediately, I would have him put in the guard-room. He did not seem to
care for this and made off in a fine old temper still issuing threats;
in fact I did receive a summons, but the Professor attended to it and
I heard no more.

Shortly after this I collided with a Short Aerial Mine at 225 mph
and the cable and bomb smashed the elevator on one side, the cable
then wrapped itself round the tail and jammed the other elevator
and I was only able to maintain control by using the trim tabs. This
was rather awkward at first as they work in the reverse sense and,
owing to their small size, I had to maintain a fair speed to keep them
effective at all. By using both hands and exerting all my strength I
finally did manage to gain some slight movement of the elevator
and so was able to make a long flat approach towards the airfield.
Just before I reached the boundary, the control seized solid again

and I was just able to maintain enough control through the tabs and use of throttle to cross the hedge. I then slammed the throttle shut and let the aircraft drop about ten or fifteen feet on to the ground, fortunately without doing any further damage.

The worst experience I had and the nearest I ever came losing all control of the aircraft occurred when I was testing the Parachute and Cable airfield defence weapon. This consisted of 1,500 feet of 3 Qr ton cable with an 8 foot parachute at either end, the whole contraption being fired into the air by a rocket into the path of low-flying enemy aircraft. To test its effectiveness, it was hung from the balloon and I collided with it at about 7,000 feet. On contact with the cable the aircraft was jerked wildly to port and turned upside down – it continued to roll and I managed to regain control as it came right side up again some 2,000 feet lower. The cable had sliced through the sixteen-gauge steel leading edge, ripped through the wing and taken about eight feet of it off. It was obvious that the damage was beyond the repair facilities at Exeter so I set course for Farnborough some hundred odd miles away. By using the 'bungee muscles' already described I was able to retain control without too much strain and landed safely at my destination.

I had another frightening experience when a demonstration of this same PAC scheme was arranged for Air Vice-Marshal Sholto Douglas, then Assistant Chief of the Air Staff and later, of course, Marshal of the RAF Lord Douglas of Kirtleside. The site chosen was a small airfield called Haldon on the top of the cliffs overlooking Torquay. I was to simulate a low-flying attack approaching from the sea, but on my first run I was to keep well to the left so that the rockets, when fired, would be on my starboard side. The object of this was to demonstrate how accurately the operator could judge the right time to press the button.

This went off successfully and I came in for the second part of the demonstration which consisted of the full battery of rockets being fired directly into my path to show what the chances were of hitting the aircraft. For the purposes of the demonstration the organizers had been considerate enough to substitute string for the cable.

I came in fast over the sea aiming to pass over the airfield at about 400 feet at 320mph. As I crossed the boundary the rockets were fired and went zigzagging up in front of me in clouds of smoke! It was a fearsome sight and I could not avoid going straight through the curtain of simulated cables. At this point it occurred to me that the great heavy rockets would now be on their way down and I fervently hoped I wouldn't meet one. Luckily, I did not. Of the strings, however, I got no less than three on the wings and there was a pronounced deceleration of the aeroplane before they broke.

As has happened all through history a weapon is no sooner devised than someone begins to develop a defence against it. The efforts of Major Hill have already been described and in the Second World War the Germans tried out a form of defence against balloon cables strangely reminiscent of Major Hill's 'snow plough'. A Heinkel HeIII, so fitted, was brought down in this country, but judging from photographs of it I think it unlikely to have been very effective. Various types of cable cutters were produced but none of them proved successful until Mr James Martin of the Martin-Baker Company produced a very simple but most effective cutter based on a shot-gun. The leading edge of the aeroplane's wing was fitted with armour plating in which slots were cut to take the cutters. When the wing struck the cable the aircraft slewed towards the cable which would then slide towards the wing tip. In doing so it would encounter one of the cutters and slip into the slot between the head of the cutter and the leading edge. It thus actuated a pair of triggers which, in turn, fired a charge in the cartridge and a 'cold chisel' was propelled forward against an 'anvil' and, on the way, cut the cable.

A suitably modified Wellington was allotted to the Flight for the cutter trials and after familiarising myself with the aircraft and trying it out against string I was ready to try it and the cutters against a real cable. While having the highest regard for Mr Martin's ingenuity and technical expertise I could not help harbouring a few doubts as to the probable effectiveness of the cutters. I rather feared that if the cutter did not work there was every possibility of the cable hanging up and tearing the wing off. Frankly I did not relish the idea of getting out of a Wellington with only one wing – it was, of course, long before the days of the ejection seat!

On arrival over the site I started my run towards the 1 Qw ton cable at an indicated 210mph at a height of 7,000 feet. Whether my uncertainty of the cutters' reliability upset my judgement I cannot say but something certainly did and I suddenly realised, too late, that

I had allowed too much for drift. Almost as soon as I realised this the cable struck the starboard propeller which cut it and lashed it back like a whip. There was a loud bang, the aeroplane careered about and a blast of cold air roared into the cockpit. The cable had slashed through the windows and fabric along the starboard side and top of the fuselage for about fifteen feet. I was very annoyed with myself for having misjudged so badly and, to make matters worse, on arriving back at the airfield I found both Sir Henry Tizard and Professor Hill waiting for me. Sir Henry, himself an ex-test pilot of no mean repute, looked over the aircraft and then said, 'I think it is quite remarkable how you manage to fly these aircraft so accurately – there, you meant to hit the cable with the left wing and you've hit it with the right!' I think he must have sensed my self-disgust and was being kind, for it wasn't in him to be sarcastic; nonetheless I felt pretty small as I had become used to errors of no more than a foot to eighteen inches. The aeroplane had suffered no structural damage so, after patching the fabric, I set off for another try. This time I approached at 220mph and braced myself for whatever was going to happen. The 2 Qr ton cable, heavier this time, seemed to approach very slowly and then, as the aiming marks grew larger, suddenly accelerated, flashed past the cockpit and struck the wing. The aeroplane gave a little twitch to port, the wing dipped almost imperceptibly, there was a slight report and the aircraft sailed serenely on; the cutters had really worked!

In a series of subsequent experiments we found that the cutters were extremely effective against the heavier cables similar to the type we considered likely to be encountered over enemy territory. Against the long aerial mines, however, the cutters occasionally proved ineffective, but as there was no evidence that the Germans were using anything like the aerial mine this occasional ineffectiveness was of no immediate importance.

As a result of our trials the cutters were adopted by the RAF and fitted to many of the bomber aircraft. There are a number of instances on record where they proved their effectiveness against enemy defences; perhaps one of the most fascinating was the occasion of the raid on the Dortmund-Ems Canal viaduct for which Wing Commander Learoyd was awarded the Victoria Cross.

It was known that the target was defended by balloons as well as the customary flak and, as the raid would of necessity be at low level, the balloons constituted a grave threat. It was decided, therefore, to adopt the Navy's technique and send in some 'mine sweepers'. Two Hampdens fitted with the Martin–Baker cutters actually flew along the line of attack ahead of the strike aircraft and cut away the enemy balloons.

After having been engaged on this work for over two years I was now posted to an operational unit and so had to hand over the Flight. By this time I had carried out a total of 300 collisions with various types of wire barrage weapons, 170 of these against the heavy cables equivalent in weight and tension to the actual mooring cables of the balloons.

Although the balloon barrage did not bring down a vast number of enemy aircraft, it did constitute an additional hazard that helped to lower the morale of the *Luftwaffe* crews and so reduced their efficiency. I think it can certainly be said that its presence forced the German aircraft to fly higher to ensure that they were out of danger of colliding with the cables; this, of course, reduced their freedom of action considerably.

4

Test Pilot

Although my work with the Defence Department and the collision experiments were my particular concern, they were not by any means all that I was required to do during my time as a test pilot at Farnborough. Not only did I carry out flight test work in connection with automatic pilots, bomb sights, blind landing systems, radio controlled target aircraft and various types of instrumentation, but I also took part in the test programmes of the other flights whenever the opportunity presented itself.

The life of a test pilot is not one of continual excitement and high adventure, although it has its moments. Quite a lot of the time the flying is rather dull and boring but, at the same time, it demands a very high degree of accuracy and one must be alert at all times. Very often, I found, one merely sat back and let the auto-pilot fly the aircraft while the flight observer checked its behaviour or made adjustments as required. As the pilot, one was there to take over in case anything went wrong and on occasions it did!

One such was a flight in a Battle – we had trouble in getting the aircraft to turn under automatics. I operated the controls from the pilot's seat while the observer made adjustments in the rear. Although we tried time and again the aeroplane just would not turn but eventually, after some further adjustments, my observer asked me to try it just once more.

I moved the controls to initiate a turn and this time the aeroplane responded and started a slow turn to port. I am not quite sure what happened next, but I think my observer attempted some further adjustments. Without warning, the aircraft 'bunted' into a violent dive. I was thrown out against my harness and, by the time I managed to reach the control lever and disengage, we were just over the vertical and I had to pull hard back on the control column to regain level flight.

My unfortunate observer, not being strapped in, was first thrown violently up against the roof of the tunnel behind the pilot's cockpit and then slammed back on to the floor as I pulled the machine out of the dive. I asked him if he was all right and he said he was, but he sounded rather dazed. I craned my neck around so that I could see him through the tiny window; there was blood all over his face and it was obvious that he was in no fit state to continue so I hurried back to the airfield where he was rushed to the Medical Officer who patched him up.

The period of which I write was really one of transition from the old biplanes, not far removed in design and performance from those of the First World War, to the monoplane era. This resulted not only in a number of new aircraft but also a wide variety of new types of equipment as it was anticipated, quite rightly, that the new aircraft would be required to operate in conditions far more critical than in the past. Such innovations as the artificial horizon and directional gyros began to put in an appearance; de-icing 'boots' were fitted to the leading edges of wings and tailplanes; new wireless equipment was being developed; the handling characteristics of the monoplane had to be investigated, likewise the effect upon both pilot and aircraft of high 'G' forces had to be explored as well as the effects of reduced atmospheric pressure upon the body.

For certain aspects of these latter considerations a new department was formed which developed into the Institute of Aviation Medicine. Under the direction of this department a great deal of invaluable research work was carried out. Some of the tests were carried out in the laboratories and in the decompression chamber but others were conducted in the air.

An example of air testing was for 'G' or acceleration tests. A Battle or Gladiator was used – there being no such thing as a centrifuge available at this time; when using the Battle, the 'subject', generally Flying Officer Stewart, sat in the rear cockpit with a cine camera trained on him to record results, while the pilot put the aeroplane into a spiral dive which he progressively tightened up. Being able to prepare himself for it, the pilot was not affected by the acceleration to the same extent as was his passenger and, on occasion, the unfortunate subject lost consciousness.

The Gladiator, being a single-seater, required a different arrangement and here a cine camera was installed so that it looked over the pilot's left shoulder and recorded the 'G' force imposed, along with the readings of other instruments, and the reflection of the pilot's face in a mirror placed just inside the windscreen. The effects were quite startling and in some pictures taken of myself I look about seventy years of age although, at the time, I was only twenty-four.

Other work not connected with the medical aspect included the investigation into the unusual behaviour of certain types of aircraft already in service. There had, for example, been several cases of Gladiators failing to recover from a spin which was unexpected as this aircraft was really most docile. Farnborough was charged with the task of investigating this strange behaviour and, with others, I found myself taking part in spinning trials of this aircraft under a wide variety of load conditions. Although at times I was quite dizzy with the spinning I never experienced any difficulty at all and recovery was always immediate.

It would be impossible to go into any great detail of the various tasks that were allotted to us or to describe all the strange experiences of the various test pilots but it might be interesting if I described just a few that illustrate how very often it is not the hazardous flight that leads to accidents or near accidents, but the seemingly dull routine flight that provides the thrills and excitement.

I had not been at Farnborough for more than a month and I had done no more than four hours flying in twin-engined aircraft when, on a flight to check on a new bomb sight, my port engine began to cough and bang and then stopped, though the propeller continued to 'windmill'. As I was at 10,000 feet I did not worry unduly – the Overstrand flew quite well on one engine. I turned back to the airfield which I could see quite clearly a few miles away. As I approached I was disconcerted to find that I had now lost my starboard engine as well! It had given no warning pops or bangs, but just lost power although it too continued to windmill.

Now I really did begin to worry as although the prospect of making a forced landing in a single-seater did not concern me, this aircraft was very much larger than anything I had ever experienced under like conditions. Fortunately it handled rather like a fighter despite its size and I was able to manoeuvre it as such and managed to scrape in over the fence and put it down safely. My disgust can be imagined when, after pulling off such a neat forced landing, both engines started immediately we touched the ground!

I never did get a proper explanation of why this should have happened, but I think it must have been carburettor icing and the touch down was just enough to jar the ice loose. My passengers, I found, were blissfully unaware that anything had happened – they hadn't even noticed the engine banging.

On another occasion I was scheduled to do some endurance flying in a Fairey Battle fitted with de-icing 'boots' which, in passing, perhaps I should explain consisted of rubber tubes running along the leading edges of the wing, the whole being covered in a protective rubber sheet. When the system was 'On', air was pumped through the tubes and then exhausted so that the rubber leading edge adopted a pulsating motion; this action broke the ice forming on the wing and it was blown away in the air flow which was thus enabled to maintain the smooth flow which was essential if the lift of the wing was to be preserved.

This equipment was relatively new to the RAF and to test its reliability a lot of flying was carried out in order to get a record of its performance under actual flight conditions. This was the purpose of my flight on this occasion, As a rule such a flight lasted about two hours, half the endurance of the aeroplane, and very often we made use of such flights to give new flight observers air experience as they were required to have a certain minimum amount of flying time before they were permitted to carry out actual experimental work in the air. On this occasion – I did not realise it at the time – I was assigned a passenger with whom I had had a first class row a few nights earlier when our cars were in collision on the North Circular Road. But if I did not recognise him, he certainly recognised me although he said nothing – this was to be his first flight!

We took off and flew hither and thither rather aimlessly until the two hours were nearly up. I checked the fuel state and found one tank was nearly empty but the other full so I decided to wait until the engine spluttered and then change tanks. A few minutes went by and then the engine duly coughed and I changed over, probably just a little too slowly, as the engine refused to pick up; I think that probably an air-lock had developed. The observer, had he known how, could have cleared it by operating something called a 'wobble pump'

– actually a hand-pumping device used when starting the engine – but, of course, he did not know and I hadn't time to tell him.

Faced with the inevitable forced-landing I selected the only available field into which I had any hope of landing, although I knew it was much too small and, despite standing orders to the contrary, I pumped down both flaps and undercarriage. It was very fortunate that I did so as on touching down I was able to steer the aircraft on its brakes and guide it between two large trees. Had I not had the undercarriage down I would have had no directional control and could well have skidded into one of these trees with possibly fatal results. But, having avoided the trees, the aircraft hurtled through a six foot hedge, a barbed wire fence, three more wire fences and finally came to rest in a pig farm.

The farm belonged to a retired naval officer who, perhaps fortunately, was not present, but no sooner had the two of us climbed out of the machine than the Commander's wife appeared on the scene with a bottle of whisky, two glasses and a soda siphon – obviously well trained in inter-service relations!

Amazingly the aircraft was undamaged except for a small tear in one de-icing boot and one or two small holes punched in the flaps by the twigs in the hedge. Unfortunately, there was no possibility of flying it out and it had to be dismantled.

I am told that my passenger held a belief for a long time that I had done the whole thing on purpose because of our earlier clash, but perhaps I have been misinformed.

One of the more interesting little aircraft we had in the flight was the Airspeed Queen Wasp, a radio-controlled cabin biplane scheduled to replace the Queen Bees in their role of target aircraft for anti-aircraft training. It was a nice looking machine and handled well; much too good, I felt, for the role it was to play.

The test schedule for the aeroplane included catapulting and, the dummy launches having proved satisfactory, preparations were made for the first live launch. Flight Lieutenant Macdougal was the pilot and when he was all ready and settled in the aeroplane, I stationed myself near the end of the catapult so that I could watch his face as he shot off the end – this was a favourite pastime amongst us as most people assumed an expression of shocked surprise as they hurtled into the air. A few seconds after Mac had signalled that he was ready the aircraft shot forward; for some reason I sensed immediately that there was something wrong and, as the aircraft passed me, I was already running. On a beautiful launch there was no sign of Mac!

The aircraft sailed into the air, then dipped very slightly touching one wheel on the ground, bounced gently into the air again, came down on to its other wheel, then into the air again, but this time when it came down it dug its wing into the ground, turned over and disintegrated. By this time I was quite close to the wreck and calling out to Mac, but not really expecting an answer. I was very relieved to hear him call, 'For Gawd's sake, get me out of here – petrol is dripping all over me.' I started to pull away at the wreckage with my bare hands and cut them quite badly in the process but in a matter of seconds others arrived and between us we managed to lift the machine sufficiently to let Mac crawl out unhurt except for minor cuts and bruises. Had it caught fire there would have been nothing we could have done but watch it burn and Mac with it.

The cause of the accident was, as usual, incredibly simple. During the static tests the weight of the pilot had been put in the seat in the form of lead shot; apparently it never occurred to the experts that pilots are not that shape and that a large proportion of the body's weight is in the upper part of the trunk and head. Naturally, when the aircraft was launched, the acceleration of some 2 Qw 'G' acting through Mac's upper body produced a 'moment' about the seat anchorage; the rivets sheared and Mac, complete with seat, had done a backward somersault into the back of the cabin and so was completely helpless throughout the whole proceedings. A most unpleasant experience.

For some considerable time now the actions of the Fascist Powers, first Italy and then Germany, indicated that war was inevitable. This became increasingly apparent as Germany settled down to precipitating crises at six-monthly intervals; it became evident that the principal protagonists would be Germany on the one side and France with Britain on the other – a continuation of the First World War.

Just what would trigger off the final explosion I did not, of course, know, but as things progressed I felt that if Germany took over the whole of Czechoslovakia, Britain and France would be forced to move. I was amazed when Germany did take this action, whilst we sat back and watched.

After the Czechoslovakian sell-out it became increasingly apparent that Poland was next and so I became convinced that the next offensive move on the part of Hitler and his armies would be Poland, and almost certainly in September 1939. I could not have been more accurate in my forecast!

The years 1938 and 1939 were a sort of transition period for the RAF and we had quite a number of prototypes of new aircraft coming into service, many of which were to make a name for themselves in the coming conflict. These included the Blenheim, Whitley, Battle, Wellington, Hampden, Spitfire, Hurricane and the Gloster and Bristol Fighters designed in competition with the Spitfire and Hurricane. I was fortunate in being able to fly all of these, along with a number of older aircraft, but I was particularly impressed with the little Gloster F.5/34, as it was known officially. It really was a delight to fly but performance-wise it was not up to either the Spitfire or the Hurricane. I believe that if it had had a bigger engine it would have proved as useful and become as famous as the other two.

During all this time I had been busy studying for my Specialisation Examination in the hopes of getting a permanent commission. Shortly after the Munich Crisis of 1938 came my crisis and I sat the exam at Odiham, the RAF Station practically next door to Farnborough. I had been interviewed by the AOC and was hoping that my work on the collision experiments might tip the scales in my favour. When the New Years Honours' list of 1939 was published, I found that I had been awarded the Air Force Cross and I feared that I had been given the decoration instead of the permanent commission – consequently I was not as pleased with my 'gong' as I should have been. Not many weeks went by, however, before the results of the examination were announced and I was gratified to find that I had been selected for appointment to a Non-Specialist Permanent Commission – just what I wanted!

His Majesty held an Investiture on 14 February 1939, to which both 'Henry' Hall of the Wireless Flight and I were summoned to receive our decorations, he having been awarded his AFC for his work with the Meteorological Flight before coming to Farnborough.

As this was peacetime we were required to attend the Investiture in full dress uniform – which few officers ever bought as it was worn only occasionally. I certainly did not possess it so, like most other people, I went to Gieves and there they fitted me out perfectly with busby, tunic, sword and belt – all for the sum of two guineas! The overalls and boots that completed the ensemble were part of our normal Mess kit.

Henry and I arrived at Buckingham Palace in a taxi, feeling a little nervous and conspicuous, but we were soon at our ease after being shown into the ante-room wherein were gathered all those attending the Investiture. Among them I was pleased to find an old friend from Sealand who had been awarded the Distinguished Flying Cross for gallantry in the Waziristan campaign. After we had been waiting a few minutes a member of the Palace staff entered and briefed us on procedure, then another member of the staff appeared and stuck hooked pins in our tunics so that the King could hang the decorations on to our tunics and avoid the trouble of pinning them on.

After waiting for what seemed an age, we eventually began to move slowly forward in order of seniority, both in rank and according to the status of the decoration or order to be received. It was a most interesting experience and the route taken to reach the room in which the Investiture was being held gave us an opportunity to see some of the many wonderful treasures in the Palace, including some of the most beautiful pictures I have ever seen hung in a long gallery through which we slowly moved.

Finally I found myself at the entrance to the Investiture room awaiting my turn. On the left stood the King, wearing the full dress uniform of a field marshal and behind him in a semi-circle stood his aides-de-camp of the three services. Directly in front of him and in line with the entrance stood the Lord Chamberlain while on the right, in line and facing His Majesty, were the Gentlemen-at-Arms. They were all very elderly and wore plumed helmets, breastplates, red tunics, white buckskin breeches, high full Wellington boots and a curved sabre. In their right hands they held and, I suspect leaned upon, a tall halberd. It was a most colourful sight and one that I shall never forget.

It was hard to believe that it was less than four years since I had left Winnipeg, not knowing to what I was coming, and not at all certain that I would even be accepted by the RAF. It was a tremendous thrill and I am not at all ashamed to admit it!

I did not have long to dwell upon the scene before the officer at the entrance said, 'Right, your turn, march in straight to the Lord

Chamberlain, halt, turn left and wait for your name to be announced. When this has been done bow to His Majesty by inclining your head and neck only, take three paces forward. After being decorated take one pace to the rear, bow, turn right and march out!' I did as I was bid and found myself standing three paces in front of the King, who was rather shorter than I had imagined, and then I heard my name being read out: 'To receive the Air Force Cross, Flying Officer John Alexander Kent, Royal Air Force!' I bowed and took the three paces forward. The King then shook me by the hand, congratulated me and then hung the cross on the little hook that had been stuck in my tunic.

I next took the one pace to the rear, bowed once more, turned right and marched out around the end of the line of Gentlemen-at-Arms feeling as proud as Lucifer with this great piece of silver dangling from my left breast. I then entered a small room and, before I knew quite what was happening, a little man wearing the dark uniform of a Government employee whipped the cross from my tunic along with the hook, slapped the cross into a case, handed it to me and said, 'This way out!' Henry and I, accompanied by Flying Officer Rodney, another Canadian who had also been awarded the AFC, set off for the Royal Air Force Club just across the park. It was really quite amusing to see the crowds around the Palace railings from the inside and to conjecture what they were conjecturing about us.

Although I had been fortunate in being awarded the AFC and successful in being selected for a Permanent Commission, I was still faced with the prospect of taking Promotion Examination 'B' for promotion to flight lieutenant in September. Despite the continuing threat of war I worked hard during all the summer preparing for the exam which was scheduled to take place on 5 September; I was saved from the ordeal by Mr Chamberlain's announcement just two days before, and instead I found myself in the throes of moving the Defence Flight to Exeter as described elsewhere.

After six months at Exeter, I handed over to Charles Hawkins and returned to Farnborough for about five weeks where I took part in the normal test programmes. Nothing very exciting occurred during this time except for a single-engined landing with the 'Rothermere Bomber' which I managed successfully.

Although at the time the Rothermere Bomber was receiving a great deal of publicity it is probably now virtually forgotten which is a pity. In the years between the end of the First World War and the beginning of the thirties very little progress had been made in the design and performance of RAF aircraft and it was becoming increasingly evident that other countries – and potential enemies at that – were making greater strides in the field of military aviation than was Britain. As a consequence there was a great deal of agitation among those in the world of aviation who were conscious of this growing disparity but very little was done until Lord Rothermere decided to take a hand in things. This enthusiast and patriot commissioned the Bristol Aeroplane Company to produce a modern high-speed aircraft with a view to stimulating interest generally and so encouraging the production and development of a number of up-to-date aircraft with which to re-equip the RAF.

The aeroplane produced by Bristol was a low-wing, twin-engined cabin monoplane which would be deemed an 'Executive' type in later days, but in those days rejoiced in the names of the 'Rothermere Bomber' or 'Britain First' – which latter name was more suitable as the aircraft was in no way a bomber.

On its appearance this aircraft created a sensation and it received a great deal of publicity. From it was developed the well-known Bristol Blenheim light bomber from which, in turn, descended a line of Bristol aircraft, including the Beaufighter and Beaufort.

But to return to my story. Hitler had by now launched his offensive in the west and I had to report to my new unit at Heston for operational duties on High Altitude Photographic Reconnaissance.

The Photographic Development Unit, to use its original name, was the brain-child of Sidney Cotton the designer of the famous Sidcot flying suit and well known for his pioneering flights immediately after the First World War. Prior to the outbreak of the second great conflict he had operated several civilian aircraft with which he had managed to photograph a fair portion of Germany without the knowledge of the Germans. He and Bob Niven, an old friend of mine from Alberta who had left the RAF to join Sidney Cotton, had a near squeak in Berlin and only just managed to overcome the many difficulties placed in their way by various officials and got away in a Lockheed Electra on the night of 2 September 1939!

Sidney Cotton could be a very persuasive person and, backed by the evidence of his photographs, he managed to get the Air Ministry to agree to the formation of this special unit at Heston with himself in command with the rank of Wing Commander. He was even successful in obtaining a sufficient number of Spitfires, of which we were desperately short, to equip four flights. In addition he acquired several Hudsons along with a variety of other aircraft. The main base was at Heston which operated one flight of long range Spitfires and the Hudsons, the other three Spitfire flights were located at Lille, Rheims and Nancy.

The Hudsons were used for low-level reconnaissance when weather conditions provided adequate cloud cover, while the Spitfires were used for high-level work and were stripped of much of their standard equipment to improve their performance and to enable them to carry the extra fuel needed for the long distances over which they operated. These modified aircraft had an extra fuel tank in the rear of the fuselage, a moulded windshield to replace the standard armoured glass and 'bubbles' on either side of the canopy. In these bubbles were placed small mirrors to take the place of the external one which was removed to help clean up the aircraft and add to its speed. The guns, armour plate, radio and even the night flying equipment were all removed, leaving the pilot with no protection except his speed and height – and with only the most elementary navigational equipment, one compass and a set of maps!

Considerable attention was given to the problem of camouflage and the Spitfires were painted a bright blue with a high gloss finish while the Hudsons were painted in shades of grey to blend with the sea; both proved very effective.

After a few flights to familiarise myself with the modified Spitfires and to get accustomed to their handling characteristics at high altitude during long cross-country flights over England, I was briefed for my first operational sortie. My target was an oil cracking depot just outside the town of Rheine not far from the Dutch border.

I left Heston and started a steady climb, the procedure being to continue climbing until the target or maximum altitude was reached then, on the return trip one could afford to put the nose down slightly so losing height gradually but adding considerably to one's speed and to the difficulties of interception. I left the English coast at

Southwold and, continuing my climb, crossed the Dutch coast near Flushing on a line running slightly to the north of Antwerp. Long before I reached the coast I could see a dense cloud of oily black smoke rising straight up from Antwerp to a height of about 25,000 feet where the wind blew it away off to the south-west giving it the appearance of a gigantic tree. It was my first sight of war.

By the time I had reached a point about midway between Antwerp and the Zuider Zee I had reached 35,000 feet. It was one of those beautiful spring days and I was able to see well into France, the whole of Belgium and Holland right along the line of Friesian Islands and I could just make out the southern part of the Jutland peninsula – this was, in fact, my first sight of the Continent and what a fabulous sight it was.

I was so enthralled with the view that at first I did not notice a slight thumping noise that seemed to come from the after part of the fuselage. It was rather intermittent and I could not think what it could be. It did not worry me particularly until it began to get louder and then, after one of these thumps, the aircraft rocked slightly fore and aft. The next thump was even louder and the aircraft gave quite a distinct rock. I could only conclude that whatever was loose in the back was affecting the controls so I decided that I had better get back somewhere near the area still held by our troops in case I had to go down or bail out. When I turned I saw what had been causing the thumps – a long line of anti-aircraft shell bursts were strung out behind me and had been gradually catching me up. It came as a bit of a shock, but after I had made one or two alterations of course the gunners' aim was completely upset and they stopped firing. They had, of course, been able to line up on the vapour trail following my machine so it was easy enough to get the line, but what surprised me was that every puff of smoke where a shell had exploded was dead on my height. I was to become very familiar with the incredible accuracy of the height estimation of the German heavy flak in the next few years, but this first experience came as a distinct shock.

By this time I had crossed the German border and identified Rheine, which was slightly north of my track so I turned port and started my first run over the target. Although I had often been to this height, 36,500 feet, in fighters I had never been required to place myself accurately over a given spot on the ground. One cannot see straight down from a Spitfire and the area of ground covered by the blind spot of wing and nose is considerable. Once I had lined up on the target and commenced the run, I lost sight of the target and had to judge when I was approaching it close enough to start the cameras. This I did and then turned and started another run. Finally I completed the number of runs that should have provided complete cover of the target and set off for home.

The return flight was quite uneventful, but I was intrigued by the fact that even at this height I could see two aircraft taking off from an airfield in Holland. They themselves were just dots but their dust clouds were very easily seen and it was this that had attracted my attention.

About two hours after landing back at Heston I was invited to see the results of my efforts. There in a large room were my photographs all spread out and overlapping to give a complete picture. They looked wonderful and I was very pleased with myself until one of the Photographic Interpreters said: 'A magnificent set of pictures, but do you mind telling us where you have been?' – I had missed Rheine altogether.

The town I had photographed turned out later to be Munster, some miles from Rheine, but slap in the middle of one plate taken on the run-up to the town was a new canal viaduct – the existence of which had been unknown until this time. It was for his attack on this viaduct some little while later that Wing Commander Learoyd was awarded his Victoria Cross. My efforts, then, were not entirely wasted but it did illustrate just how difficult it is to tell exactly where you are in relation to the ground when one is at this sort of altitude.

I managed to get in a bit more practice in the art and made several other sorties over the Continent, including one to Bremen, but all were uneventful.

About two weeks after my first sortie I flew over to France in a Hudson to visit our sole remaining base at Meaux, some forty miles east of Paris. On the way over we could see the long lines of refugees as they made their way south away from the invading Germans; it was a horrible sight and one that made our blood boil.

On arriving at Meaux I was welcomed by Bob Niven who declared that I was just the chap they wanted and I had better stay. I pointed out that I had no kit of any kind and I would have to go back and get some, which I did, and returned to France the next day.

The sorties flown during the incredible period of confusion immediately prior to the French collapse were, for the most part, of relatively short range and were concerned more with tactical reconnaissance than strategic. I made very few flights while I was at Meaux and these were only as far as Givet and Namur, the object of the sorties was to find a large tank army that was rumoured to be somewhere in the area – it was. In fact, the country was so thickly wooded that high level photography was of little value.

Early in June and shortly after landing from a sortie the sirens sounded and the low hum of approaching aircraft could be heard. It turned out to be the first mass raid of the war and some 250 German aircraft took part. Their targets were various factories on the outskirts of Paris but, just for the hell of it, they dropped a number of visiting cards on us at Meaux both on their way to Paris and on their way back.

In the middle of all the attendant hullabaloo I managed to get most of the airmen into shelters, but several were unaccounted for, so I set out to find them in case they had been wounded. By this time there was quite a fight going on overhead and jettisoned bombs, spent bullets and cartridge cases were exploding and spattering around all over the place. It was sickening to be stuck on the ground and unable to do anything about it.

I found most of the men taking shelter in a slit trench, but there were still two or three more adrift so I set out again. At this point one of our aircraft, returning from a sortie, ran slap into the fight and got shot up, the pilot being wounded in the leg. I was just in time to see the Spitfire come in and land while bombs were bursting all over the airfield. The pilot taxied to the hangar and switched off and at the same time another officer, Tim Craxton, ran out. Seeing that the pilot was wounded, he helped him out of the aeroplane, got him into a car and shot off down the road with bombs dropping on either side of them and succeeded in getting the wounded pilot to hospital.

The casualties were not all on one side, however, and just as the Spitfire was crossing the boundary, a Ju88 shot past it, crossed the airfield and belly-landed in the next field. The pilot was the only one of the crew alive and he was very badly hit, having had his knee and pelvis smashed by bullets from a Morane 406 based on nearby Coullomiers.

The Germans were advancing more and more rapidly and it was not long before we were ordered to clear out and go south to the airfield at Bricy near Orleans. Two of us remained behind after the main party had gone to finish clearing up and then, on 9 June, we departed in the sole remaining aircraft – two Tiger Moths! I was seated in mine warming up the engine in the approved manner when the airman at the wing tip rocked the machine, I looked at him and he pointed up. I followed his gesture and there was a formation of German aircraft just approaching the airfield at about 8,000 feet; as I looked I caught the glisten of bombs on their way down. The chocks had by now been pulled away so I opened the throttle wide and took off straight ahead. As I left the ground and started an immediate turn the first bombs were bursting on the edge of the aerodrome – I was quite petrified and kept the little Tiger at tree-top height and headed south closely followed by the second Tiger. For some reason the Germans completely ignored us, but I was expecting one or two of the escort fighters to swoop down on us at any moment. It was a most unpleasant experience and we were very glad to arrive safely at Bricy a little over an hour later.

Although operating from Bricy, most of us were accommodated in Orleans and the city was filled with refugees all desperately trying to keep ahead of the advancing Germans. Some of the sights were so pathetic that it was impossible to avoid a moist eye – one old lady, I recall particularly, apparently had all her possessions piled into a pram and, swinging from the handle, was a parrot cage with her pet cat inside it. She herself just wandered on as though she was unaware of the crush of people around her, all moving south.

One day French tanks and guns came rumbling through the city and the locals were convinced that they had arrived to make a stand on the Loire and turn the Germans back. The disappointment of the people was painful to see when this force which, by its appearance, had not seen action at all, crossed the Loire and continued on south. The troops themselves looked utterly dejected.

During this period anxiety was felt about the bridges over the Seine – had they been destroyed or not? To get some information I was sent out on a flight to cover the river from Paris to Le Havre.

The westward run I made at 32,000 feet but it was obvious that not much would be gained from the photographs as much of the area was obscured by the dense clouds of smoke from the many fires burning to the north of the river. In Rouen the flames from the burning oil installations came gulping up through the smoke, deep red in colour and clearly visible even from this height of six miles.

My return run was made at 19,000 feet and I kept a watchful eye open for enemy aircraft but saw none. We had realised for some time that high-level reconnaissance did not really meet the present requirements and that sooner or later we were going to have to resort to low-level. This was not so amusing as we depended entirely on our speed and altitude for defence.

With the prospect of this low-level role we re-equipped one of the Spitfires with its eight guns and I flew this machine on another reconnaissance of the bridges. There was a considerable amount of cumulus cloud over the area and some cumulo-nimbus; I did not fancy my chances of getting any photographs at all. Initially I climbed to 15,000 feet, but gradually let down as I approached the river. When I had reached 10,000 feet I saw, about a mile away, eleven Messerschmitts Flying in line astern formation and on a course that would cross my bows. They did not appear to have seen me and I turned and flew almost parallel to them but on a slightly converging course, gained a couple of thousand feet, and continued to watch them. These were the first German aircraft I had seen whilst on a sortie and I was not going to rush into anything.

Without warning four Hurricanes swept from behind one of the towering cumulus straight down on to the leading five Messerschmitts. Instantly everyone seemed to go mad and aeroplanes whirled around in crazy gyrations. Then the rest of the 109s joined in and I latched on to the last one. We went diving down towards the swarm already engaged. I was determined to get as close as possible to make sure of my man and I lost sight of the others, but at about 3,000 feet my 109 pulled out of his dive and started a turn to the right – I was now only about fifty yards behind him and just about to open fire. I think the pilot must have seen me then for the first time as he made a sudden wild half-roll into which I followed him – and immediately regretted it as the ground was much too close. I lost interest in my intended victim and concentrated on getting out of the jam I was in. Luckily the Spitfire is very forgiving and also I was fortunate in being directly over the river. I was able to recover literally between the banks. As I was rushing downwards, I saw a red flash out of the corner of my eye and as I climbed away I saw a column of smoke coming out of what looked like a bomb crater about 100 yards from the river bank. Of the 109 there was no sign and although I could not claim this as an enemy aircraft destroyed I have always been satisfied that the flash and the crater were caused by the German machine.

I have often wondered why he took such violent evasive action as at that time the German pilots were, for the most part, pretty experienced and I can only conclude that this one got the shock of his life to find a Spitfire on his tail, as there were no squadrons of them in France, and a bright blue one at that. Perhaps he thought that he had met the British ace of aces!

After this brief encounter I carried out a visual reconnaissance at about 1,000 feet for some sixty miles along the river. The smoke was very dense in places and it was difficult to see whether any damage had been done to the bridges. Every so often I came under heavy anti-aircraft fire and several times my machine was bounced by the explosions, but luckily no actual hits were scored. Who was shooting at me I could not make out, it may have been the Germans, the French or both.

I returned to base at about 500 feet past Evreux, Dreux and Chartres. Just beyond Evreux I came on a stationary train with one tanker car blazing, but could see no sign of any people; in fact, the whole way back to Bricy I saw only one vehicle moving and that appeared to be a staff car.

This same day an Australian pilot and his gunner arrived at Bricy in a Battle which looked rather like a colander it was so full of holes. The pilot said that as far as he knew they were the sole survivors of six that had set out about an hour before. They had bombed their target but had been set upon by some 109s. He had had a running fight with one and in endeavouring to evade it he had actually hit a tree. He was, understandably, in a very bad state of nerves and we arranged to send him and his gunner back to their squadron which was not far away. We asked what he wanted done about the aeroplane and he replied that we could do anything we liked with it; he didn't want it and anyway it was a write-off.

When they had departed we pushed the Battle into the one remaining hangar to examine it. As we were doing so someone in the cockpit pressed the control for opening the bomb doors and to our horror out came the racks with one bomb hung up. At the same moment I noticed a slight wisp of smoke coming out of the wing above the port petrol tank and immediately above the bomb. It turned out to be an incendiary bullet that was still burning, but I managed to fish it out with a pair of long-nosed pliers, while the plane was hurriedly pushed outside again. Some gallant chaps then came along and removed the bomb.

Far from being written off, this particular machine, with its bashed in leading edge repaired with a piece of tree trunk and some fabric, was flown back to Heston a few days later carrying not only the pilot, Flight Lieutenant Wilson, but six airmen and their kit!

The day after the Australian episode I was instructed to take the armed Spitfire back to Heston while the others moved on to Poitiers. I flew back via Cherbourg and the Isle of Wight as instructed. The actual location of the Germans being uncertain, I was briefed to keep as far to the west as practicable. The flight was quite uneventful and I only saw one other machine, but it was too far away to be able to identify it as friend or foe.

When I left Bricy the German forward troops were only some thirty miles away while the nearest French forces were, as far as I know, some forty miles from us in the other direction. Those who went on to Poitiers had, almost on arrival, to start preparing to evacuate and make their way back to England. A ground party was despatched to Bordeaux and the air party set off for Heston, some of them via Nantes. 'Cowboy' Blatchford, yet another Canadian, who later in the year was to lead the squadron that decimated the first Italian air attack on Britain, was stuck with a Tiger Moth and he was not at all sure of his chances of getting home. On landing at Nantes he found some RAF men pushing a number of perfectly serviceable Battles into a heap. Cowboy walked over and asked what they were doing; he was told that they had orders to burn them as there were no pilots to fly them out. 'OK,' Cowboy replied. 'Then burn this thing, I'll have one of those.' And he duly arrived at Heston in the Battle.

The ground party got to Bordeaux and shipped aboard a coal barge, which eventually got them back to England; they turned up with the leader of the party, Flight Lieutenant George Belcher, as black as ink but very cheerful and extremely glad to be home.

Although enthusiastic enough to start with, I had found the photographic work very frustrating and I longed to get back on to fighters where one could immediately see the results of one's efforts. Unfortunately, it was not easy to get a posting from the photographic role as it took time to train pilots and there were not all that many available. It was, therefore, only after a lot of pestering that I managed to get myself back to fighters. First of all, however, I had to attend an Operational Training Unit at Hawarden in North Wales only a few miles from my Flying school – Sealand.

5

Battle of Britain

My arrival at Hawarden coincided with that of 'Babe' McArthur, another Farnborough test pilot itching to get back on to fighters. Neither of us were too impressed with the station, which was a sea of mud, and the accommodation was all under canvas which we both loathed, so it came as a horrible shock when the CO said he felt that there had been a mistake and we must have been posted in as instructors and not pupils. Mac and I talked very fast and managed to convince the CO that we really were pupils. We did not mind the discomfort of the place for a few days if it was to get us on to operations, but the thought of being based there for an indefinite period was too much.

I quite understood the Station Commander's reasoning when I met the instructors as hardly any of them had been on operations and mine had not served in a squadron for over three years. Fortunately the Flight Commander, Bill Kain, had been in France with 73 Squadron and really knew what the score was. He rather apologetically explained that the rules required both Mac and I to be given a dual check before being allowed to fly Hurricanes. As he was pushed for time and short of instructors, he felt that the best thing to do was for us to check out one another in a Miles Master. This took about fifteen minutes and then we transferred ourselves into a couple of Hurricanes and went off on a 'dog-fighting' exercise.

Everything was confused during this period and the training syllabus was very sketchy – it consisted mostly of formation flying and dog-fighting exercises. I kept after Bill Kain about air firing, explaining that I had never fired eight guns and I wanted to find out what they sounded like – and what effect they had on the aircraft.

Finally, in desperation, he allowed me one shoot. My target was a spit of sand in the Dee Estuary and, on my first attack, I got a neat group with a half-second burst, but on my second dive the guns failed to fire. I tried several more times, but just nothing happened so, in a bit of a temper, I returned to the airfield and told Bill Kain what I thought of an installation which could produce stoppages in all eight guns at once. Bill then explained that there had been no stoppage – that was all the ammunition they could spare me!

I knew that both the country and the Air Force were in a pretty bad way, but this brought home to me just how desperate the situation was. It did not matter so much in my particular case as I had done so much front-gun firing before, although it was with only two guns, but many of the new boys never fired their guns at all until they went into action for the first time – a sobering thought when one considers the task before them. It was a great tribute to their grit and determination that they carried themselves into the violent battles of the next few months, and inflicted the damage they did, with virtually no instruction or practice in air-firing at all. One wonders what the results might have been if it had been possible to thoroughly train every pilot before he went into action.

It was thought at this time that the Germans either were, or were considering, using captured British aircraft to fly unmolested over England; overnight, therefore, all British aircraft were required to have their markings changed as outlined in instructions sent to all units. Any aircraft found after this with the old markings were to be considered as hostile; the types of aircraft thought most likely to be used by the Germans were Whitleys and Lysanders.

A few days after this instruction was implemented, I was carrying out some formation practice with two others using the defence Section aircraft, three Hurricanes with fully loaded guns. As we were over the Irish Sea and flying westward, I saw a Whitley. I decided to investigate and, sure enough, it had the old markings. I would have been quite justified in shooting it down but, knowing how often correspondence goes astray or is delayed, I gave this machine the benefit of the doubt and did not attack immediately. Instead, I put the section into line-astern and flew past the Whitley on the port side motioning the pilot to turn back towards land. He ignored this, so I got into position to attack; he immediately turned back, but as soon as my section went into vic formation he again turned west. Again I got into position to attack so he turned back. This went on for some minutes and I was just about to attack in earnest when he continued on his course for land while my section and I escorted him.

About three miles from Hawarden the navigator of the Whitley started to flash the 'Letter of the day' at me with an Aldis lamp, but he was a bit late so I stayed with the Whitley until it touched down and then I landed behind it – to find a very irate Australian flying officer calling me everything under the sun. I pointed out that apart from my being senior in rank to him and therefore not prepared to stand for his attitude, his aircraft had the wrong markings and he had acted in a suspicious manner from the time I first saw him.

He countered this by saying that his navigator had signalled the letter of the day and that should have been good enough.

I then asked why he had taken so long to give any recognition signal and why had he not fired a signal cartridge giving the colour of the day – I could see that the pockets of his overalls were full of them. His answer was a classic: 'My instructions are that I am not to use these cartridges except in cases of emergency!'

I looked at him in disbelief and then, pointing to the three Hurricanes, said: 'Look – you had twenty-four fully loaded Brownings up your "chuff" and it only needed one more false move on your part and you would have had the lot – now, if that is not an emergency, I'm damned if I know what is!'

Very disgruntled and, I think, a little shaken, he finally left for his home base at Abingdon to break the news before any of his friends met someone with less patience than I had.

After a hectic four days of intensive flying, postings came through for both Mac and myself; he was to go to 238 at Middle Wallop on Hurricanes whilst I was to report to 54 Squadron at Hornchurch which was equipped with Spitfires. I had a couple of free days before I was due at Hornchurch and I called in at Farnborough where I met Henry Hall, who had been commanding a flight in 257 Squadron at Northolt but had just been posted back to Farnborough as the Air Force, apparently, had decided that it could not afford to risk the loss of test pilots on operations. He then informed me that I had been posted to fill the vacancy created by his being posted back to the RAE.

I immediately telephoned the Squadron Commander at Hornchurch, who confirmed that my posting had been changed and that I was now to report to No. 257 as Henry had said. I didn't like the sound of this at all – if they had dragged Henry back, it was a fair bet that I would be brought back, too.

As I had expected, the signal had overtaken me by the time I reported to 257 the next day: it stated that I was not permitted to fly on operations. That meant only one thing, back to Farnborough; all I could do was to sit and wait for the next signal and dwell upon the extraordinary difference between the First World War and this one – in the first you had to fight like hell to keep out of it, while in this one you had to fight like hell to get into it!

The follow-up signal arrived and back I went to join all the other re-called and fed up test pilots. Everything was at sixes and sevens, and there was virtually nothing for us to do except pester our long-suffering CO with requests to be sent back to a squadron. Whether it was our pestering or a change in Air Ministry policy I don't know, but after a week we were all posted away again, Henry Hall returning to 257 whilst I, having no squadron to return to, was posted to a new one due to form at Northolt, this was No. 303 (Polish) Squadron!

It was just about the last straw to find myself after all my efforts posted to a foreign squadron that had not even been formed and I was thoroughly fed up and despondent. All I knew about the Polish Air Force was that it had only lasted about three days against the *Luftwaffe* and I had no reason to suppose that they would shine any more brightly operating from England. My new Squadron Commander, Squadron Leader R.G. Kellett, was not as despondent as I was, but was becoming very irritated at being left to command a squadron which consisted of two Flight Commanders, an Intelligence Officer, an Orderly Room Corporal and three Senior NCO ground crew. There were no Poles, no troops, and no operational aeroplanes. All these were due to arrive any day and we busied ourselves preparing to receive them and to train both air and ground crews in British methods and to turn out a fully operational squadron in a minimum of time.

Although we in the squadrons did not fully appreciate it, the preliminaries for the Battle of Britain had already begun and the first attacks on the Channel convoys and ports were taking place. On our side, frantic efforts were being made to build up a force capable of standing up to and defeating the full fury of the German offensive that was bound to come. With our problems of language superimposed upon the general problems we were, perhaps, more muddled and confused than most, but somehow, we managed to cope.

It was only a few days after returning to 257 Squadron that Henry Hall was lost in a battle over one of the convoys. These early combats were, in my opinion, the most deadly of all and many a good fighter pilot was lost who would have been invaluable in the days that followed. Fighting over England one always had the comfort of knowing that if one was forced to jump one would come down on land where medical attention, if required, could rapidly be obtained. Over the sea it was a different matter as we were only equipped with archaic Mae Wests, the buoyancy of which depended upon wads of kapok and a rubber bladder that had to be inflated by mouth. The chances of being picked up during a convoy attack if one had to bale out were very remote and this may well have happened to Henry as it did to so many others.

Not long after Henry's death, No. 257 was moved out of line for a rest and was replaced by No. 1 Squadron. Having known the squadron before the war and in France, it was nice to greet a number of old friends again. Hilly Brown, a fellow countryman and particular friend of mine, was now commanding 'A' Flight in his squadron as I was in mine. He was one of the finest fighter pilots of the war and even at this early stage he had already chalked up a score of seventeen enemy aircraft destroyed.

Eventually the Poles arrived and, fortunately, so did some aircraft; one Master, one dual Battle and eight Hurricanes. Out of all the Poles there were only two who had any English at all, one, an Engineer Officer, had visited England some years previously and had a smattering of the language; the other one could say 'Come on, boys!' – and that was all.

In the Polish Air Force the squadrons were slightly smaller than those in the RAF, but slightly larger than a flight. Consequently No. 303 RAF Squadron, being formed of two Polish squadrons, No. 111 which became 'A' Flight and No. 112 which became 'B' Flight, was somewhat larger than an ordinary RAF squadron. The two Polish squadrons were both Warsaw squadrons and No. 111 had originally been, like the Lafayette Escadrille in the French Air Force, an American Volunteer Squadron and formed during the Polish-Russian War of 1919-21; again, as in the case of the French Squadron, it was named after a national hero who had fought for the Americans in their War of Independence – in this case after Kosciusko who had been General Washington's Adjutant and later became Dictator of Poland.

All the senior appointments, both among officers and men, were duplicated so that under Squadron Leader Kellett was a Polish Squadron Leader Krasnodemski; under me, as the Polish Flight Commander, was originally Flight Lieutenant Henneberg – ironically a friend of the Italian Foreign Minister, Count Ciano – and later Flight Lieutenant Urbanowicz. In 'B' Flight, Atholl Forbes had as his deputy Flight Lieutenant Lapkowski.

I was pleasantly surprised to find in my flight one of the Poles who had been stationed at Meaux with a Dewoitine Squadron and he was quite pleased to find someone with whom he had something in common, however slight, in this strange country.

Although a knowledge of English was practically non-existent amongst the Poles, they all spoke French. Ronald Kellett also spoke quite good French while Atholl Forbes was completely bilingual which helped enormously. Unfortunately my French was very poor and consequently I had to learn some Polish; this I did by taking one or two of the pilots out of the aircraft and pointing to it, saying, 'aeroplane' slowly and distinctly. They got the idea and answered '*samolot*' which I wrote down phonetically. I then went round the aircraft giving the English names for the various parts and getting the Polish in return. Gradually I worked out a complete procedure in Polish and had it all written down phonetically on my knee pad and used it when giving instructions in the air. It worked very well and amused the Poles a lot.

The officer from Meaux, Flying Officer Januszewicz, I checked out first and he got away in the Hurricane quite happily, but after this we began to have troubles. Some of the pilots had never flown aircraft with retractable undercarriages and, both in Poland and in France, they had been used to opening the throttle by pulling it back instead of pushing it forward. As can be imagined these differences caused confusion and we had several of the aircraft landed with their undercarriages retracted. One of these was put down by a Sergeant Frantisek and I tore him off a first class strip – he didn't know what I was saying but knew he had to answer in a foreign tongue and kept repeating: '*Oui, mon commandant*,' over and over.

Among some of the things I said to him was: 'How in hell do you think you are going to fight the Germans if you can't even fly the ruddy aeroplanes?' At this time we really knew nothing of the background of the Poles or of their experiences so it made me feel rather foolish to learn later that, in fact, Frantisek was a Czech, not a Pole, and when Hitler invaded his country he took off and strafed the German troops and then flew on to Poland where he dropped his rank of lieutenant to that of corporal. When Germany attacked Poland, he succeeded in shooting down three enemy aircraft with the old outdated PZL fighter before he himself was shot down. He escaped through Romania and made his way to France where he was sent to a Caudron Cyclone squadron. This little aeroplane was really a converted sports plane and had the machine guns literally strapped under the wing, but with this aircraft Frantisek shot down a further eleven German aircraft during the fighting in France. Within the next six weeks he was to go on and destroy another seventeen of the enemy before being killed in an accident the cause of which was never determined. It is no wonder I feel a bit foolish when I think of my ticking him off.

Because of our lack of knowledge of the Poles' experience and their general background we had to be very careful about their training, especially as regards R/T; we could not expect them to remember even what little English we were able to teach them during the excitement of combat. Whereas they could speak to one another, the Controller could neither understand them nor they him. It was necessary, therefore, to have at least one of the British pilots flying with them on all exercises and, later of course, in combat.

I think perhaps the training period was unnecessarily prolonged and this certainly irked the Poles, who kept remonstrating with us that the best training was over France, but we still had to be quite sure they knew exactly how we operated. This was not always easy to get across as illustrated on one occasion when 'A' Flight was scheduled to act as a formation of 'bombers' while 'B' Flight was to carry out an interception and make dummy attacks on us. I explained this very carefully and impressed upon them that no evasive action was to be taken as we were simulating bombers depending upon crossfire for defence. They all said that they fully understood and off we went.

I led the flight off to the west and climbed to height, then set course for Northolt. Just east of Reading I saw the other flight diving down to attack and then, as they completed the attack and started their break away, I was horrified to see my number three, Flying

Officer Feric, pull up into a violent barrel-roll and get right on to the tail of one of the attacking Hurricanes. Fortunately he recognised it just in time as he was on the point of shooting it down – he had completely misunderstood what I had said during briefing, even though I had used an interpreter, and thought that we were to be the attacking force.

During this training period we British pilots were scrambled individually on several occasions but failed to achieve any decisive results as we generally arrived in the battle area as combat was being broken off and the enemy were streaking for home. At this time Northolt was a two-squadron Station; however we had heard rumours that a third would soon be moving in and, in mid-August, it arrived. I was delighted when it turned out to be No. 1 Royal Canadian Air Force Squadron, commanded by Ernie McNab whom I had known well since 1931. It was a nice feeling to have one's fellow countrymen as next-door neighbours at such a time in history and now we had three different Air Forces on the station, first, No. 1 RAF, next No. 1 RCAF and then No. 303 Polish – and there were Canadians in all three of them.

On 30 August the squadron was taking part in another exercise; this time a formation of Blenheims was acting as target and the interception had just been effected. Then, just to the north of London, there appeared a whole formation of German aircraft – the Poles quickly changed their role to that of escort and, fortunately, the German fighters apparently did not see our formations as they made no attempt to attack. The sight of these enemy machines was too much for Flying Officer Paskewicz of 'B' Flight and he broke formation and shot down a Dornier 17, following it right down to the ground to ensure that it crashed.

This was the Squadron's first victory and the Poles were absolutely cock-a-hoop over it. Ronald Kellett was so pleased with the way they had behaved that he immediately asked for permission to declare the Squadron 'Operational'. This was granted and the squadron was placed on 'Readiness' for the first time the following morning, 31 August, just a year after the German attack on their country. There was not long to wait until the first 'Scramble' order came through and away went the Squadron led by Ronald Kellett. After some vectoring about, they intercepted a formation of Messerschmitt 109s.

Kellett immediately attacked and in a matter of minutes six German fighters were destroyed. It was a wonderful opening to what was to be a fantastic six weeks.

It is my everlasting regret that I did not take part in either of these two flights as I had been given two days off by the CO because he did not expect anything much to happen. Naturally I was very put out when I returned to hear the news and I got a lot of good-natured ribbing, chiefly from Hilly Brown, for missing the party. I did not mind the ribbing itself, but I was fed up with myself for not being in on things.

After this effort I stayed on duty every day, but every patrol and every scramble ended the same way, not a sign of the enemy. Of course, everything was happening so rapidly that a day felt like a week and a week a year; in fact, it was only two days later that I had my first real brush with a number of our opponents.

The first part of the day was quiet and it was not until about tea-time that we were scrambled after a raid; I was leading the squadron and we were soon over Manston at 19,000 feet – having the greatest difficulty in hearing the Controller as we were at extreme range. I did hear a warning of 'bandits' (any enemy aircraft, as opposed to a 'bogey' which was an unidentified subject) in our vicinity, but as I almost immediately intercepted a squadron of Hurricanes I put it down to mistaken identity. Within a minute or two I turned south and, looking up, saw nine 109s diving on us out of the sun. I turned into the attack and Sergeant Rogowski, who was doing search formation behind, pulled up and went head-on into the middle of them, closely followed by Frantisek. The German formation split up and a general mêlée ensued, grey shapes with black crosses on them flashed past only feet away, next the brown and green of a Hurricane flashed across the sights. Streams of grey tracer smoke criss-crossed the sky in all directions. It was impossible to hold a steady aim and snap shooting was the order of the day, but so confused was the fight that one had little or no chance to see if one's fire had taken effect before having to take wild evasive action to avoid either the enemy's fire or a collision.

Even more suddenly than it had started the fight was over and the sky was empty, except for a long trail of oily black smoke to the north and a trail of white vapour to the south, while a parachute drifted lazily down towards the waiting sea – I was alone. A minute went by, perhaps two, and then I saw three aircraft approaching rapidly. Not recognising them immediately, I watched carefully with my thumb on the gun button ready for instant action should they prove hostile. I could not help being reminded of how like strange dogs we must appear, cautiously approaching each other, stiff-legged. These were, however, my own aircraft and we joined up and flew home, not having any idea where the others had got to.

The missing ones came drifting in at intervals after we had landed, three of them doing victory rolls as they pulled up over the dispersal. Rogowski and Frantisek had got one each which I had witnessed just before the two formations really tangled. Heaneberg had chased a 109 ten miles into France before he managed to shoot it down; he then had to turn for home, but found his victim's number two was on to him. After a brief encounter, Henneberg succeeded in destroying this 109 also.

It was all very satisfactory as, despite the tactical advantage the enemy had enjoyed, they had lost four destroyed and one probably destroyed, this one by Feric who had then suffered engine failure and had had to land near Manston. As he glided down, Rogowski saw that he was in trouble and went down with him to protect him from attack. This readiness to help a stricken comrade was a feature amongst the Poles that I was to witness on several occasions and it was good to know they possessed it.

The following day the situation became confused in the Operations Room by the large number of raids on the board and the Controller ordered both 'A' Flight and 'B' Flight to 'Stand by', but separately. Within a minute or two he scrambled first one and then the other without realising what he had done. He kept giving me vectors to intercept and it dawned on me that, from his instructions he thought the two flights were together as a squadron. I did not want to compromise security by telling him this on the R/T in clear but – when he said: 'Garta to Apany Red Leader, vector one-four-zero Angels one-five, one hundred and fifty plus twenty miles ahead – over!' – I felt that the time had come. 'Apany Red Leader to Garta,' I replied, 'Understand one-fifty plus twenty miles ahead – you realise we are only six, I repeat six – over.' 'Apany Red Leader from Garta,' came the cheery reply. 'Understand you are only six; very well, be careful!' – I could have shot him!

As things turned out, we did not intercept this particular raid as it had been turned back before we got to it, but I continued to look for trouble although the sky seemed empty. When we had reached 24,000 feet over Dungeness I turned and flew west prior to returning to base. Still the sky appeared to be empty when, suddenly, a black cross appeared right in front of me. It was on the fuselage of a 109 and so close I don't know to this day how we did not collide. I am sure the German pilot was as surprised as I was, if he ever did see me. I turned violently after the German and was gratified to see, out of the corner of my eye, that my number two, Johnny Zumbach, was still in tight formation. Although I fired one or two bursts I could not get near enough to my quarry to do him any visible harm and he was well out of range by the time we reached mid-Channel.

It was not until I got back to Northolt that I learned that the propeller I had seen turning at my wing tip during my initial violent turn belonged to another 109 and not to Zumbach at all. Fortunately he had seen the German formating on me, so he attacked and drove him off. Sergeant Wojtowicz got several bursts into a 109 from close range, but while he was still shooting he had his own propeller and a large piece of cowling shot off; he had to crash-land near Ashford but was himself unhurt.

Altogether it was quite a day. Henneberg had tangled with four Messerschmitts and his aeroplane was pretty badly shot up although he himself was all right. Poor Frantisek, however, had begun to wonder whose side he was on, during an early patrol he was attacked by a Spitfire and later in the day by a Hurricane! Even so he did manage to destroy one enemy machine which he was pretty certain was a Heinkel 113. These aircraft were one of the mysteries of the war – I personally never came across one, but I have met a number of pilots who claim to have encountered them, while some experts claim they were never used operationally. Be that as it may, there are photographs of a line-up of them apparently in squadron service.

Early in September the *Luftwaffe* started its raids on London's dock-land and in the evenings when we had been released from Readiness we used to sit outside the Mess and watch the flares drifting down and the tiny red fireflies that were bursting anti-aircraft shells, too far away to be heard. Things were reasonably quiet for a day or two, and then they really hotted up as the *Luftwaffe* began to concentrate its attacks on the fighter airfields. Being situated to the north-west of London we were spared these concentrated attacks, but at the same time it took us longer to get into the battle area. During this period the situation was often highly confused with Germans and British scattered all over the sky; it was difficult to mount a really concentrated attack and we tended to become split up as well. During one of these confused battles Ronald Kellett was badly hit, having practically all the fabric shot off the rear of his aircraft and he himself received a minor wound in the leg. His aeroplane was barely controllable and he had to make a very fast landing at Biggin Hill where he was somewhat unceremoniously dragged out of the cockpit and into a shelter as they were still receiving some attention from the Germans. On the same day, Atholl Forbes was wounded in the neck and got a crease across the bridge of the nose, but was not seriously injured; Squadron Leader Krasnodemski, Sergeant Karubin and Sergeant Rogowski were not so fortunate all three being shot down and badly burned. By the evening the squadron was reduced to three serviceable aeroplanes and – this was just when No. 12 Group was trying to force its wing philosophy on to No. 11 Group – the Northolt 'Wing' was scrambled with myself leading all three squadrons with a grand total of nine aeroplanes, all that were left on the airfield!

We took off, my section being followed by one from No. 1 Canadian and another from No. 1 bringing up the rear. We climbed to about 11,000 feet and then, without any warning, there was a loud bang as my engine blew up and caught fire. Flames were licking around the canopy and sparks darted around inside the cockpit. I switched off the ignition, turned off the fuel, turned up my oxygen supply and started side-slipping in an effort to keep the flames from reaching the reserve petrol tank situated just behind the firewall bulkhead. My aircraft rapidly lost speed and the other aircraft shot past me, or all except one which came in to tight formation – it was Hilly Brown who called me on the R/T saying: 'Haw, bloody haw! You gettin' hot in there, Bud?' This was a reprisal for a lot of ribbing I had been giving him for having been shot down and burnt a few days before, but I thought he could at least have waited until I got down!

I was, in fact, in a bit of a predicament as I was right over the centre of London and, if I baled out, the machine would crash into a densely populated area – though why I should think that this would be worse than the bombs already falling there, I don't quite know! Anyway, I decided to stay with the aircraft and hoped that the fire would be blown out and that I might reach open country or possibly even my own airfield.

I called the Controller and told him what had happened and what I was trying to do. Nothing much was said for some minutes and then the Station Commander, Stanley Vincent, came on to the radio and asked if I was going to bale out. By this time it was too late and I was already starting the final approach and had pumped down both wheels and flaps. Although the smoke had died away quite a bit I was far from happy, but it was good to see two beautifully sited fire engines converging on me as I touched down. They started to throw foam at me as I was completing my landing roll but the operators had never been given instructions in deflection shooting – while they were aiming at the engine, they managed to hit me, so after stopping ten yards from the spot where I had started my take-off, I got out looking rather like a snowman.

Later in the evening Januszewicz went off with the Canadians in a machine he had borrowed from No. 1 Squadron; they got into combat with some Messerschmitt 109s and 110s. Januszewicz got one probable, but was himself shot down, fortunately without being wounded. Altogether it had been an expensive day and 303 Squadron ended the day with only two of the eighteen aircraft with which it had started. Happily no one was killed although several had been wounded and burned. It reflects great credit upon those who were responsible for the supply of replacements and upon the Air Transport Auxiliary who delivered them, that, by ten o'clock the following morning, the Squadron was again up to strength and fully operational.

Although we had been hard hit there was also the credit side to be considered; the squadron had inflicted more damage on the Germans than it had itself suffered, but for my part I felt that I was still in the red, as I had not contributed one 'confirmable' hit to the score of the squadron. Instead, I had delivered it one very unserviceable aeroplane with an engine that had two connecting rods stuck through the side of the crankcase, the cause of the fire, and no cowling on the front end – otherwise the airframe was all right!

As a result of all three British officers having been knocked out in the course of one day, it was decided that, henceforth, only one

British officer was to fly with the squadron at a time and he must, of course, always be the leader. This had two results: one was that it reduced the individual's opportunities of increasing his personal bag; but at the same time it reduced the chances of his being killed, allowed him time to analyse what was going on, and I think, form a more balanced view of the air fighting as a whole than many others who did not have time to regard the matter dispassionately.

The day following that upon which the squadron had lost so many aircraft was again an active one. The squadron was scrambled to intercept a large raid and was led by Atholl Forbes whilst I was left to sit on the ground and wait for the next piece of activity. They successfully intercepted the raid and attacked with their usual aggressiveness which resulted in the destruction of fourteen enemy aircraft and the probable destruction of another four, but Dasziewski and Lapkowski of 'B' Flight were badly wounded and Pisarek had to abandon his aircraft; Forbes himself was quite badly wounded in the leg – I had to help him out of the cockpit on his return and then take his place at Readiness with the squadron.

In the evening we were scrambled after a raid that turned back. It was probably a 'spoof' raid to get our fighters into the air but, in any case, we saw no sign of it. After being rather aimlessly vectored about and foolishly put up to 28,000 feet where a Hurricane was no match for a 109, we were recalled to base. On the way home, it was just about dusk, I could see the fires in London that the *Luftwaffe* had started on this, their first raid on London itself. I don't think I have ever been so angry and I found myself beating my fists against the sides of the cockpit in a fury. It was a strange experience, I had not realised that I could feel so deeply, but at that moment I would have butchered any German I could lay my hands on.

That night I looked at the red glow over London and brooded – I was beginning to understand the attitude of the Poles.

9 September was quiet and nothing happened until about five o'clock when we were ordered off in company with No. 1 Canadian. At first we saw nothing but Spitfires and 109s high above us and I thought that it was to be another abortive sortie, but just then there appeared a formation of about forty or fifty bombers with a 109 escort heading south-east towards France. They were in a shallow dive and moving fast so I picked on a Ju88 and gave chase. It took some little

time to accelerate so I pulled the boost over-ride plug and opened
the throttle wide. Very slowly I began to gain on the German but, at
the same time, I could see one of the 109 escort fighters diving down
after me. I kept on in the hope of catching the Junkers before the 109
caught me, but it looked very much as though I was going to lose
the race; I was on the point of breaking away as the 109 was getting
uncomfortably close when a Hurricane flashed across in front of the
109 and forced its pilot to pull up. As the Hurricane climbed above me
to reposition itself I recognised Henneberg's machine and so, with him
as my protector, I carried on after the Junkers and opened fire from
400 yards while Henneberg repeatedly chased the Messerschmitt off
my tail. After two bursts the starboard engine of the 88 burst into flame
and the aircraft rolled over and dived into cloud. I followed the trail
of black smoke hoping it would guide me to the 88 under the clouds
where I could finish it off but, on breaking cloud, I found myself over
the Channel and not a sign of a German machine.

The light was poor so I set off towards the French coast hoping
that I might find the damaged bomber when, quite unexpectedly, I
saw a twin-engined aircraft that, at first looked like a Hampden. I
could not think what a Hampden would be doing over the Channel
so I approached it rather cautiously to make a positive identification.
As I got closer it began to look less familiar and then its rear gunner
opened fire so, even though it was not the Ju88 I was looking for,
I immediately attacked. It was quite fascinating and made a pretty
sight in the gloom watching my tracer sail gracefully towards the
German while at the same time his came streaming back at me
like a string of gleaming red beads. After my third burst the enemy
made a sharp turn to port and the silhouette it presented was that
of a 110. I can remember the picture it made so terribly clearly, it
was like a picture out of a book on air firing – 'At this angle place
your sights there and FIRE!' which is precisely what I did and
his starboard engine flew to bits. He was obviously badly hit and
turned back towards England while I flew alongside but out of
range of the rear gunner just in case he was still alive and active. As
I followed the stricken machine smoky fingers streamed past on my
port side, I did a fast turn and found a 109 intent on evening the
score. Fortunately I could out-turn him easily at this low altitude
and got two bursts into him after which he quickly disengaged and

flew off towards France. Although I think I hit him I could not be sure as light was so bad.

By this time the 110 was getting very low and the smoke from its starboard motor was getting thicker and thicker, finally, about ten miles from Dungeness, it hit the water and exploded. I came down low and could see the twin tail sticking out of the water and what appeared to be an empty dinghy floating nearby, but of the crew I could see nothing at all.

This was my first confirmed victory and I flew home beside myself with excitement and a sense of achievement. On landing and taxiing in to the dispersal the usual greeting was afforded me when it was seen that my guns had been fired. I waved back confirmation of success in the boxers' traditional style and then, happening to look out to my left, I was just in time to see the C-in-C, Air Marshal 'Stuffy' Dowding, and the Station Commander ducking wildly to avoid having their heads taken off by my wingtip! Years later I reminded Lord Dowding of the occasion and told him that it had given me the opportunity of saying that I was probably the only fighter pilot in the Battle of Britain to whom the C-in-C bowed as he passed. He rather took the wind out of my sails by saying that he remembered the incident well and that he could think of 'no more noble cause in which to bow!'

I still had a shock to come, however; I thanked Henneberg for 'keeping that Hun off my tail' and he really jolted me when he replied: 'Not *one* Messerschmitt – *six*!'

In the battle my number two, Zumbach, got a 109 destroyed and one probable while Frantisek shot down a Heinkel 111 and probably destroyed a 109 – but he also got a bullet through his radiator and had to land near Brighton. He was particularly pleased because he had been given a bar of chocolate by a bystander as he waited at the station for a train back to base.

On 11 September we suffered our first fatalities when, in a battle over Horsham, Flying Officer Cebrzynski and Sergeant Wojtowicz were killed. It was strange really, as Cebrzynski knew he would be killed and he told me quite dispassionately only two days before that he would not survive long enough to see the end of the month. He was not morbid about it, he was just stating a fact which he accepted and merely wondered vaguely when it might be.

Sergeant Wojtowicz became separated from his flight and fought a long drawn out battle with six 109s single-handed and managed to shoot down two of his opponents before he himself was shot down near Westerham in Kent, not far from the Prime Minister's home. The fight came down to quite low altitude and was clearly witnessed from the ground. A very gallant young man, Sergeant Wojtowicz, who, because he was a foreigner, we could not recommend for our only posthumous decoration, the Victoria Cross. Later his own Government awarded him the Polish equivalent, the *Virtuti Militari* – which is, I believe, the oldest military decoration in Europe.

The next three days were fairly quiet but then came the culminating point of the whole of the Battle of Britain, 15 September, a Sunday!

I led the first scramble of the day in company with 229 Squadron, which had replaced No. 1 a few days previously. We were vectored towards the south-east and when we arrived over the area to the south of Croydon No. 229, which was the leading Squadron, started a gentle turn to starboard. At the same time I saw a large formation of enemy aircraft approaching from the south which put us in a perfect position for a head-on attack. I waited for the Wing Leader to attack the bombers with 229 Squadron while I prepared to give him protection from the German fighter escort. It suddenly dawned on me that he had not seen the enemy as he continued his turn away from them and here we experienced one of those incidents which indicated just how impractical the wing theory was under the circumstances obtaining at the time.

At this point perhaps I had best make my position quite clear regarding the wing theory and why I opposed it. No one would have been happier than I if we could have completely overwhelmed the German formations, but it was quite impossible to do so at this time and there were many reasons why.

First and foremost, of course, was the fact that we did not have a sufficient number of fighter aircraft and many a time individual flights, usually of six aircraft each, were scrambled separately in order to ensure that as many as possible of the raids received some attention.

Although there were more fighter aircraft in the adjoining Groups full use of these could not be made because of the distance they were based away from the usual combat area over Kent, Surrey and Sussex. Also the amount of warning we in 11 Group received of an approaching raid was generally insufficient to enable a two or three squadron wing to make an interception as can be appreciated when it is realised that, at full strength, a squadron operated twelve aircraft: a formation of twenty-four to thirty-six fighters therefore took some assembling and manoeuvring.

These, however, were by no means the only problems and the following was perhaps the worst of the lot – the appalling communication system. Despite the magnificent work that had been done in the development of Radio Direction Finding equipment, later to become known as RADAR, the High Frequency radio communication equipment with which nearly all the fighter squadrons were equipped was so bad that the full benefit of the RDF was never realised during the battle.

This particular sortie to which I have been referring provided a perfect example of this. We, No. 303 Squadron, were equipped with H/F radio communication equipment as was No. 229 Squadron but the two squadrons were on different frequencies and while we could both speak to the Controller in the Operations Room and receive messages from him we could not speak to one another! In this instance, when it became evident to me that John Banham, leading 229, had not seen the German formation I tried to relay a message to him via the Controller but he could not understand me as we were just at about the extreme range of the radio which was only about forty miles!

I feel that I should also make it clear that the radio frequencies upon which the radios would operate were set on the ground by Wireless Mechanics and the sets could not be readjusted in the air even if the pilot did know how to do it.

In this instance I had less than one minute in which to make up my mind as to what action I must take if this enemy formation was not to get away scot-free. I realised that it was hopeless endeavouring to get 229 into action at this stage so I sent down three sections of my squadron, nine aircraft, to attack the bombers while I and my section went for the fightcrs. By this time we were, unfortunately, in nowhere near as good a position and the bombers were already dropping their bombs.

As there were about fifty enemy fighters, we three Hurricanes could not do very much except interfere with their attempts to go to the help of their charges, so our combat – while fast and furious – was still indecisive. Zumbach and I both got a lot of smoke out of a couple of 109s but the pace was too fast for us to see what happened to them.

The wild mêlée suddenly came to an end and the only enemy machines to be seen were away in the distance heading for France. Amazingly none of us three had received so much as one bullet in our aircraft, so we went off on a patrol of the south coast where we turned westward over the Rye area. As we completed the turn. I just caught a glimpse of two 109s diving down on our starboard quarter. Mike Feric, my number three, also saw them and whirled to meet them, firing as he did so, but at the same moment his own aircraft was hit. I dived after the other which had overshot its attack. As I followed, the German rolled on to his back just before I opened fire and then rolled back again and on round until he was inverted again, then once more he rolled right side up and I saw a large piece of the aircraft come off and spin away over the top of my aircraft. We were both diving almost vertically by this time and he was outdistancing me, so I ceased fire and waited to catch him as he pulled out of the dive. To my surprise the aircraft dived straight into the sea just a few hundred yards off the tip of Dungeness; there was a vivid flash as it hit, a large cloud of black smoke billowed up and the petrol continued to blaze upon the surface of the water.

I was told later by the Intelligence Officer that the large piece that had nearly hit my aircraft was the pilot who had baled out but whose parachute had failed to open. He was found lying dead on the beach at Dungeness.

A few days later Zumbach, Feric and I were scrambled after one enemy aircraft that was reported at 15,000 feet. We had a long climb through cloud before breaking out at 12,000 feet; the cloud formation was unusual – a flat carpet at this height, but with large cumulo-nimbus towering through and above it with an overcast of very high cirrus. We were given various vectors by the Controller but saw nothing except four anti-aircraft shells that burst some little way ahead of us so I presumed that we must be over London. Finally I was given a vector that would have taken us straight into one of the huge thunderclouds so I called the Controller and tried to give him the hint that this vector was no good. He went on pushing it for a time and sounded as though he was getting angry. Suddenly he gave me another vector that took us eastward; we swept on over the undulating cloud surface that had the appearance of a roll of soft fleece and made a perfect interception on two Spitfires. They were probably chasing the same aircraft as we were.

By now we were out of R/T range and my mental navigation told me we were well to the east of London and probably over the Thames Estuary, so I decided to make a cautious descent. After what seemed an age we broke cloud at about 1,000 feet over water; with my two wingmen tucked in tightly I flew westward and before long I could see land to starboard, but the weather was so murky I could not distinguish any features. Then I saw more land to port and I was reasonably certain that this was the Thames. This was almost immediately confirmed as suddenly I saw a number of close-hauled balloons just clear of the clouds. I didn't like this at all and did a very gentle turn back towards the east and now found I was right in the middle of the barrage. Despite my previous experience I had no wish to hit a cable at 1,000 feet in a Hurricane! All I could do was to hope that we would continue to be lucky. I led my section along the northern shore of the estuary until I picked up some landmarks which I recognised and from there began to map-read our way home.

When about fifteen miles from base I called up the Controller again, we had been out of contact for the best part of half an hour, and his immediate reaction was, 'Bandit, ten miles ahead of you, Angels one-five.'

'Good, he can stay there,' I replied. 'I am at Angels one half!'

Back he came, 'Apany Red Leader, increase Angels at once!'

I replied: 'Apany Red Leader to Garta – to hell with that, I'm nearly out of fuel and you've already nearly had me into the balloons in this filthy weather so I'm coming home!'

On landing and getting into the Dispersal Hut I was called to the telephone and subjected to a terrific tirade from the Controller – a certain Squadron Leader who never flew on operations – principally because I had compromised the secret of our weather conditions to the enemy. He would not listen to any explanation so I hung up – I would very much have liked to go along to the Operations Room and clouted him. He hadn't been wandering around in the murk, lost and out of radio contact – and as for compromising the secrecy of the weather conditions I couldn't understand his stupidity! Aside from the fact that, if he had not been able to hear me, it was very unlikely that the Germans would, if there was an enemy reconnaissance aircraft over England, then its crew would know just as much about the weather as I did.

The next day was fine and all three squadrons were sent off as a wing with myself leading. There was very little activity and we stayed on our patrol line and watched a number of small formations of 109s that were scattered about above us. Every now and then they would start down as though to attack but always pulled up immediately we turned towards them. Then, for no apparent reason, one 109 dived right across my nose and to help him on his way I fired a short burst at him. He immediately went into an almost vertical dive and I followed waiting for him to pull out so that I could cut the corner and finish him off. He pulled out at about 4,000 feet and I was able to catch him easily and opened fire at fifty yards.

My first burst riddled his radiators and a cloud of glycol enveloped my aircraft and splattered over my windscreen. The smell was so strong that I thought for a moment that my own engine had a glycol leak and I pulled out to one side. I saw then that it was the 109 only that was spewing forth the coolant so I commenced another attack and, this time, shot away part of the tailplane and pulled up on the other side of him. All this time the pilot had taken no evasive action whatever and I did not know whether he was dead or not. He just kept straight on towards the sea although he must have known that he could not hope to cross the Channel as he had been at least six miles inland from our coast when I first hit him. Although there were any number of fields in which he could have crash-landed he stubbornly kept on.

I kept attacking and shooting various pieces off the aircraft including the canopy and, finally, when almost half way across the Channel, a large piece of engine cowling. At this point I was getting exasperated and pulled up well above him and started a quarter attack to administer the *coup de grace*. I could see him sitting rigidly in the cockpit hanging on to the control column and still flying straight and level but, as I started my dive, his engine stopped and he looked up at me, rolled the aircraft on to its back and appeared from behind the tail, looking for all the world like a rag doll that had been thrown out. The 109 dived straight into the sea, while he, apparently unhurt, drifted down in his parachute. I circled round him a couple of times and felt it might be kinder to shoot him as he had one hell of a long swim, but I could not bring myself to do it.

Without waiting for him to hit the water I turned for home. As I approached Dungeness I saw an aircraft low over the water and about five miles off shore. I flew towards it to investigate. It was with some surprise that I discovered it was a German machine – just what type I have never been absolutely sure, but from the recognition manuals it most closely resembled a Focke-Wulf 158 – although I can't imagine what such a machine would have been doing there unless it was somehow connected with an air-sea rescue system. At any rate, it had large black crosses on it and that made it fair game. I immediately attacked, my first burst splattering around the rear cockpit, but I got no return fire so I had probably killed the rear gunner. On my second attack only a few bullets were left and my guns stopped almost immediately after I pressed the gun button. To my disgust I could do nothing but watch as the German headed towards France as fast as he could go.

The Poles were fed up with me when I admitted that I could not bring myself to shoot the chap in the parachute and they reminded me of events earlier in the month when we were told that one or two pilots of No. 1 Squadron had baled out and had then been shot by German fighters. At the time the Poles had asked me if it was true that this was happening. I had to tell them that, as far as I knew, it was, at which they asked, 'Oh, can we?' I explained that, distasteful as it was, the Germans were within their rights in shooting our pilots over this country and that, if one of us shot down a German aircraft over France and the pilot baled out, then we were quite entitled to shoot him. But this was not so over England as, aside from anything else, he would be out of the war and might even be a very useful source of information for us. They thought about this for a bit and then said: 'Yes, we understand – but what if he is over the Channel?' – to which I had jokingly replied: 'Well, you can't let the poor bugger drown, can you?' This remark was quite seriously thrown in my teeth when they heard about the 109 pilot I had just shot down. There was no doubt about it, the Poles were playing the game for keeps far more than we were.

On 26 September the Squadron was honoured by a visit from
His Majesty, King George VI, to whom the pilots were presented.
He very graciously signed the carefully kept history book of the
squadron on the page adjacent to that upon which I had done a
drawing introducing the British phase of the history. He was very
complimentary about the Squadron's record and the pilots were
thrilled. In the middle of the afternoon of the next day 'A' Flight
was scrambled with myself leading. Almost immediately after take-
off I could see the enemy formations approaching. London and the
anti-aircraft bursts were thick amongst them. We could not intercept
them before they got to London as they were well above us but as
they turned for home they started a shallow dive to increase their
speed. I levelled off and took up a course to intercept them as they
came lower.

The formation I picked on was one of Ju88s and as I chased them
I noticed a lone Heinkel being attacked by a single Spitfire; as I
gradually overhauled the 88s I kept a fascinated eye on this combat
and before long I noticed a dull red glow in the belly of the Heinkel
but, strangely enough, very little smoke. The Spitfire made another
pass and a little black figure appeared behind the tail of the Heinkel
and a parachute blossomed forth while the bomber steepened its
dive, the glow growing brighter and then, quite without warning,
the German machine exploded with such violence that I think the
bombs must still have been aboard. There was nothing left but tiny
flaming pieces falling to the ground.

By this time I had caught up with the 88s and manoeuvred into
position under the tail of one of them while still some miles from the
south coast. I could see the rear gun pointing upwards and I think the
gunner must have been watching two Spitfires that were overhead.
I got to within thirty yards before he saw me. Then his gun came
down and I found myself looking straight up the barrel. I crouched
behind the armoured windscreen as his bullets zipped all round the
cockpit; oddly enough, I could not help thinking how closely it
resembled the high pressure jet of a garden hose. This fantasy was
rapidly dispelled by a loud bang beside my head as a bullet crashed
through the canopy. I opened fire with a very short burst directly at
the gunner who, poor devil, had no armour plate and only one gun
to my eight. That one short burst was enough to kill him and I saw

him slump over his gun. With the gunner disposed of, I then got on with finishing off the aircraft relatively undisturbed.

I dropped back to about 50 yards and concentrated on the starboard engine which, after a longish burst, threw off chunks of cowling and bits of engine and stopped dead. Although I had oil on the windscreen and the front of my aeroplane, none of the bits of the enemy machine hit me. I then opened up on the port engine, which burst into flames, the smoke enveloping my aircraft and momentarily blinding me.

Although the Junkers was doomed, I was anxious to set the whole aircraft alight and fired directly into the fuselage. Just as I was firing a very long burst, a Hurricane suddenly shot between us going almost vertically upwards – where he came from and what happened to him I have no idea but he must have collected some of my bullets. I noticed that he pulled away to the right, but I was now really concentrating on the Junkers so I do not know whether he had been badly hit or not.

By this time we were getting very low and I was afraid that the German was going to crash into the houses at Bexhill which we were approaching. As we got to the outskirts I fired another long burst into it and then, to my horror, my eyes focused beyond it and I saw a whole group of people standing watching. I had the ghastly thought that I must have fired straight into them. I discovered later, to my relief, that no one was hit, but how they escaped I have never been able to understand.

The German carried straight on, pulled up over the buildings on the front and went into the sea about a hundred yards out. The machine skipped like a flat stone twice and then sank – I circled over the spot and up popped one man who turned out to be the pilot, the only member of the crew with any armour plate; the rest had all been killed.

As I climbed away to look for more business the whole south coast seemed to be swarming with our fighters, all looking for something to shoot at. All I could see of the enemy were a number of ominous looking streaks of oily black smoke where one after another of the raiders had gone down. Then, from nowhere, appeared a lone Dornier going as fast as he could, straight through the screen of fighters. It reminded me of the comedian who, in the middle of an act, appears from the wings, walks quickly across the stage and into the opposite wings, while the people on stage do a quick double take, shrug their shoulders and carry on. In this instance the double take resulted in two fighters reacting in such a manner that they seemed literally to leap on to the Dornier and claw it from the sky, sending it crashing into the sea in flames.

When I got back to Northolt I went over my machine very carefully and found, to my surprise, that despite the amount of tracer that the unfortunate rear gunner had sent in my direction only two bullets had hit my aircraft, one through the hood and the other right on the tip of the propeller! These were to be the only bullets that ever hit my machine during my whole time on operations.

Although there had been only six of us on this particular sortie we had succeeded in destroying four enemy aircraft for no losses which – in the words of the great Mannock of First World War fame – is 'good arithmetic'.

A couple of days later we were scrambled in company with No. 1 Canadian and after some vectoring around we saw, in the distance, quite a large number of enemy aircraft stepped up with the lower aircraft in what appeared to be the usual bomber formation. The role of 303 was to attack the bombers while No. 1 Canadian was to provide protection from the German fighter escort. Consequently, while keeping an eye on the fighters above us, I opened the throttle and started a wide curving attack on what I had taken to be the bomber formation. In doing so I outdistanced my own squadron and, at the same time, failed to see that the Canadians had turned away to meet an attack from some more German fighters which I had not seen. The leader of the squadron, being on a different frequency, could not tell me what he was doing and the Poles, being somewhat excited, forgot their English and could not tell me either. It came as a distinct shock, therefore, when just as I was closing with the enemy, which I had now recognised as 109s in an unusual formation, a stream of tracer bullets streaked past just above the top of my cockpit canopy. I immediately broke right; I did this as nine people out of ten – I am speaking of pilots, of course – will turn left if suddenly told to turn. An attacking pilot subconsciously expects his target to turn in that direction and when it doesn't he is, for a split second, upset. He does, of course, recover extremely rapidly but there is that split second of hesitation which can make all the difference between death and survival.

In this instance I discovered that I was all alone with a mass of enemy fighters; I could not dive away as they would easily catch me before I could reach cloud cover, which was many thousands of feet below. I had, therefore, no alternative but to stay and fight. I kept in a steep right-hand turn with enough rudder on to keep the machine skidding while various 109s attacked, though none succeeded in hitting me. When the tracer stopped flying past I straightened up. Four of the enemy passed close in front of me, I opened fire and the rearmost one went down with smoke pouring out of it. The Germans started to mill around above me while I circled, watched and waited and at this point the Controller called me and asked if I had engaged the enemy yet! I replied, 'No, but I think *they* are going to engage *me* at any moment and – here they come!'

In a way I suppose I had the advantage of being in a position where I could fire at anything that came past, whilst they had to take care not to hit one another. In any case I managed to get a good burst into another 109 from fifty yards on this attack and it disappeared in a bright sheet of flame. The Germans again pulled away and I continued to circle hoping that they would get short of fuel and go home. Then some of them started another attack and I turned to meet them; as I did so the leader pulled up and I rolled underneath him, reversing my turn in a manner similar to what became known as the 'Derry Turn' after the war, and I managed to fire into his belly; I saw some strikes but no other results. With this they climbed away, formed up and headed for France. I was by this time in a cold fury and all thought of personal danger had disappeared. I followed them hoping that some of them would return and renew the contest. I could not climb up to them but as I followed I counted thirty-eight aircraft in the formation so I must have been up against forty; probably the reason I survived was that they kept getting in one another's way!

I left them somewhere about mid-Channel and came down to the top of the cloud where I met a lone 109 heading for home, I fired at it but it dived away into cloud and I lost it, which was probably as well as I was practically out of ammunition. When I got back to Northolt the Station Commander, Stanley Vincent, who had heard my remark on the R/T about the attack coming, was very complimentary indeed as was Ronald Kellett. I tried to explain that I had no idea that I was alone when I went into the attack and that I wasn't really foolhardy enough to take on that lot on my own. They said that wasn't the point, it was what I did when I found myself in the spot that counted. Ten days later I was awarded the Distinguished Flying Cross for my leadership of the squadron and for this combat in particular. Although I flew again that day and on numerous other occasions, I did not personally succeed in destroying any more of the enemy while with the now famous 303 Squadron. Activity was dying out and it seemed that the Germans had at last realised the futility of their attacks. And then on 11 October we were moved north to Leconfield for a rest.

It was with a very proud record that No. 303 Squadron left Northolt, the place of its rebirth. In six hectic weeks, perhaps the most important in our history, the Squadron had destroyed 126 enemy aircraft for the loss of only 8 pilots killed, although a much greater number had suffered wounds of greater or less severity. It was a record unrivalled by any other squadron.

Frantisek had been, perhaps, the most outstandingly successful of all the pilots in the squadron, destroying 17 of the enemy in a little over a month. His death came as a great shock to us all – it was totally unexpected and even now we do not know what actually happened.

On 8 October, the squadron was ordered off and was given the usual vectoring around, but nothing was seen or encountered. Before long the squadron was recalled to base. As we approached Northolt, we closed up into a tight formation of four vics of three in line astern from which we normally did a break over the airfield and put the sections into echelon prior to landing. On this occasion we were letting down in a shallow dive and were just over the Staines Reservoirs when Frantisek, who was in the rear section, pulled out and flew alongside the squadron. Someone called him on the R/T and told him to get back into formation at which he turned slowly away to the east and disappeared. Some time later we heard that he had crashed near Sutton and was dead when the rescuers got to the wreckage. He was seen approaching an open space apparently trying to make a forced-landing when suddenly his aircraft flicked on to its back and dived into the ground. We never did find out why this happened as we had not been in action and there were no bullet holes in either him or the aeroplane. It was not only a very great loss, it was a very worrying one.

Almost as soon as we arrived at Leconfield we began to receive a number of replacements for those who had been killed or wounded and also for a number who were being posted to Operational Training Units to pass on to others the benefit of their experience. This meant quite an extensive training programme for the newcomers and, in Ronald Kellett's absence, I worked with Squadron Leader Urbanowicz who had taken over as Polish CO when Krasnodemski was shot down. And then came a telephone call to inform me that I had been given command of No. 92 Squadron at Biggin Hill and that I was to report as soon as I possibly could.

Although I was sorry to leave the Polish Squadron, I was very pleased with my promotion and the fact that I would have command of my own squadron. Atholl Forbes had already been given command of 66 Squadron which was also at Biggin Hill.

Before I left, the squadron gave me a most magnificent party in the Mess at Leconfield and, at the same time, informed me that I had been awarded a Polish decoration; they presented me with the ribbon of the *Krzyz Walecznych* and insisted that I have it sewn on my tunic immediately. The party was quite fantastic, but I managed to hold my own and at three o'clock in the morning the only two left on their feet were Johnny Zumbach, my number two, and myself – and I saw him to bed! This feat boosted my reputation with the Poles quite considerably.

The next day I set off for Biggin Hill and arrived there just at tea-time. The Mess Sergeant pointed out the officers of my new squadron who were all sitting together at one table so I joined them without telling them who I was. My first impressions were not favourable and their general attitude and lack of manners indicated a lack of control and discipline. I began to realise that I was probably going to have my hands full – and how right I was.

A formation of Avro Tutor primary training aircraft, 1935.

A Junkers 88 shot down near Meaux in France, 1940.

Hawker Fury advanced trainer.

Bristol Bulldog fighters.

The Gloster Gauntlet which failed to make a formation landing – the pilot was unhurt.

The display team of Gloster Gauntlets led by 'Broadie' Broadhurst, 1936.

Johnny Kent flies a 19 Squadron Gauntlet, Duxford, 1936.

A Queen Wasp which crashed after a catapult launch, Farnborough, 1938. The pilot was only slightly injured.

Johnny Kent makes his first landing with the twin-engined Boulton and Paul Overstrand, Farnborough, 1938.

Johnny Kent in his photo-reconnaissance Spitfire with special streamlined canopy, at Heston, 1940.

Flying Officer Henneberg (left), Johnny Kent and Flight Lieutenant Pisarek, No. 303 Kosciusko Squadron, October 1940.

No. 92 East India Squadron with a Spitfire behind, Manston, 1941.

Johnny Kent flies a Spitfire from Farnborough as Chief Test Pilot after the war.

Flying test bed – the Nene Lancastrian with two Merlin piston engines and two Nene jets, 1948.

The Avro Delta at Farnborough, 1950.

Johnny Kent at the controls of a 1911 Deperdussin from the Shuttleworth Trust, White Waltham, 1949.

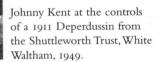

The first Hawker Hunter at Tangmere, 1955.

6

Squadron Commander

I soon discovered that 92 Squadron, my new command, had not only lost four Commanding Officers, three of them in the past month, but the total losses had been more than double those of 303 Squadron in the same period. Not unnaturally morale was at a pretty low ebb, which was reflected in the inevitable lack of discipline resulting from the fact that the squadron had been virtually leaderless.

The first CO had been an Auxiliary Air Force Officer, Roger Bushell, who had been shot down and taken prisoner at Dunkirk. He later distinguished himself as a leader of the POWs in their resistance to the Germans. He also played a major part in their many escapes, culminating in the famous mass escape from Stalag Luft III, for which effort he was murdered by the Germans. Squadron Leader 'Sandy' Sanders then assumed command and remained as CO until he was rather badly burned in an accident not long after the squadron arrived at Biggin Hill from South Wales. He was succeeded by Squadron Leader Lister who lasted two days, being shot down on both of them – he was most unfortunate as he arrived at the squadron in a supernumerary capacity to get some fighter experience before being given command of a squadron; before he had managed to get any experience Sandy met with his accident and Lister found himself the boss. It was a very rough introduction to the fighter world. A few days after Lister had been put out of action, command was taken by Squadron Leader Maclachlan but, within a week, he too was shot down and wounded. It was then intended to promote the senior Flight Commander, Flight Lieutenant Brian Kingcome, and put him in command but, before this recommendation got beyond Group Headquarters he also had been shot down – he maintained, by Spitfires!

The upshot of all this was that I was appointed to take over a disorganized, undisciplined and demoralised collection of first class material. Although they had suffered terrific casualties they had also inflicted severe losses upon the enemy and, under the circumstances, they felt they knew far more about air fighting than any Squadron Leader who might occupy the chair of office for a day or two.

The Station Commander, Group Captain Dick Grice, who really was a first class commander, told me that the Air Officer Commanding had decided to move No. 92 to the north for a well-earned rest. I argued that if this was done, the squadron would be finished and I begged to be allowed to keep it at Biggin as that would give me the chance I needed to get it into shape – while the stigma of having 'had it' could not be attached to it. I pointed out that the activity of the *Luftwaffe* was decreasing and I felt that it was unlikely to increase again until the spring. He saw my point of view and agreed with it; he also managed to persuade the AOC to agree, for which I have always been extremely grateful.

The remainder of the month was, on the whole, very quiet and I did not myself make any contact with the enemy. One Flight led by Flight Lieutenant Villa tangled with some 110s one evening and shot down several of them.

Although 31 October was later chosen as the date upon which the Battle of Britain came to an end, we taking part noticed no change in the situation when Friday 1 November arrived. It came as no surprise then when the telephone orderly stuck his head round the corner and yelled: 'Garrick Squadron – scramble base – Angels one-five!' and off we went climbing, on fresh orders from the Controller, towards Dover.

After a lot of vectoring about and being told that the raid consisted of fifty Junkers, although no height could be given, I caught sight of a flash of yellow and then saw a number of yellow-nosed 109s just above cloud near Rochester, and about 6,000 feet below us – an unusual situation. I immediately gave 'Tally ho!' to the Operations Room and told the squadron that we were going in to attack. We closed in very rapidly, I opened fire from 150 yards and could see my De Wilde ammunition bursting all around the cockpit of the rearmost 109. The pilot immediately started to take violent evasive action and I had difficulty staying with him. Out of the corner of my eye, I saw another aircraft within feet of me and closing fast, and I had to pull up to avoid a collision. The German I had attacked dived away into cloud and I followed breaking out at about 2,000 feet, but could not at first see my man. Suddenly I spotted a 109 about 1,000 feet below streaking eastwards and I am fairly certain that it was the one that I had already hit. I managed to catch up with him and after another burst he dived into the water not far from Whitstable.

I climbed back through cloud, saw three 109s pop up out of cloud some two or three miles to the south so I gave chase and was gaining on them when, right in front of me and between me and the German aircraft, burst a lot of our own anti-aircraft shells! I rapidly changed direction and so lost the chance of catching the enemy machines – I was furious but, of course, the gunners were firing blind and could not know that one of their targets was British.

On returning to base I found that Flying Officers Holland and Bartley had each destroyed a 109 while Pilot Officers Saunders and Kinder, being in the rear section, had seen, through a gap in the clouds, a number of bomb bursts in the water. They had, therefore, ignored the fighters and gone on down to find the fifty Junkers, Stukas, at about 1,500 feet. It was a great surprise as these aircraft had suffered such heavy losses early on that they had not been seen for many weeks. As soon as they saw the Spitfires they jettisoned their bombs and turned for home, but Saunders and Kinder got one each in flames. Immediately afterwards Saunders was attacked and shot down, crash-landing at Eastchurch. Although a bullet had creased his helmet and gone through his goggles he was unhurt.

Kinder, a hefty New Zealander, was shooting at a second Stuka when he too was attacked. A few days later I received a letter from him written in hospital and I think it is one of the most perfect examples of unwitting understatement I have ever come across. The purpose of the letter was to lay claim to one Stuka destroyed and one probably destroyed and he followed up with a description of what had happened.

I was firing at the second Ju87 [he wrote], which began to smoke heavily at the starboard wing root, but at this point my attention was distracted by a cannon shell which entered the left wing and blew the end off. I turned and chased the 109 that had hit me and I last saw it going down smoking near Herne Bay. I did not feel very well so I decided to return to Biggin, but after a while I felt worse so I landed in a field, I regret to say, with my undercarriage retracted. After a little while I felt better so I phoned the nearest RAF Station and they came and collected me from the farmhouse from which I had phoned.

'Tiny' Kinder was not the sort of man to try to impress me with his coolness, he was just stating plain facts. He did not mention, because to him it had no bearing on the matter, that the shell that 'blew the end off' had also badly wounded him in the left arm and leg. Despite this he clamped his arm on to his leg in an effort to stop the bleeding in both, turned his partly disabled aircraft and succeeded in out-manoeuvring the German and, I was able to establish later, shot it down. It was no wonder that he 'felt ill' but again he did not mention that he had had to walk nearly a mile from where he had landed to the farmhouse. A remarkable person.

In the afternoon we were on patrol when I experienced the first really serious result of the squadron's losses and lack of leadership. There were a number of small formations of 109s high above us over the south coast and every now and then one or two of them would start to dive towards us but I always turned to meet them head-on and they would break off their attack. For some reason the German pilots seemed to loathe head-on attacks and would invariably break away if one turned and flew straight at them – later on in the war, they overcame this and carried out some very daring head-on attacks, particularly against the American bomber formations.

On this occasion, after a number of these abortive passes had been made, I found that several of my pilots had broken formation and were heading for home. It was clearly a case of what was called '109-itis' and it was apparent that these pilots had lost all confidence in their ability to cope with the German fighters. I knew that this confidence had to be restored as rapidly as possible and the place to do it was in a combat area and not when on a so-called rest.

When we returned to our airfield I had all the pilots in and gave them a really good talking to and announced that if I had any more people breaking away – and by so doing exposing not only them-selves to attack but the rest of the squadron – I would not wait for the Germans to shoot down the offender but would do it myself. They all looked a bit glum and there was little doubt that they loathed my guts – I didn't care as I felt that they needed a bit of straight talking. Although they obviously disliked me, they were beginning to appreciate the fact that I was, after all, the first CO they had had who was more experienced in war than they were.

In the evening another patrol was carried out but the only signs of enemy that I saw were the big guns on Cap Gris Nez firing on Dover. The squadron stayed in nice tight formation but whether this was because of my tirade or the fact that there were no 109s in evidence I could not tell.

On returning from this last patrol we were greeted by the Squadron Intelligence Officer, Flight Lieutenant Tom Wiesse, the only Norwegian in the RAF, who announced that in shooting down the 109 that morning I had brought the squadron score to a round hundred!

Our differences temporarily forgotten, we all decided that this needed celebrating, but as we were scheduled for Dawn Readiness the next day we felt it advisable to check with the Meteorological Office. They, at first, thought we were being frightfully keen and said that they were terribly sorry but there was no hope of our flying the next day as the weather would be far too bad. That, of course, was just what we wanted and preparations continued.

The usual ritual was observed and we all went down to the White Hart at Brasted, presided over by that inimitable pair, Kath and Teddy Preston. After a 'swing round' we returned to the Mess for dinner and the continuation of the party in which we were joined by a number of the pilots from the other two squadrons – No. 66, commanded by Atholl Forbes and No. 74 whose CO was another old friend, Sailor Malan. After we had all drunk far more than was good for us we all retired to bed. I, fortunately, had a room in the Mess but the others had to drive about six miles to the big country house that served as our dispersed Mess. At this time the pilots were not allowed to sleep on the airfield in case they were killed by bombs of which Biggin Hill had its fair share, both by day and night.

I slept like a log and the next thing I knew I was being shaken awake by my batman. I told him, rather roughly as I felt ghastly, to bog off and leave me alone. He protested that I was due at dispersal shortly as the Squadron was on Readiness. Impatiently I told him not to be a clot, the weather was far too bad. He replied rather quietly and, I like to think, sympathetically, 'It looks all right to me, sir!'

I pulled the black-out curtains back and – Oh, perfidious Met Officers – it was bright starlight – not a sign of a cloud anywhere.

Somehow I got dressed, shaved, downed a cup of coffee, felt sick at the sight of breakfast, left it and struggled down to the Dispersal and into my flying kit and then collapsed into a chair surrounded by eleven other sufferers, all hoping we would not die before being released at eight o'clock.

Once or twice the telephone rang and everyone groaned hoping against hope that it would not be Ops ordering a scramble. Providence was kind – until ten minutes before we were due to be released and then it came. The orderly took the call and yelled his all too familiar message 'Garrick Squadron, scramble base, Angels one-five!' It was cruel and how we got to our aircraft I do not know, but we did and were away well within the prescribed time.

As we climbed and were vectored about by the Controller one pilot after another called up to say that his oil pressure was low, his engine was running rough, even that the radio wasn't working. This, however, was no result of what became known as 'Battle Fatigue' – it was purely and simply the father and mother of all collective hangovers!

We had been airborne for perhaps forty minutes and had climbed to 27,000 feet on the Maidstone patrol line with only five of the original twelve left when I had a call from one of the stouter pilots to the effect that there was 'Anti-aircraft fire, ten o'clock below!' I glanced in the direction indicated and there, about 7,000 feet below us, were around sixty 109s – it was just at the time the Germans were sending over these fighters carrying bombs and I think this must have been such a raid with their escort fighters. We had the advantage of being in the sun and I was able to lead the squadron, or what was left of it, into a perfect astern attack without the enemy being aware of our presence.

I held my fire until I was about 150 yards from one of the rear pair of Messerschmitts and then let go with a long burst and the aircraft immediately dived straight down trailing a great cloud of smoke. I was travelling very fast and was likely to overshoot the other one of the pair, but by skidding my machine and throttling back I was able to lose speed, pass under the 109's tail and come into formation with it on the starboard side. I could see the pilot looking out to the left presumably to see what had happened to his late comrade but still flying straight and level. I could not help saying to myself 'What a stupid clot!' – by which time I had slowed down enough to get underneath him and give him a burst from about 100 yards. He immediately poured forth clouds of smoke in the midst of which I could see a flicker of flame, rolled on to his back and dived vertically. Both these aircraft were found outside Ashford in Kent within half a mile of each other.

The rest of the German formation dived for the coast and did not attempt to turn and fight, at least all but one. We chased after the fleeing Germans and I caught up with this one and attacked. I found that I had picked an old hand; instead of just running away he waited until I was very close and then suddenly broke to the right and into the sun. I momentarily lost sight of him but as he continued to turn he moved out of the glare of the sun and the contest developed into a tail-chase. As we came round full circle he repeated his manoeuvre but this time I pulled my sights through him and, although losing him under the nose of my aircraft, gave a short burst in the hopes that I might get some tracer near enough to him to frighten him into running for home. I misjudged my man, however, and he continued his tactics and, apparently had no intention of running at all but finally after the fourth or fifth circle I drew my sights through him again, gave a longish burst and was startled when he suddenly appeared from under my nose and we very nearly collided. I still have a very vivid mental picture of him looking up at me as we flashed past not twenty feet apart. I distinctly remember that he had his goggles up on his helmet and his oxygen mask in place.

I also recall the gashes along the side of the fuselage where my bullets had struck and the tail of the aircraft with practically no fabric left on it and a control cable streaming back with a small piece of metal whirling around on the end of it. It is one of those pictures of a split-seconds action that remains indelibly imprinted upon one's mind. I *did* not, in the heat of the moment, fully appreciate the significance of all this and was jubilant when I saw that my opponent was reversing his turn, a fatal move in a fight, and gave him one last burst from a 'fine quarter' into his left side. A thin trail of grey smoke appeared and the aircraft rolled quite slowly on to its back and started down. I immediately thought that he was getting away and followed with throttle wide open hoping to catch him as he levelled out.

The last time I glanced at the airspeed indicator it was registering something like 450mph but still the 109 outdistanced me and finally I lost it against the ground. While continuing my dive and waiting to see the grey plan-form of it as it pulled out I was startled to see a vivid red flash and a great cloud of jet black smoke appear as the machine hit the ground and exploded.

I came down low to see where the aircraft had struck but could see no sign of it, until I noticed some soldiers running across the fields and waving to me. Then I saw it, a gaping hole that looked just like a bomb crater and hundreds of little bits scattered around.

A few days later the Intelligence Officer told me that the pilot had been quite a highly decorated Major but it had not been possible to establish his identity. Apparently I had shot away his controls and he was on the point of baling out when my last burst killed him. This was deduced from the fact that his fighting harness was picked up undone and undamaged and the left half of his tunic was found with six bullet holes in it. Of the pilot himself they found very little, he was under the engine which was found thirty feet down in the ground; not surprising considering the aircraft had gone in vertically from about 16,000 feet.

Our operations became very tame as the time went on and consisted of numerous patrols but only one other contact with the enemy as far as I was concerned. On these patrols we came across numerous small formations of high-flying German fighters but we were never lucky enough to get above them and except on one occasion they only made feint attacks.

We had been scrambled and were climbing for height when I saw a formation of 109s a few thousand feet above and to my right. I turned and climbed as rapidly as possible in an endeavour to inter-cept them or to entice them to come down. At this point another squadron appeared above us, between us and the Germans. As they were Hurricanes I did not think they had much chance of catching the 109s and so continued climbing.

Suddenly, without any warning tracer bullets came streaming past my aircraft and just above my head. I yelled, 'Break!' to the squadron, doing so myself at the same instant and there followed the usual mix-up of aircraft all seemingly going in different directions. I could not get my sights on an enemy, but I saw one going down though I did not see who had bagged it. Then, as usual, it was all over and we made our separate ways back to Biggin.

On arrival I found that two were missing, however, it was not long before we received word that both pilots were unhurt but that their aircraft were pretty badly shot up and both had been forced to crash-land.

At this particular time we flew in sections of three aircraft in vic formation, each section keeping station in line astern. The rearmost vic acted as the defence section to protect the squadron from an astern attack and this was accomplished by the number two and three of the section weaving back and forth across and behind the squadron so that they could maintain a good lookout astern and counter any attack. This left the Squadron Leader free to concentrate upon the instructions given him by the Controller, search for the enemy and position his squadron. This type of formation was not ideal by any means, but it was manoeuvrable and facilitated the squadron leader's task of positioning his force for an attack. While this was a legitimate reason for using the formation against enemy bomber forces it certainly did not suit fighter versus fighter operations. At the same time we were still not at all certain that our role had changed permanently and that we had seen the last of the large daylight raids.

On this particular occasion only eleven aircraft had been available and, therefore, we had only one weaver. Whilst I was concentrating on the 109s I was hoping to intercept, four others had attacked from the rear – the one weaver, who had had quite a rough time during the preceding weeks, instead of turning into these four and splitting them up, which would have been by far the safest thing to do in any case, merely called: 'Garrick Squadron, Snappers behind!' and then half-rolled and dived away. Unfortunately nobody heard him and, consequently, the two rearmost aircraft were shot down.

In fact the Germans came off worst as two of the attacking four were destroyed, but this did not prevent me getting into a flaming temper and even more so a few days later when I met the squadron commander of the Hurricane squadron who had watched the whole thing and done nothing about it – despite the fact that it was a perfect set up to draw the higher 109s into battle. All he had had to do was to have turned over the top of my squadron, taken the four 109s head-on and, by turning tail to the upper formation, enticed them to attack. If they had done so I would have been in the ideal position to take them head-on. But, no – he just watched and thought it was a huge joke to see us get jumped. I advised him that it would probably be much healthier for him if he kept out of my way in the air as I could just possibly mistake him for a 109; in fact, it would be a pleasure to do so! At the time I really meant it, too.

But what really worried me was my own squadron and I took this opportunity of telling them exactly what I thought of them, what I proposed to do about it and what would happen to anyone who thought he knew better and disobeyed my orders. As it was evident that the whole Squadron was affected, I assembled all the senior NCOs, pilots and ground crew, and all the officers, and then let fly; firstly at the sergeants and dismissed them; next the flight sergeants and dismissed them; and so on right through to the flight commanders. By the time I had finished there was nobody who did not know just exactly where he stood.

This action made me even more unpopular and I am sure many dire threats were made behind my back, but nothing came of them and gradually it began to dawn on them all that the squadron had become more efficient and that perhaps my tirade had not been delivered simply because I was an unpleasant bastard but because I had done it for their own good. Bit by bit the ice began to thaw, as I knew it would.

After the intense activity had died down Air Marshal Dowding was succeeded as Commander-in-Chief by Air Marshal Sholto Douglas, and Air Vice-Marshal Park handed over No. 11 Group, which had borne the brunt of the Battle, to Air Vice-Marshal Leigh-Mallory from No. 12 Group. Both of the new commanders had been in favour of the wing formation during the Battle and both favoured a more offensive policy. It was now deemed possible to do this as the training schemes were beginning to produce a flow of pilots which was eventually to achieve vast proportions and the squadrons had all been brought up to strength. The terrific fighter production programme planned and set in motion by Lord Beaverbrook and his predecessors was also now getting into gear and there was no shortage of aircraft.

As the Battle had progressed it became increasingly apparent that the Germans were badly shaken by the fire-power of our fighters and they were frantically trying to protect their aircraft by armouring them. They, like some theorists in our own Air Force, had held the view that the bomber could outrun the fighter – a fatal mistake on both sides, although I think we learned our lesson first.

At any rate it was getting more difficult to shoot down the German machines and even the Dornier, which usually only needed one good burst, was standing up to some very heavy punishment. It became evident that the .303 machine gun was too light a weapon for the task. Earlier in the year one squadron of Spitfires had been armed with 20mm Hispano cannons but, for a variety of reasons, they had not proved successful and the pilots, fed up with the continual stoppages, cried out for a return to the .303 which was duly agreed.

Discussions were held at both Group and Command Headquarters at which the views of various Squadron Commanders and Staff Officers were expressed as to how best to meet the new problem of the armour on the German machines. For the most part the Squadron Commanders were in favour of the re-introduction of the cannons if they could be made reliable; I personally was quite certain that we must have cannon and must make them work. I was, perhaps, rather outspoken about this. Certain notable Squadron Commanders were, however, almost as outspoken against them and begged to be given more .303s.

The new C-in-C listened to all the arguments for and against cannon and then with his usual common sense approach to a problem decided to have a small number of Spitfires modified to take two Hispano cannons and four .303 machine guns. This gave us six seconds' fire with the cannons while retaining the seventeen seconds of the machine guns.

In order to get a good cross-section of opinion as unbiased as possible he had three of these modified aircraft allotted to four selected Squadrons. This was important, as it precluded the experience of one squadron, good or bad, unduly influencing the opinions of others. The *Luftwaffe* had a saying which was very true: 'If you have two pilots – you have got three opinions!' – which was just what the Air Marshal was trying to avoid.

Probably because I had spoken up so strongly for cannons, my squadron was one of those selected and in a very short time we received our modified Spitfire Is and set about making the cannons work. In this we were most successful and by far the greatest part of the credit for this must go to the Squadron Armament Officer, Warrant Officer Stewart, who worked like a slave to ensure that they were a success.

It was not very long after we received these aircraft that one of the flights was scrambled after a small force of 109s. The Flight Commander, 'Pancho' Villa, got to within 300 yards of one of the Germans and opened fire with his machine guns. Although he could see a number of strikes on the enemy aircraft, his fire was having no visible effect. He then remembered his cannons and, slipping his thumb on to the cannon button, gave a very short burst and was more than a little startled, as was everybody else, when the 109 exploded. As he described it, it looked just like an anti-aircraft shell bursting and there was nothing left but a cloud of black smoke and tiny pieces tumbling to the ground.

This success made us all the more enthusiastic and it was with satisfaction that I received a call from the C-in-C, Air Marshal Sir Sholto Douglas, the following day to congratulate the Squadron as a whole and the Armament Officer and pilot in particular on this demonstration of gun reliability and effectiveness. He asked me if I was still convinced that we really needed cannons and when I replied in the affirmative he asked if I felt cannons were sufficient or would mixed armament be better.

My reply was to the effect that, as I had stressed before, we must have cannon to combat effectively the renewed onslaught that we expected would commence in the spring but, as each cannon only carried sixty rounds in its magazine, giving a bare six seconds' fire, I was of the opinion that mixed armour was the answer as the .303 would still be useful in deflection shooting where the bullets could get past the armour plate into the vital parts of the aircraft. He said this was precisely his own thinking and, with that, he hung up.

A few days later I was most gratified to receive notification that 92 Squadron was to be re-equipped immediately with the latest Mark of Spitfire, the Vb, which carried the mixed armament I had advocated.

On Christmas Day accompanied by Sailor Malan and Atholl Forbes I drove over to Hornchurch to attend a conference being held by the new AOC, the purpose of which was to discuss an offensive operation scheduled for the following day when we hoped to catch the Germans while they were still feeling 'Christmassy'. The plan was to escort a few bombers over the Pas de Calais area to bomb some installations in the Foret de Guines and shoot up any enemy aircraft sighted in the air or on the ground. The role of the Biggin Hill squadrons was to sweep in behind the main force as they crossed the French coast on their way home and tackle any pursuing German fighters. The whole plan seemed somewhat at variance with the spirit of Christmas – but we were at war! I need have had no qualms as the weather put paid to the operation by producing thick fog that persisted for days on end; the first offensive operation to be mounted by Fighter Command since Dunkirk had, of necessity, to be postponed.

One of the achievements of the *Luftwaffe* during the early part of the Battle of Britain was effectively to deny us the use of Manston and Hawkinge airfields except as forward bases for particular operations and for the re-arming and refuelling of fighters. With the decrease in activity it was now decided to re-occupy them and we found that we had been chosen to do the first stint at Manston – which did not please us too much.

We moved into Manston early in January 1941 and found the accommodation to be rather on the rough side; many of the services were still out of order as a result of the pounding the Station had taken during the summer and autumn. It was wet, muddy and cold, and most of the time we were engaged on soul-destroying convoy patrol work covering shipping as it was shepherded through Bomb Alley past Dover and Ramsgate into the Thames Estuary. Altogether we were rather unhappy with the situation and the middle of February, when No. 74 Squadron was to relieve us, seemed a long way off.

On one of these patrols the formation leader was startled to see one of the ships explode; his first thought was that it must have struck a mine but then, to his amazement, he saw one lone Stuka low on the water heading for France. He and the other three dived to the attack and the German pilot, seeing the Spitfires after him, turned and made for Manston – presumably to give himself up, as he had no hope of survival in a fight.

The night before this episode some of the officers had been saying that if they brought down a German in one piece the thing to do would be to take him to the Mess and entertain him before bundling him off to a POW camp. I did not feel that there was any place for the chivalry displayed in the First World War and I gave the boys a little lecture on the reasons they were there, this boiled down to first defending the country and secondly to killing as many of the enemy as possible – and they had better get that firmly into their heads. They learned their lesson very well.

Having been on the first patrol of the morning, I had been back to the Mess for breakfast and was just returning to Dispersal when I heard gunfire. I stopped the car and got out to stare in amazement at the sight of one lone Stuka weaving madly in an attempt to avoid the attentions of four Spitfires. All five were coming towards me and it occurred to me that I was in the line of fire so I hid behind a vehicle that was handy. Then I saw a notice on it reading '100 Octane' – it was one of the refuelling bowsers. So I darted back to my car! Just as I reached it the Stuka reached the edge of the airfield almost directly above me at about a hundred feet. Here he was headed off by one of the Spitfires and I could clearly see both gunner and pilot in their cockpits with the De Wilde ammunition bursting around them.

The Spitfire overshot and pulled away and the German made another desperate attempt to land and turned violently to port but at this instant Pilot Officer Folkes, in my aeroplane, flashed past me and gave a short burst with the cannons. I can still hear the 'thump-thump-thump' of them followed by the terrific 'whoosh' as the Stuka blew up and crashed just outside the boundary of the airfield.

My words had been taken rather too literally, as it would have been better to have let him land; at that time we did not possess an intact Stuka and it would have been very useful, particularly in setting at rest the minds of those vociferous Members of Parliament who complained so long and so loudly about the fact that the RAF had no comparable dive-bomber and in so doing gave the Stuka an importance it did not deserve – certainly not in attacks on England.

The German crew, both of whom were killed, were a very brave, if foolhardy, pair. They had come over alone from their base in Belgium, bombed and sunk the ship right under the noses of the fighters while they must have known that their chances of getting home were practically non-existent.

These dreary patrols were occasionally relieved by interception sorties after single reconnaissance aircraft and Tony Bartley was fortunate in catching a Heinkel just over Southend Pier in full view of an admiring public. His aircraft also had cannons and his wildly excited voice on the radio yelling: 'Christ! He's coming to pieces, there are bits flying off everywhere. Boy! What a sight!' bore witness to the devastating effect of these new weapons.

On 9 January, we were warned that the operation planned for Boxing Day was now scheduled for the 10th, and that 92 Squadron would lead the Biggin Hill Wing, meeting up with the other two squadrons over Dungeness.

January the 10th dawned clear and it was evident that the show was on; this was soon confirmed by Ops at Biggin. At the appointed time we took off and set course for Dungeness where we arrived right on time with the other Squadrons, formed up and set course for Le Touquet where we were to turn and fly north, sweeping in behind the main force, or 'Beehive' as it was called, just over the French coast.

As we approached Boulogne I had no difficulty in picking up the raiding party as my attention was drawn to it by the mass of anti-aircraft shell bursts that followed it – the German had certainly recovered from his Christmas hangover.

Although the German flak gunners were on their toes, there seemed to be little or no reaction on the part of the fighters – we did not see any at all – so I led the wing back to our own coast and let down towards Manston while the other two squadrons carried on to Biggin Hill.

Although this operation was on a very small scale and did not achieve very much from a material point of view, it did mark the turning point where Fighter Command began its swing from a purely defensive role to one that was to become more and more offensive in character. I thought it was a great honour to have led the Biggin Hill Wing – which was to achieve such fame under the leadership of Malan, Rankin and Deere – on this, its very first offensive operation.

After the 10th the weather again became quite foul and the ground at Manston was so soft that it was practically impossible for the refuelling bowsers to drive anywhere on the grass without sinking in and getting stuck. We did find one reasonably solid bit of ground, and, weather conditions being what they were, I ruled out the possibility of any air attack and took the calculated risk of concentrating the aircraft on this fairly hard piece of ground so that the refuelling bowsers could get to them.

A day or two later while the weather was still bad and I had kept the aircraft grouped in this way; I was endeavouring to catch up on a lot of paperwork in my office, which was a little wooden hut on the opposite side of the airfield from the Dispersal hut. Tom Wiesse was with me when we heard an aeroplane somewhere in the murk above. I had just made the remark that he would be lucky to get down safely when I heard machine gun fire and, looking out of the window, I stared straight at the nose of a rapidly approaching 109. As I gaped at it the pilot dropped his bomb which came straight towards the hut as the plane zoomed over the top, the black crosses looking enormous.

Just as I started to dive under the table I saw a second 109 drop its bomb right into the middle of the parked aircraft. I hit the floor under the table, but Tom had beaten me to it – there followed a shattering explosion and the whole office rocked. Nothing fell down and so, after waiting to make sure that that was the end of the attack, we crawled out and with sinking hearts went over to see what damage had been done and how many aircraft we had lost.

The bomb that had appeared to have my name on it actually burst out on the airfield and aside from very minor splinter damage had been very ineffective. It was the second bomb that worried me, so I was more thankful than I can say when I discovered that the ground, being so wet, had saved the day. The bomb penetrated deep into the ground and when it exploded it merely shot a great shower of earth almost straight up. The result was a lot of mud on the aeroplanes – and a small hole in the fabric of one elevator. It was really quite remarkable and for once I was very thankful for all the rain we had had.

We remained at Manston until relieved by No. 74 Squadron late in February. During this period we carried out normal patrol work, but we did not encounter any enemy aircraft. Unfortunately, it was while based at Manston that the squadron suffered the only fatality during the period it was under my command, nearly six months in all. This occurred during a weather test when one of the Flight Commanders took off with his number two, Pilot Officer Bill Watling; the fog closed in and they lost contact. The Flight Commander was extremely lucky and managed to land back safely at Manston, but Bill Watling flew into a hill near St Margaret's Bay and was killed instantly. It was a sad loss as he was a most likeable and promising young officer and the whole thing was such an unnecessary waste.

Shortly after my arrival at Biggin Hill in October I was summoned to an Investiture to be held by His Majesty at Buckingham Palace when I was to receive the Distinguished Flying Cross. On the appointed day I arrived at the Palace where I met ex-Station Commander Stanley Vincent, who was also to receive the same decoration. He is one of the very few officers to have flown operationally in both world wars and, I think, the only one to have shot down enemy aircraft in both. Also attending was a lad called Alan Edey from Winnipeg who used to sit next to me at school. The ceremony itself was very impressive and exciting but, of course, had none of the colour and glitter of the peacetime Investiture.

It now turned out that the Polish decoration that the squadron pilots had informed me I had been awarded was the wrong one! I received orders to attend an Investiture to be held by General Sikorski at the Polish Headquarters in the Rubens Hotel where Ronald Kellett, Atholl Forbes and I were to receive the *Virtuti Militari* for our operations with the 'Kosciusko Eskadra' or, as it was known officially in the RAF, No. 303 Squadron.

This decoration is Poland's highest military award, ranking, in Polish eyes, with our Victoria Cross; it is a very attractive silver Maltese Cross with the white Polish Eagle in its centre, suspended from a royal blue ribbon with black vertical stripes near the edges. It used to carry a number of very useful privileges and a small estate with its award, but since the advent of a Communist government this has all been done away with – a pity!

The three of us met at the hotel where we were taken to a room upstairs to find a crowd of people and a whole battery of cameras – all for us! A Staff Officer briefed us and then positioned us in front of the cameras. A few minutes elapsed and then the General arrived and the cameras started clicking, flashing and whirring.

A senior staff officer read out an announcement first in Polish and then in English, but I cannot remember what he said. The General then moved towards us, halting in front of Kellett, the same staff officer read out the citation in Polish and then in English and the General next took the cross handed to him by yet another officer and pinned it well and truly to Ronald's tunic. There was no question of using convenient hooks and rings as at Buckingham Palace! The General then shook him by the hand and kissed him on both cheeks; after this the performance was repeated with myself and then Atholl.

Next came a series of posed photographs, some with the General and Air Marshal Babington who, as the British Director General of Personnel, also attended. Others were taken with Urbanowicz, the Polish CO of 303. Then, it was all over and I went downstairs to collect my things preparatory to leaving. At the bottom of the stairs I was stopped and directed along a corridor towards the rear of the hotel. I thought 'well, at least you are shown out of the front door of the Palace!' Just as I reached some swing-doors the General and his retinue appeared through another door on my left. I stood back to let them pass but the General motioned me to go ahead saying: 'The hero first, please!' With that I straightened my tie and swept in – it appeared we had been invited to lunch.

There was a great profusion of Polish delicacies set out on shelves; the others followed and we were all given a liqueur glass of vodka and briefed on how to drink it, the drill being to eat one of the rather greasy snacks, drink the vodka in one gulp and then quickly eat another of the snacks. Despite the number of times the toast '*Naz drovia*' was given we managed to cope amazingly well for the best part of an hour and a half, and by then we had put away a remarkable amount of both food and drink; then there came a rap on the table and we turned to find the General announcing that lunch was about to be served and would we please take our places!

Even by peacetime standards the lunch was quite fantastic, but in this period of all-round shortages it was nothing short of fabulous. There was a magnificent selection of the most delicious wines, smoked salmon, venison, fresh fruits, cheeses and the lord knows what! The last really clear recollection I have of this fantastic feast is of the General, at about five o'clock in the afternoon, pushing himself back from the table, raising his glass to me and saying: 'Squadron Leader – *a votre sante!*' I replied, also forgetting my English, with: 'Here's the skin off your nose, General!'

In the evening the squadron took us out on the town; we started with dinner at the Grosvenor House, but the whole party became very involved and a few of us ended up at five o'clock in the morning in somebody's flat off Park Lane drinking pink champagne which was being poured out for us by a Polish army officer serving from behind a bar made of mirrors. I don't know to this day who the place belonged to, but it was a most memorable and enjoyable day.

While I was at Biggin the Station's Permanent Duty Pilot (operational pilots were not called upon to carry out the function of Duty Pilot) was a certain Douglas Stephenson, an American who had served with the RAF in the First World War and later joined the staff of the Beaverbrook newspapers. Through him and his most charming wife, the well known actress Jeanne de Casalis, a great many of the leading figures in the theatrical world came to Biggin and often would put on an impromptu show. Not being subjected to censorship a very free rein was given to their talents, the results being appreciated by all.

The Stephensons were generous to a fault and often acted as hosts to we 'fighter boys', not only in their own home, but in London's West End.

On one occasion Steve introduced me to a fellow Canadian, Sir Beverly Baxter, who seemed very interested to hear my account of the war as I had seen it. To my surprise he wrote an account of our meeting and it was published in one of the national newspapers headed 'Not a Poet', the general theme being that my hands and the way I used them made him think of me as a poetic type, but as conversation progressed it became abundantly clear to him that I was not. His final comments were: 'From his appearance he might have been a poet – but I would hate to be a German looking at those eyes and mouth behind a gun!'

I must have needed a haircut to give a first impression like that and as for my hands I, like any other fighter pilot, would have been practically tongue-tied if I had had to sit on them and so not use them to describe and illustrate an action.

We had not been back at Biggin Hill from Manston more than a few days when the Station Commander, Group Captain Soden, who had replaced Dick Grice, announced that the wing organization was to be established permanently. A Wing Leader would be appointed whose responsibility would be to ensure the operational efficiency of the squadrons within the wing and to lead the wing on operations. He would not have any administrative duties and the Squadron Commanders would still be responsible for these. In short, the Wing Leader would relieve the Station Commander, invariably a much older man, of all direct and detailed operational worries allowing the Station Com-mander to concentrate more on administrative matters.

Group Captain 'Mongoose' Soden further announced that Sailor Malan had been chosen for the post of Wing Leader of the Biggin Hill Wing while I was to be taken off operational flying and sent to take over as Wing Commander Flying at a new Operational Training Unit about to form at Heston, the PRU organization having moved to Benson near Oxford. My new CO was to be that redoubtable ace of the First World War, Group Captain J.I.T. Jones DSO, MC, DFC★, MM who was a great disciple of Mannock's and who was himself credited with forty victories.

It was with great regret that I handed over command of the 'Ninety-Second Foot and Mouth' as the Squadron called itself, on the eve of what we expected to be a renewal of the German offensive. I handed over early in March to a more than worthy successor, Squadron Leader Jamie Rankin, who was to make a great name for himself in the ensuing months eventually falling heir to the wing when Sailor Malan was sent on rest.

Despite my regret, I did have the satisfaction of having taken over what was something approaching an undisciplined, leaderless mob and, six months later, handing over a first class fighting unit composed almost entirely of the same individuals as when I had arrived. Whereas, on my first assuming command the squadron was on the point of being moved north out of the line, I was not only successful in stopping this but the squadron was to go on and complete fifteen months in the line at Biggin Hill, the longest tour of any squadron. Finally at the end of the war it was credited with a greater number of kills than any other fighter squadron even including 303 (Kosciusko) Squadron!

What is even more important is that we had proved that the 20mm Hispano could be made to give reliable service and in destroying several enemy aircraft with these weapons gave ample proof of their effectiveness.

On reporting to my new CO, I was promptly charged with the task of organizing the Training Wing of this unit, still in the process of formation, and known officially as No. 53 (Fighter) Operational Training Unit. The organizing of the wing into flights and picking suitable flight commanders took a little time as it was essential to check the qualifications and qualities of all the officers to make sure that as few mistakes as possible were made during the selection.

The fact that I knew quite a number of the officers who had been posted in as instructors helped greatly. I was pleased to find amongst them the irrepressible Billy Drake, a veteran of the French campaign with No. 1 Squadron and the Battle of Britain in No. 91 (Jim Crow) Squadron. Because of his experience I appointed him Chief Flying Instructor.

To keep myself fully *au fait* with all aspects of the unit's task, I took part in the actual training myself both lecturing and instructing in the air, but I must admit I did not much enjoy giving dual instruction in the Masters. These aircraft were used to test the pupil's ability before letting him loose in the precious Spitfires. After a short period of familiarisation on the Spitfire, pupils were put through a training syllabus included in which were aerobatics, air firing, navigation and formation flying. On occasion we would come across a pupil who just would not fly close enough. To cure this an instructor would take the cautious one down to the south coast and, placing the pupil so that he was on the side nearer the cliffs, he would then edge in closer and closer to the cliffs giving the pupil the option of either coming in close or flying into the cliff which, of course, he could see out of the corner of his eye – I never met or heard of a pupil who didn't prefer to fly closer!

By and large the standard of pupil was very high both in flying ability and eagerness to get into the fray – these two qualities did not necessarily always go together by any manner of means. There were a few lemons of course, and one Sergeant came to ask me if he could be taken off the course and sent to Training Command to become an Instructor. When I asked the reason for this request, he announced that he wanted to 'get married and lead a normal life'.

My reply is not printable! Fortunately such types were extremely rare.

Heston had been a very active civilian airfield before the war and the hangars still contained a variety of civil aircraft including two old Avro 504Ns, identical, except for the engine, to the standard training aeroplane of the First World War. These particular machines had been used for towing banners advertising various pills and such like things in the piping days of peace. I had them pushed out and checked over; as they seemed perfectly sound, two of us went off and amused ourselves buzzing around the airfield, much to the delight of the pupils.

The airfield was not ideally situated for training as we were right in the operational area and much too close to the balloons over London to the east, Langley to the north-west and Weybridge in the south-west. Unfortunately we did not have the help of the operations room staff at Northolt as had the squadrons at Northolt, so it was not long before we lost a pilot who flew into the Langley barrage and was killed; another hit one of the Weybridge balloon cables but, very fortunately, survived.

The accident rate during training was considerably higher than it was on an operational unit and, although always regrettable, some of them had their amusing side. One was the result of engine failure immediately after take-off and the pilot had no option but to come down in Osterley Park where he hit a tree and literally wrapped the aeroplane around it. When we got there we could not move the machine and had to wait for the Crash Crew, in the meantime we examined the wreckage and could see that the pilot was himself jammed tightly up against the tree. Judging from the angle of his head, his neck appeared to be broken and there was no sign of life at all.

On arrival, the Crash Crew rapidly got a chain around the aeroplane and, using their lorry, quickly pulled it clear – as it did so the pilot's head snapped back into its normal position and he said: 'Thank you very much!'

Apparently he had been so tightly jammed up against the tree that he could neither move nor speak, but he had been able to hear all the comments as we surveyed his 'dead' body. Actually his injuries were confined to a few scratches and bruises.

Being so close to Northolt and having a direct line to the Operations Room there, I had my radio fitted with the right crystals and quite often went off on my own under control from Northolt to see if I could find the odd German aircraft that might venture close to our shores. There was very little activity at this time, however, and only on one occasion did I come across any enemy aircraft. I had climbed steadily from Heston and arrived over Beachy Head at 20,000 feet at the same time as ten 109s arrived from the south, but they were about 5,000 feet above me. We all turned east and flew along the coast to Dover where the Germans turned away and made off over the Channel towards home. I had been hoping that they would attack me, as I felt quite confident of being able to handle the situation, but they paid no attention to me at all and I rather doubt if they ever saw me – although at the time, still a bit cock-a-hoop after the Battle of Britain, I thought they just didn't want to tangle with a Spitfire – confidence is a great thing!

The OTU had not been in operation very long when a very unusual intake of pupils arrived, these were officers of the United States Army Air Corps. Pearl Harbor was still eight months off and they were officially known as 'Observers of the War' – all seventeen of them, at a training station! They were a very fine bunch and fitted into things extremely well and we, naturally, put them through the complete course.

The spirit of the unit's pilots was terrific and many were the hilarious parties that were held. The Americans were very intrigued with our Mess life, customs and games and: they joined in wholeheartedly – it was something that had no parallel in their Service. On one such impromptu party somebody got the idea of putting a motorcycle in Billy Drake's bath to see what his reaction would be when he returned from London where, it was suspected, he had been 'poodle faking' round the West End. Everyone thought it was a good idea and after a bit of a struggle we managed to manoeuvre the motorcycle up the narrow stairs and into Billy's bath.

He returned about eleven o'clock and, as we expected, went up to his room. Then he came tearing down crying: 'Hey, there's a motorbike in my bath!'

We all looked blandly at him and said: 'Yes, we know!'

The joke went off very well until the next morning when we found that we could not get it out – after a long struggle we eventually had to dismantle it and bring it down in pieces, so the joke was really on us.

'Taffy' Jones, the CO, was always a leading light in these escapades and he did all he could to build up morale. One of his efforts was a song that he and Billy Drake had written and called '*The Brave Old Fifty-Third*' to be sung to the tune of '*The Grand Old Duke of York*'. It proved very popular indeed, especially among our Yanks who were always in the forefront when it was time to roar out the chorus. Another favourite was '*The Bombing of the Military Objective at Bembridge*'. This was the story of an imaginary raid on England, recited in a phoney German accent with words that, if they weren't German, certainly should have been. The whole was accompanied by suitable noises such as starting up, the take-off, the droning flight to the target, the shriek of the bombs followed by the chatter of the machine guns as the fighters appeared; finally the German aircraft was shot down and, with a suitable whine, hurtled towards the ground. By this time Taffy would be standing on the bar with his arms full of as much of the Mess cutlery as he could get hold of and then, at the moment the enemy 'hit the deck', he dropped the lot! The resulting din had to be heard to be believed, but it was extraordinarily realistic and the Americans loved it!

As the OTU was scheduled to move to Llandow in South Wales I flew over one day to have a look at the station. Just before leaving I got a message from the local Ops Room asking me to keep an eye open for a Ju88 that had been reported near Cardiff. I took off and set course for Heston. Then, just as I crossed the coast, I caught a glimpse of a twin-engined aircraft just nipping in and out of cloud the base of which was about 800 feet. I stalked the aeroplane and got to within 50 yards without being seen.

There seemed no mistake; it was a Ju88. The tail was the right shape, the raised 'greenhouse' over the crew positions was pure 88 and I took careful aim, but just as I was about to open fire something, I don't know what, made me look again. I crept closer, we were both now in and out of cloud, and then I got right under his tail, slid to one side and, on the side of the fuselage, I saw, not the black cross I had expected, but the RAF roundel! The aircraft was a Coastal Command Beaufort!

I turned away and headed for Heston again rather disappointed that it was not a Ju88 but thankful that I had had a second look. The crew of the Beaufort never knew how lucky they were as they had no idea that I was there. I was so close that I could have blown the machine to pieces.

After only three months at Heston I was again posted, this time as Wing Leader of the Polish Wing at Northolt. I was very pleased indeed and, although I was sorry to leave Taffy and the others, I looked forward to getting back on ops, particularly with the Poles whom I knew so well. This time, however, I was to have, not just a flight, but four whole squadrons of them!

7

Wing Leader

My Station Commander at Northolt was Group Captain McEvoy who had taken over from Stanley Vincent. I had known him for a number of years and I had the highest regard for him. After reporting to the Group Captain, I set off round the Dispersals with the Polish Wing Commander, Philip Laguna, who had been the Polish CO of 302 Squadron. I knew very few of the pilots I met, but they all seemed to have the same spirit that had been so marked in 303 Squadron and I felt confident that I would be quite at home with them.

Nothing very much happened on the first few occasions I flew with the wing but then we were called upon to escort some Blenheims which were to bomb the airfield at St Omer. As we approached the target I saw two 109s climbing to attack the bombers head-on. Almost at the same moment they opened fire and one of the Blenheims burst into flames and dived towards the ground, two of the crew escaping by parachute.

The German fighters then passed under the bombers and one was shot down by a Hurricane of the close escort squadron. I lost sight of the second 109 for a few seconds and then it reappeared, climbing on a course parallel to my own and about 500 feet below at 'eleven o'clock'. I attacked and opened fire at about 100 yards; it was the first time I had fired cannons for three or four months and I was not prepared for the vibration and loud *thud-thud-thud* as I pressed the gun button. I quickly let go as if I had been stung! I do not know how many shells I fired, it could not have been many, but it was enough – there was a brilliant flash on the starboard wing root of the 109 and the whole wing came off. The rest of the aircraft hurtled down twisting madly round and round giving the pilot no chance to escape even if he had still been alive, which I rather doubt.

Over the target more 109s put in an appearance and in the result-ing mêlée I became separated from the rest of the formation. I chased one lone 109, but could not get within range, so I turned for home. Not wishing to expose myself unduly to the attentions of the flak gunners on the coast I came down very low and slipped over the seashore at Gravelines. Just crossing my path was a small convoy so I put a burst into the stern of one of the ships which started a fire. On my return to Northolt I discovered that I had only fired sixteen rounds out of each cannon – I had not used my machine guns – and I became more convinced than ever of the validity of my argument as to the cannon's effectiveness.

Despite our offensive operations we were still half expecting the Germans to renew their assault of the previous year. Events were shaping in other ways, however, and the very day following that on which I had gained my first cannon victory Hitler committed the supreme blunder and launched his attack on Russia.

This fateful day, 22 June 1941, turned out to be a particularly pleas-ant one for me as it was on this day that I had been invited to go to Windsor Castle with Taffy and the Americans from Heston.

We were met on our arrival and conducted on a tour of the castle which absolutely thrilled the Americans – and me, too. Then, as we rounded a corner, we found ourselves in the presence of the King and Queen, who were accompanied by the two Princesses. We were all presented and, after chatting for a while, Queen Elizabeth explained that they were on their way to listen to the Guards band playing just outside the castle and she asked us to accompany them. It was both a pleasant surprise and a great honour.

Taffy walked with the King whilst I accompanied Her Majesty a short distance behind. As we reached the gate which looks out upon the Great Park, the band struck up the National Anthem while we all stood to attention and saluted. I shall never forget the sight of Taffy's little figure not only right alongside the King instead of slightly behind, but on his right instead of his left! Nobody seemed to mind but I couldn't help feeling that only Taffy would have got away with it.

There was a large crowd outside the castle waiting to see the Royal family and when they emerged the people broke into spontane-ous cheering and clapping. It was a most touching demonstration of loyalty and affection that brought quite a lump to my throat, a sentimentality inherited from my Scottish forebears, no doubt. I felt very proud indeed to be there and our Yanks could hardly believe that they were!

When the band had finished its recital we all went back to the castle grounds taking a route that brought us close to the crowd. One man had his very young baby in his arms and suddenly the Queen stopped, went over to him and placed her hand on the baby's head, gently chiding the father for having such a young baby out in the hot sun without a bonnet. The man loved it and grinned all over his face and the crowd too appreciated this very human gesture and laughed at his proud discomfiture.

After saying goodbye to our royal hosts, we were entertained to tea by the King's Equerry and then we all went back to Heston where we had something stronger to drink in celebration of a wonderful experience.

The next day I was over France again, escorting bombers attacking Hardelot.

This was one of the strange things about the air war in Europe; the fact that one could be in the thick of it one day, the next at Windsor in an atmosphere entirely divorced from war, and the following day back into action again. This fantastic situation had, I think, two main effects. One was that it imposed a very severe strain on the nerves, by bringing home most forcibly if subconsciously, just what you were risking. The soldier or sailor was already divorced from this peacetime existence long before he met the enemy and, if taken prisoner, was already mentally conditioned to some extent to this state. In many cases being taken prisoner must, initially, have come as a relief, particularly when an action had dragged on for hours or even days. The noise alone must have had a most wearing effect upon the system and the reaction to its cessation could be nothing less than a feeling of great relief.

The pilot, on the other hand – and particularly the fighter pilot based near London – had no such conditioning. One evening he could be disporting himself in a London nightclub and by lunchtime the next day be in the hands of the enemy. He did not suffer the long drawn out action or the noise, everything was swift, sudden and relatively quiet. The resultant reaction then was not a sense of relief but rather one of resentment at being deprived of the comforts and pleasures of home and this led to a determination to escape. I am sure that this is the primary reason why Air Force prisoners-of-war were so noted for their refusal to accept the situation in which they found themselves.

I do not in any way intend to suggest that the sailors and soldiers were more lacking in initiative or courage than the airmen. I think it was the circumstances leading up to capture, coupled with the fact that the airmen ran a much greater risk of being captured and were, therefore, probably more 'escape minded', that developed this most marked determination to get away, best illustrated perhaps by the mass escape from Stalag-Luft III.

Our offensive operations continued against targets at St Omer, Lille, Hazebrouck, Boulogne and Bethune, along with others less well known. In addition, fighter sweeps were carried out with the express purpose of bringing the *Luftwaffe* to battle. Generally speaking, the German pilots seemed anxious to avoid combat which was strange considering the aggressiveness they had displayed over France and England the previous year. It is probable that the withdrawal of many of the more experienced pilots from the Pas de Calais for service in Russia coupled with the serious losses suffered over England lowered the general standard of the German fighter pilots we were meeting. There were some, of course, who were very good indeed as I found out on several occasions but, overall, they were not up to the standard of the previous year.

There were, in fact, several instances where our Operations Board showed quite a number of hostile plots over France as our formations approached. On the order from the German controllers: 'Large enemy forces approaching from the north-west, all fighters to intercept over Calais!' it was noticed that often the hostile plots would make off in practically every direction except that towards Calais.

Transcripts of the radio-telephone conversations between German pilots and the ground stations picked up by our listening service are very revealing:

'There is a Spitfire behind me. There is something going on away in front!'

'There are some more again, behind and to the left.'

'There are three Spitfires.'

'Enemy aircraft retiring near Calais.'

'Are you about, Hermann?'

'What the devil's the matter?'

'My oxygen is running out.'

'I've got to pancake.'

'Just a minute there's a Spitfire behind you!'

'There is a single machine to the left.'

'Where?'

'Behind you.'

'That's me!'

'Are *you* over there?'

'How much petrol have you still got?'

'Spitfires – look out!'

'Our own machines – no, what are those? What the devil's happened? Spitfire to the right behind us in Direction 3. I'm being shot down!'

The note of panic can be detected even in cold print and it is very interesting to note that the Spitfire seems to have been a major factor in producing this panic. It is a pity that we were not able to hear and understand it at the time as it would have boosted our morale every bit as much as the Spitfire seems to have depressed the Germans.

Late in June we were scheduled to carry out a sweep from Le Touquet over St Omer, the main fighter base, and to cross the coast homeward bound at Gravelines. Philip Laguna, my Polish counterpart, who was to fly as my number two, was in great spirits as he had just received word that his wife had managed to get out of Poland and was on her way to England.

The weather over France was not very suitable for our purposes there being a lot of broken cloud about and the visibility was poor. Two 109s appeared briefly but dived away to the cast when they saw us. We continued on our way losing height gradually and travelling fast when suddenly I saw Calais right in front of us. We were too far to the west; I immediately started a turn to port and at the same time the flak batteries clustered around the town opened up. We were down to about 3,000 feet by this time and made tempting targets; one of the first shells scored a direct hit on Philip Laguna flying alongside me – a sickeningly tragic end to a day that had started with so much promise for him.

To avoid presenting ourselves as such tempting targets again, I led the wing back inland towards the south-east for ten to fifteen miles and then turning north-west once more; coming down to tree-top level we streaked in to attack the airfield just outside Calais. We were not expected and caught the defenders by surprise. I managed to destroy a 109 on the ground, blast in the front of a small building and blow up a petrol bowser.

In the small intervening piece of land between the airfield and the coast was a farm and as I streaked over it I caught sight of the farmer, he had a white horse pulling a plough and wearing a straw hat with its ears sticking through. Both the farmer and the horse seemed to be looking up at me as if to say: 'What in hell's going on?' – while the shells and bullets flew all around them. It was only a momentary glimpse, but the picture is as clear in my mind as though I had seen it yesterday.

On the shore just ahead of me a flak post was firing at one of the other aircraft so I emptied my guns into it which effectively silenced it. With that I was across the coast, under fire from two other posts, their tracer converging right in my path. I had no chance of evading it and flew straight through the mass of glowing red 'cricket balls' that flashed all around me but, amazingly, not one touched me!

We must have really upset the Germans as they put up a barrage above and in front of us and also fired their coastal guns, the shells sending up great spouts of water. No doubt the Germans were hoping we would fly into them. At the same time tracer shells were ricocheting off the water under my wing and disappearing in front of me. Also I distinctly saw the splash of big shells, fired at too low a trajectory, skipping off the water like great flat stones.

When I reached our own coast I realised that I was roaring with laughter – an odd reaction to which I have found I am prone after being subjected to considerable stress. Probably it serves as a good safety valve.

I circled over the coast until the wing reformed and then I led them back to Northolt; it was not until after we had all landed that I learned of Laguna's death. I had not seen him hit and in the confusion of the attack had not missed him. Apart from his loss, and nine bullet holes through the rudder of one Spitfire, we had been untouched but had managed to inflict quite a considerable amount of damage. Militarily I suppose the operation was a success, but Philip's loss was keenly felt by us all as, apart from his ability as a fighter pilot, he was a very popular officer and an able leader. I felt particularly bad about it as I felt that to some extent I was to blame, although I do not know what I could have done to avoid it.

The vacancy left by this tragedy was filled by promoting one of the Squadron Commanders, Squadron Leader Rolski of 306 Squadron, a diminutive but very tough officer. I had an unpleasant experience a few days later when, after shooting down a 109 in a mix-up near St Omer, I became separated from the wing and my number two and so set off for home on my own. I had not gone far before I was attacked by five Messerschmitts. Luckily I saw them in plenty of time and was able to turn into the attack at which the leader pulled up over the top of my machine taking up position on my port side. The others remained on my starboard side and then attacks began from alternate sides forcing me to turn first one way and then the other to meet them. They did not seem anxious to press home their attacks and it dawned on me that they were waiting for me to run out of petrol. We were already over Belgium and I began to get into a bit of a sweat.

Just as I was beginning to think that I was in for a protracted stay in Germany, two of them mistimed their attacks; the 109 on my port or seaward side having to pull up sharply to avoid a collision with one attacking from my starboard side. Like a flash I whipped into a left-hand turn, rolled on to my back to accelerate more rapidly and then as I gained speed rolled right way up again diving for the sea at full throttle. The 109s followed, firing but at extreme range. They continued to chase me out over the sea and some of their tracers bounced off the water under me, but none hit me. Eventually they gave up the chase, much to my relief, and I returned thankfully home.

One evening after being released – we had done two operations that day – I met the CO at the entrance to the Mess and was telling him about the events of the day when a large car drew up and in it were the Prime Minister and Mrs Churchill. I was rather embarrassed as I was pretty dirty and tired, wearing battle dress, a scarf, battered hat and flying boots into which were thrust maps and a revolver. I was duly introduced and could only hope that they did not notice my battered appearance. After chatting about generalities for a while they took their leave and departed for Chequers.

On the follow Monday the Wing was stood down and not required for operations that day. I was about to set off for London and was all dressed up in my best uniform when the telephone orderly came rushing to me in the Mess to tell me that I was wanted at the Headquarters building at once. Cursing my luck I hurried down and found a group of officers, including the CO, standing around Mr Churchill. It was apparent that the PM was not in too good a mood so I discreetly positioned myself in the background to see what would happen.

I learned later that, as was his custom, the PM had certain of his Senior Commanders down to Chequers for weekend and, as usual, they had all been discussing various aspects of the war. Among the subjects that came up was the question of how prepared the airfields were to beat off an airborne attack. Although the Air Chief Marshal present assured him that every station had its own special plan for dealing with such an eventuality and the necessary forces were trained and available on site, the PM was not at all convinced.

On the way back to London, accompanied by the Air Chief Marshal, the discussion had continued and as they approached Northolt Mr Churchill suddenly ordered the driver to turn in to the Station. Now, here he was, and he wanted to see for himself! The Guards Major in command of the defending forces had been sent for, but had not arrived when I got there.

Mr Churchill began to walk up and down as he waited; as he passed me he looked up, continued on his way, came back, stopped in front of me and, taking the cigar from his mouth, growled: 'Met you the other night, didn't I?'

'Yes, sir, that's right!' I answered brightly, pleased that I had been recognised.

He looked at me for a moment or two and then grunted: 'Look a bloody sight cleaner today!' It was hardly the remark I had expected and it left me somewhat deflated.

The Major appeared at this juncture and Churchill, gesturing towards the sky, snapped: 'There are 5,000 paratroops coming down – what are you going to do?'

'I'd sound the alarm, sir,' answered the Major and waited – only to be blasted by the PM with: 'Well, get on with it, man, don't just stand there!'

Very taken aback the Major saluted, dashed off and sounded the alarm. Much to everyone's surprise, certainly mine, things did happen. Men appeared like magic and took up their allotted positions, guns at the ready and obviously quite clear as to what was expected of them.

After checking on a number of details the PM said he wanted to go round the Dispersals to see how they were defended. Unfortunately the news that the Great Man was on the station had got around and all the pilots, to whom Churchill was practically God, had come down to the Dispersals in the hopes of getting a glimpse of him.

The first Dispersal we came to was that of 303 Squadron and I was pleased to see the airmen wearing tin hats and in position to beat off an attack – rifles at the ready. After a quick cursory glance Churchill made for the Dispersal Hut and there, sure enough, were all the pilots. He paused and then snapped, 'What are all these people doing here?' I had to say something so I explained that we had been released from operations for the day and that these were the pilots who were being given a lecture on tactics.

'All right, but what would they be doing in an attack?' he snapped back at me.

'Well, sir, they'd be in the air!' I answered.

He took one look at the group of about eighteen pilots who were by now beginning to crowd round him, then looked out at the twelve aeroplanes and shot out: 'All of them?'

I had to say: 'No, sir, the others would be helping to man the defences using their own personal weapons.'

There was, of course, no evidence that such weapons existed and he suddenly turned on one and barked: 'You got a gun?'

Poor Zumbach, the pilot picked upon, did not fully understand so I had to tell him in my best Polish what was wanted. Realisation spread over his face and he pulled forth a small cannon! The others all got the idea and in no time there was a veritable arsenal on display.

Churchill grunted, bit into his cigar, turned and made to pass Feric who very deftly whipped his gun into his hip pocket and at the same time produced the Squadron History Book and a pen, handed them to the PM and said: 'Please to sign, sair!'

The Great Man looked furious and, turning to me, rapped out: 'What's all this?'

I then explained that it was a history book they had kept up ever since the start of the war in Poland and they liked to get the signatures of every notable person who visited squadron.

'Why should I sign it?' he practically snarled.

By this time I'd had enough of him; I thought his attitude and grumpiness quite uncalled for, so I replied with some bite in my words: 'Well, sir, His Majesty saw fit to sign it on the preceding page!'

He looked at me for a second, turned back the page and there it was – *George, R.I.* The PM glanced back at me and I think I detected a faint amused twinkle come into his eye and he said: 'All right!' – and signed.

Quietly, and to myself, I marked one up.

Our offensive operations continued against varying opposition and we engaged in numerous brief combats and managed to keep on the credit side by destroying more of the enemy than we lost of our own, although I feel even now that a goodly percentage of our losses could have been avoided. Of the enemy aircraft destroyed only one more fell to my guns before the end of the month. This came at the end of a running fight between St Omer and Gravelines; after firing at several with no result I finally got a good burst into a Messerschmitt from 200 yards and it went into the sea a few hundred yards from the shore.

The wing provided close escort for three Stirlings raiding Lille and, never having seen bombs actually leaving an aircraft, I got into quite close formation with one of the Stirlings as he started his bombing run. The bomb doors opened and then the bombs came tumbling out – on such a short flight these aircraft carried over 17,000 pounds of bombs and these were all 500-pounders. I thought they would never stop coming out.

I was most intrigued and watched fascinated as the bombs hurtled down towards their target but I was taken aback when the tail gunner swung his turret around so that his guns were pointing almost straight at me and then commenced firing. Almost at the same instant a stream of tracer flew over my canopy from behind! I broke wildly, realising as I did so that it was the German – he had so nearly got me – whom the rear gunner had been firing at. Allowing for deflection it looked as though he was shooting at me.

It taught me a very sharp lesson to keep a constant lookout even when one was surrounded by one's own aircraft. On this occasion the German must have dived straight through a mass of our fighters in order to get anywhere near me. Actually I never did see him – just his tracer and that was quite enough.

The fact that such an attack could be made without any effective interference from any one of the large number of our fighters illustrates two major mistakes we were making during this phase of the air war. One was that we had learned little or nothing from the German mistakes of 1940 and, like them, we tied our fighters to the bombers, their mere proximity supposedly giving protection. As we ourselves had found, a few fighters travelling fast can flash through a screen of escorting fighters, do their damage and get away while the escort is trying to accelerate and at the same time look around to see if any more of the enemy are about.

The second mistake was really very similar in its effect to the first but, if anything, was accentuated in that operations carried out as far afield as Lille necessitated the fighters flying slowly not only to stay with the bombers but also to conserve fuel. The fact is that one could not afford to fight on such an operation as to do so properly meant that you would have insufficient fuel to get back across the Channel. All that we could do was to defend ourselves, but by so doing one failed to give adequate protection to the bombers. This was something that we had noticed with the Germans in 1940 – the fighters were loath to join combat when escorting their bombers on the more deeply penetrating raids. The significance was not appreciated by us – or at least not by those who were more concerned with planning our operations than carrying them out.

The advantages of speed which allowed the Spitfire to be used to its best advantage against the enemy was proven on the fighter sweeps of relatively shallow penetration. This was demonstrated with particular emphasis by the Biggin Hill Wing under the leadership of first Malan and later Rankin. The aircraft were already travelling fast when they met the enemy and so could easily catch the 109s which were shot out of the sky in large numbers with very little loss to the Biggin Wing. This could not be said of the wings, any of them, when employed on close escort work.

Regular conferences were held at Northolt to discuss our various problems; the AOC presided and, among others, the leaders of the fighter wings and the bomber leaders attended. On one such occasion I raised the question of just what our purpose was in carrying out these operations. If it was to destroy the industrial potential of the various targets and so reduce the contribution of industry in the Occupied Countries to Germany's war effort I maintained that it would require a far greater bomber force than we had so far escorted.

If, I continued, the bombers were merely there as bait to bring up the fighters so that they could be destroyed then we should restrict our radius of activity to that which would permit us to fight without the nagging fear of running out of fuel. This mental obstacle seriously interfered with a pilot's fighting spirit and it was my opinion that we had already lost far too many first class men because these factors were not receiving sufficient consideration.

Air Vice-Marshal Leigh-Mallory looked rather taken aback at this and he turned to his Group Captain Operations, Victor Beamish, who was a very experienced and successful fighter pilot, and asked him what he thought. Victor said that he agreed with me so the AOC turned to another of his staff officers and asked his opinion. 'My answer to Kent is – we've done it!' he replied.

Although this officer had a very fine record in the First World War he had not operated in the second conflict – I was furious and was quite rude in the remarks I flung back, but it was no good; the AOC preferred the second opinion and we continued to go to Lille and lose good men, all to little purpose.

After leading the Polish Wing for over two months the Wing Leader at Kenley, Johnny Peel, was shot down into the Channel but was rescued and taken off operational flying and sent on rest. I was then posted to fill the vacancy he left. It was a sensible decision as there was no longer any point in duplicating the Wing Leader's post at Northolt as the Poles were quite capable of leading their own units; their English had improved so much that there was no longer any difficulty in their understanding instructions passed to them in the air from the Operations Room; we even had Polish Controllers by this time. I had, therefore, no qualms about handing over to Rolski whom I knew to be perfectly capable and reliable.

On arrival at Kenley I found that there were three squadrons in the wing, No. 602, commanded by a New Zealander, Alan Deere, and No. 452 (Australian) at Kenley with No. 485 (New Zealand) at the satellite airfield – Redhill. Also I was operationally responsible for a RCAF Tomahawk Squadron based at Gatwick. This latter squadron had been trained on Army Co-operation work and was not suitable either by training or equipment for use in fighter operations. I could make no use of them, which was a great pity as I would have liked to have had some of my own countrymen flying with the other squadrons and so make up quite a Commonwealth force.

The operations we were engaged upon were identical to those of the Polish Wing and on my first sortie with the wing we ran into some 109s over St Omer. We had quite a successful engagement, three of the enemy being destroyed with another two probably destroyed and only one Spitfire slightly damaged.

A few days later we were scheduled to provide the target support wing for a raid on Bethune. This required us to be high over the target before the bombers arrived so we took off and climbed on course crossing the coast of France at Gravelines at 25,000 feet. Shortly after passing Hazebrouck I heard someone, I could not make out who, calling 'mayday', the distress call.

We continued on our way weaving in the usual manner with my number two maintaining position about 30 yards or so behind me. When we got over the target and started to make a wide sweep around it I noticed a 109 diving away about 100 yards off on my left. I considered chasing it but decided against it as we were too far inside enemy territory. Aside from this one aircraft I had seen no sign of a hostile machine and even the flak had been light.

On my return to base I got the rest of the story – apparently my number two had left me just after crossing the coast as he had oxygen trouble and something wrong with his R/T and I was unaware of his departure. Then, near Hazebrouck, some 109s passed just under Al Deere's Squadron and he immediately attacked. As he did so he was badly hit by one he did not see and his canopy was shot off, his instrument panel shattered and his top tank riddled, the cockpit flooding with petrol. He immediately turned for home with, we found later, thirty-seven bullets through the radiator, coolant header tank and tyres. It had been Al I had heard calling 'mayday' – and he had good reason.

The conditions were such that even if his aircraft did not catch fire the engine would have to stop in a matter of minutes, but for Al neither of these things happened and for some unknown reason he was able to keep going and make a successful landing at Manston in an aeroplane that looked like the proverbial colander.

It must have been at the time Al was hit that one of the other 109s joined our formation and took up his position as my number two! It was not until we were over Bethune that the leader of the section on my right suddenly realised that my wingman was, in fact, a 109. He immediately opened fire and the enemy aircraft dived away, which was when I saw it.

The distance from Hazebrouck to Bethune is quite considerable and all this time I had had this German aircraft behind me, in fact, I was even looking back straight into its gun muzzles without recognising it! Just why he did not open fire I will never know but all I can think is that he was a new boy who joined our formation by mistake, thinking it was his own, or having found himself by accident in the midst of a whole wing of the much feared Spitfires he just did not know how to break away without being immediately shot down.

Although it still gives me the creeps, it is interesting to speculate on what would have happened if he had not been fired at – perhaps he might even have landed back at Kenley with us!

About a week later we carried out a sweep over Dunkirk, St Omer and Gravelines. We did not encounter anything until we were approaching the coast on our way out then I noticed that the number three of a section on my left was intermittently 'trailing'. I thought it was strange, as no vapour trails were being formed by any of the other aircraft, so I had a closer look and to my horror realised that numbers three and four in the section were 109s and the 'vapour trail' I had noticed against the brilliant blue of the sky was, in fact, smoke from his guns as he fired at the number two of the section. He must have been a terribly bad shot as he failed to score a hit.

I called out a warning and climbed towards the 109s opening fire as I did so. The Germans dived away and I latched on to the tail of the leader, his number two latched on to me and my number two on to him – and down we hurtled towards the beaches of Gravelines.

I was in the fortunate position of being the only one who could fire as the German number two could not fire at me for fear of hitting his leader and my number two could not shoot in case he hit me! As we got lower the 109 I was shooting at pulled out of its dive and started a climbing turn to starboard and I noticed that we were now about 3,000 feet right over the flak batteries so, having failed to hit the 109, as I thought, I broke violently to port and dived away out to sea weaving gently. A certain amount of flak came up but it was very wide of the mark.

It was not until debriefing at Kenley that I learned from my number two that 'my' 109 had continued its turn to starboard, rolling on to its back and diving straight into the sand dunes where it exploded.

The next day I had a very unpleasant experience – all the more so as it was to some extent my own stupidity that caused it. We were again acting as target support wing and although we saw quite a number of 109s we were never in the proper position to attack and they kept their distance. On arriving over the target I noticed a single 109 flying on a course that would take him across my bows at a 200 yards. I tracked him and instinctively throttled back little to tighten my turn and then opened fire. Unfortunately I did not take into consideration the fact that we were at 36,000 feet and this coupled with the turn and reduced power produced a situation wherein the recoil of the guns was enough to stall the aircraft. I was in a gentle turn to the left when I fired: the aeroplane juddered violently, flickered the other way and went spinning madly down through the squadrons below. How we did not collide with any of these aircraft I am at a loss to understand but at one point Spitfires seemed to be flashing by at all angles. I was unable to get the machine under control again until I was down to 18,000 feet. My number two, I found, had faithfully followed me wondering what on earth I was doing.

Operations continued but I was unsuccessful in my attempts to obtain any further decisive results although I fired at a number of enemy aircraft. Some, I feel certain in my own mind, were badly hit but there was insufficient evidence upon which to base a claim. This was bound to happen when operating around the 30,000 foot level, as we usually were at this time, because one rapidly lost sight of an aeroplane diving away as it blended so well with the colour of the ground. Also even if one had exceptional eye-sight it would be far too dangerous to keep one's eye on an aircraft during all the time it would take to strike the ground from this sort of altitude.

Early in October I was awarded a Bar to my Distinguished Flying Cross and a few days later taken off operational flying for a rest and posted to 53 OTU again which, by now, had moved to Llandow in South Wales. Taffy was still in command so, although I protested about the move, I was pleased to know I was rejoining an old comrade.

One always *did* object to all moves that took one off operational flying, the ridiculous thing being that although one quickly recognised the signs of 'battle fatigue' in others, one did not notice it in oneself. Looking back on it now, and looking at photographs of myself taken about this time, there is no doubt that I had just about had it.

It took a few days to resign myself to the inevitable, but I was still upset, taking it all as a personal affront which, of course, it was not. I have no doubt now that, had I been allowed to continue, I would almost certainly have been killed as I know I was taking stupid and needless risks. It came, therefore, as a shock when, having bowed to the inevitable, I was told that my posting had been changed and I was now going as Wing Leader to, of all places, Malta! At this time there were only twelve Hurricanes on the Island.

Naturally this created a storm and in the end Air Vice-Marshal Leigh-Mallory flatly refused to allow me to go and had the posting stopped. Hilly Brown, who was on rest up north, was sent in my place. My feelings can be imagined when I heard that he had been killed just three weeks after taking over the Wing – I doubt if I would have lasted one week.

My successor at Kenley, Norman Ryder, did not last much longer and he was shot down and taken prisoner near Dunkirk when escorting some 'ship-busting' Hurricanes. Al Deere who had also taken part in the operation wrote to me about it and I reproduce his letter in part as I think it gives such a clear picture of the event and of his personal feelings.

Dear Johnny

I had intended writing to you about Norman but with my usual thoroughness, overlooked it. However, 602 with me leading and 485 with Norman leading rendezvoused at Manston with nine Hurricane bombers for the first low-flying attack under this bloody scheme we are now working on. We 'peed' out to Dunkirk of all places, at 50 feet and there's no need to explain the reception we received from ground defences. Could have stepped out of the machine and walked on the Bofors shells. Quite a few people received hits and we lost two Hurricanes and Norman. No 109s appeared at any time there or coming back. Norman was last seen at 500 feet by his number two, who was hit fairly badly, just near Dunkirk and inland. No one saw what happened to him and we can only guess he collected a packet from a post firing at his section who were split up.

Personally I think that there is a very small chance because any hit at that height would probably be fatal. Both Hurricanes went straight in.

That's the story and I consider it a bloody poor way for an experienced pilot to buy it. How the hell any of us got back is a miracle. To cap the party off we were ordered off at five minutes notice from thirty minutes availability not even having done a similar show before. I can tell you, Johnny, we are all pretty sore about it and Group received no soft soap from me in my report...'

It was most unfortunate that I was tired and nervy when I rejoined Taffy and I fear that I was unable to give him all the help and support that he needed. It was a difficult time and Group Headquarters and Taffy did not see eye to eye on a number of points. I probably made matters worse by being intolerant of what I considered complete lack of understanding on the part of many of the Group Staff Officers, very few of whom had any operational experience.

Our biggest headache was an appalling lack of flying discipline among the pupils going through the OTU and in an endeavour to improve things I paraded the whole course and announced that I would Court Martial the next one caught low-flying against orders. I was prompted to do this as I found that practically the whole course had, at one time or another, flown under the suspension bridge over the Menai Straits. While I applauded their spirit I deplored the fact that the same disregard for orders had resulted in far too many fatalities.

It is interesting to note at this point that at one time the accident rate was so high on both sides that it became a major factor in the air war. Göring even issued an edict to the effect that *Luftwaffe* pilots killed in accidents caused by a disregard for orders would be stripped of all military honours and refused a military funeral.

Despite my tirade and threats, within an hour and a half of my having issued my ultimatum a sergeant in the Free French Air Force, practising formation flying, broke away from his leader and went down into the valleys of South Wales, presumably to wave to his girlfriend. While doing so he failed to notice a mountain that inconveniently got in his way. The result was a loud bang and little was left of the sergeant.

I was furious when this was reported to me and even more so when within another half hour, an American member of the RCAF also disregarded my orders and warnings and 'beat up' some friends near Barry. He too went in and killed himself.

When I heard this I went to see Taffy and said: 'Quite frankly, Chief, I reckon we ought to shoot 'em. At least it will save the aeroplanes!'

Taffy thought for a while and then in his funny stuttering way said: 'Johnny – you leave this to me!'

I was only too glad to do so but I was completely unprepared for his next action.

He had the entire course assembled and then, pointing to a small building with a door at each end, he announced that they were to march in, one at a time, halt, turn left, salute as a way of paying respect to their friends, then, one pace to the rear, turn right and march out!

He had arranged for the American boy to be laid out on the slab in the mortuary, for that is what it was, just as he had come out of the crash. Alongside was a small box which contained the charred remains of the Frenchman. Well – fresh-faced young men marched in and rather green-complexioned old men came out. It was very rough treatment, believe me, but it did stop the low-flying and undoubtedly saved a good many lives which, after all, was Taffy's aim. It did not go down well with higher authority however as it was, in fact, political dynamite.

An enquiry was held and cognizance was taken of the fact that we were, in effect, operating under front line conditions and Taffy's action was, therefore, accepted as fully justified. Despite this, however, he was never reinstated to the rank of Acting Group Captain which he had to relinquish when the Court of Enquiry was convened and it was not very long before he was called upon to retire from the RAF in the rank of Wing Commander.

To me this was a great injustice as, although the action he took could be described as brutal, it was what was required. Many years later I was approached in the RAF Club in London by an Ex-Canadian Air Force officer who introduced himself by saying: 'You won't remember me, sir, but I was one of your students at Llandow in 1941, and I just want to say that I reckon you and Taffy saved one hell of a lot of lives when you held that parade after the crashes – most of us hated your guts at the time but later, when we began to understand what it was all about, we really appreciated what had been done for us!'

The fact that this officer, more than twenty-five years after the event, took the trouble to approach me out of the blue to express these sentiments is more than ample justification of Taffy's action and proves how right and understanding he was.

In my case it was considered that, as I had just come off two tours of Operational Flying, I was, perhaps, to be excused my callous exterior and it was decided to send me on a six months lecture tour of Canada and the United States – I have often wondered if it was meant as a reward or a penance!

8

Lecture Tour

Although I welcomed the opportunity of going home and seeing my parents and friends I was not all that keen on the idea of a lecture tour and even less on the prospect of the journey by sea. Eventually the time came for me to join the ship at Greenock and I made the journey via London, a most tedious and uncomfortable trip in overcrowded trains. The ship I was to travel in turned out to be the *Montrose*, a Canadian Pacific liner of some 12,000 tons that had been converted into an armed merchant cruiser. And our first port of call after leaving Greenock was Milford Haven – not all that far from Llandow! It was a reassuring place – the harbour was full of the funnels and masts of sunken ships sticking out of the water. We only stayed here a few hours and then set off for Canada in company with a Dutch liner, the *Van Damm*, and two 'tin cans' – old four-funnelled American destroyers of First World War vintage.

The second day out one of the escorts turned back and we were left to face the fury of the Atlantic and the German *Kriegsmarine Unterseebooten* with one antiquated destroyer for protection. The ship was terribly overcrowded and the weather was quite appalling, all of which added to the joys of the trip. The seas were so great that we did not go anywhere for two days, the ship only just managing to hold its own. The Captain swore that it was the worst weather he had ever experienced.

The storm, having blown itself out, allowed us eventually to make some sort of headway, but it was not long before the destroyer 'wink-winked' a message to us to the effect that it was running short of fuel and would have to leave us and put in to St John's, Newfoundland. The message went on to give us the cheering news that a U-boat pack was waiting for us, but that Halifax had been informed that we were without escort: it was hoped that the RCN would send out destroyers to shepherd us in.

On the morning of our arrival at Halifax we could hear gunfire and depth-charging going on behind us. Later we were told that our RCN escort had located the U-boats and had sunk one while another surfaced and surrendered. I was very pleased to hear the news, but even more pleased to get my feet back on solid earth after seventeen days at sea.

From Halifax I went on by train to Ottawa, where I was briefed on what was expected of me, and a day or two later I started my tour at Toronto. From there I went to various stations around Toronto, Kingston and London after which I flew to Winnipeg where I had two weeks leave at home.

Even during my leave I was asked to give two or three lectures to civilian and military organizations that were not on my schedule. One of these was to the Canadian Club at one of the better known hotels in the city and most of the prominent citizens were present including the Lieutenant-Governor of the Province. I do not think that he could have been too impressed with my after-lunch speech though, as, at the end of it, he rose to his feet and, turning away from me, congratulated a non-flying RCAF Squadron Leader on a magnificent speech!

On completion of my leave I visited a number of flying training schools in Manitoba and Saskatchewan and then went on to Calgary in Alberta. On the flight from Saskatoon I was flying a borrowed Oxford and made the last hundred miles on one engine.

I visited a number of units in the Calgary and Lethbridge area and also managed to make a trip to that beautiful place Banff, but did not have the time to participate in any of the winter sports.

From Calgary I flew over to Vancouver and Vancouver Island and gave lectures to two or three units. Whilst visiting Patricia Bay on the island I was pleased to run into a number of old friends from No. 1 Canadian Squadron and they very kindly arranged for me to fly a little Grumman Goose amphibian, the first of this class I had flown. I was even allowed to ferry it over to Jericho Beach in Vancouver on my way back east.

From Vancouver I flew back to Winnipeg and had the good fortune to be just about halfway across the Rockies as the dawn arrived, almost stealthily. The snow-peaks below gradually took on a most beautiful rosy blush whilst the valleys below were still in deep darkness where tiny lights twinkled in an unreal world.

I was permitted a few more days at home before setting out for the east again. This was the last time I ever saw my mother and I feel that she had a premonition of it, as she clung to me so tightly when saying goodbye at the airport. As a parent myself, now, I can begin to understand just what it all meant to her and I marvel all the more at her courage and unselfishness – a truly wonderful person of whom I am very proud.

From Winnipeg I flew to Montreal and a day or so later flew to Halifax where Hartland Molson, who had been a member of No. 1 Canadian Squadron, and his charming wife looked after me extremely well and insisted that I stay with them during my time there. On my way back to Ottawa I paid visits to Stations in Nova Scotia, New Brunswick and Prince Edward Island at all of which I gave one or two lectures and, by this time, I could practically give the lecture in my sleep.

After a few days in Ottawa I was sent on a tour of the United States, first reporting to Washington for briefing and then to Rhode Island and back to Washington via New York. After this I visited US Naval and Air Corps Stations in the south-eastern States before going on through Texas, Oklahoma and Arizona to California. It was a most interesting experience but there was too much to see and absorb in too short a time.

I was rather surprised to find that quite a number of Americans were not altogether as anti-German as I had expected. It was, of course, only a few months after the Japanese attack on Pearl Harbor and, understandably, many people were regarding the Japanese threat as of more immediate importance than the menace of Germany. Also people were very remote from the war and were only just beginning to realise that America was in it at all. While appreciating this I was still rather unprepared for the question of an Air Corps Captain in Alabama who came up to me and, pointing to the ribbons on my tunic said: 'Say, are them shootin' medals?' I assured him that they were, but refrained from saying what at.

After about six weeks I returned to Washington where I met a lot of RAF friends and acquaintances; one of these, a Medical

Officer, was an old friend from Farnborough. One night we went out together to the Mayflower Hotel and got a table near the band. I was doing a bit of a line with the singer who, whenever she could, joined us at the table. My medical friend I don't think cared too much for this arrangement as he felt a little out of it. However, from time to time a chap from another table came over and invited us to join his party – being otherwise occupied I was not interested, but my companion eventually succumbed and joined up with them while I concentrated on Roberta, the singer.

The next morning I was awakened by the telephone ringing and when I answered it a voice asked: 'Is that Wing Commander Kent?'

I admitted that it was and asked what did the voice want.

'This is the FBI here,' it said, so I promptly said 'Nuts!' and hung up, thinking that it was one of my joker friends.

In a matter of moments the telephone rang again and the same voice said: 'Look, this *is* the FBI and we're not foolin'.'

A little taken aback I thought for a moment and then asked what on earth they wanted with me. The voice then said: 'You were at the Mayflower last night!' I admitted that I had been. He then said: 'You joined a table of about six people and you were dancing with a blonde girl.'

At that I said, 'Oh no! Not me – I was otherwise engaged!' – to which the voice replied: 'OK, you were asked to join them but you did not; but your Wing Commander friend did, didn't he?'

All I could say was: 'Well, yes, I believe he did, but so what?'

'Just this,' replied the voice. 'We've had him here all night and, for your information, those hospitable people were German agents!'

A few days later I returned to Ottawa and luckily managed to secure a seat in one of BOAC's converted Liberators and crossed the Atlantic in that – frozen stiff but not half so frightened – and was back in London only eighteen hours after leaving Montreal, whereas it had taken me nineteen days to go the other way by ship and rail.

The tour was a marvellous experience and I wouldn't have missed it, but it was too long and, much as I enjoyed it all, I was rather glad to get back to a nice quiet war for a rest.

On my return from Canada I reported to the Air Ministry and was instructed to present myself at Headquarters Fighter Command,

where I was pleased to find that I was to command a fighter station
a few miles south of Taunton by the name of Churchstanton which
came under No. 10 Group. The officer from whom I was to take
over was an old test pilot friend, Wing Commander Ramsbottom-
Isherwood, a New Zealander who had taken the RAF Fighter Wing
to Russia earlier in the war. Now he was off again on another special
assignment – he did not know where he was going, but strongly
suspected that it would be the Caucasus.

As we were signing the Handing Over and Taking Over Certificates
I heard a roar and snarl as an aircraft screamed low over the airfield.
Looking out I saw that it was a Battle – one that I had had at Exeter.
I asked 'Ish' what it was doing there and he said: 'Oh, Hell, I'd forgot-
ten; your old flight is here. It was moved up here from Exeter when
the wing moved in!'

I was pleased to hear this and suggested that we drive around and
see the chaps – Ish promptly obliged and in a few minutes we were
at the Dispersal where we were greeted by 'Tiger' Hawkins, now a
Squadron Leader; he just looked at me and said: 'You bastard!'

So I replied, pointing to the three broad stripes on my sleeve:
'Watch it, Tiger!'

Quite unabashed he retorted: 'All right, then – Sir Bastard!'

He had not altogether forgiven me for having told him that the
Wellington stood up to the collision experiments quite happily. As
he had experienced the complete disintegration of the aircraft, he
felt that I had perhaps led him up the garden path – perhaps I had,
but it was quite unintentional. Anyway, it was not really a seriously
held conviction and we remained good friends.

The Squadron on the station was No. 313 (Czechoslovakian) so I
was again among the Slavs; a second squadron arrived a few weeks
later. The Czech Wing operated under the control of the Sector
Station at Exeter where the third Czech squadron was based.

Operationally things were very quiet in No. 10 Group and although
we did a few sorties over the Cherbourg and Brest Peninsulas we
did not see much action. On one occasion we were followed back
and attacked by some Fw190s over Exmouth and a couple of our
aircraft were shot down, but one of the German pilots lost his way
and landed a perfectly good 190 on an airfield in South Wales – the
first such aircraft to fall into our hands.

Operations over enemy territory being rather few and far between, the squadrons spent most of their time at Bolt Head to the south of Torquay in the hopes of catching some of the tip and run raiders that came in practically at sea level to bomb the coastal towns. I spent quite some time on these duties myself and caught sight of the raiders several times but could not close the range sufficiently to make sure of a kill. All I could do was to fire at long range and hope for the best. Once or twice I saw traces of smoke coming from aircraft I had fired at but I was never able to claim even a 'damaged' to my own satisfaction.

Orders came through one day for the squadrons to paint the aircraft with black and white stripes in preparation for a special operation. It was very hush-hush indeed and I could get no information about the operation at all. The squadrons moved to an 11 Group Station and then all was cancelled and they returned – still I was not told what had been planned.

Suddenly the operation was on again and the disaster of Dieppe took place. Apparently the security in the ground forces was not as effective as that of the air forces and the plan was known to the Germans.

Early in September I was ordered to report to the Air Ministry at a certain time and date, but no explanation was given as to what was to take place. On my arrival I found a group of others including Max Aitken, Sailor Malan, Al Deere, Brian Kingcome, Richard Hillary and Tony Bartley. None of us had the faintest idea of what it was all about and we just stood around talking and waiting. We did not have too long to wait, however, before Air Marshal Sir Richard Peck appeared and briefed us on what was to happen. Apparently it was a press conference to be held by Lord Dowding to celebrate the second anniversary of the Battle of Britain and we had been selected to represent 'The Few'.

After lunch, which was at the Savoy, we were whisked off to the Ministry of Information where the Conference was to take place. We were all seated on a platform behind Lord Dowding who had some very complimentary things to say. After this we all went outside where a number of press photographs were taken.

When our services were no longer required, several of us decided to 'beat up' the West End and went off to a variety of clubs and late spots in search of further refreshment. It was quite a memorable day, although perhaps the term is not strictly accurate as applied to the later stages of it.

Shortly after this I was posted to Fighter Command Headquarters as Wing Commander Training under Group Captain 'Doggie' Oliver who welcomed me enthusiastically. 'Glad you've arrived,' he said. 'Just the chap I want – I was meant to present some proficiency certificates to a number of ATC Cadets at a Cinema in Hendon tonight, but you can do it better than I can. Here is the name of the Squadron Commander who will brief you – good luck!'

What a welcome – I had no option but to obey orders and go! Somehow I managed to survive the ordeal and was even able to oblige when, without warning, I was called upon to give a short speech to the audience extolling the virtues of the ATC about which, at that time, I knew very little. My lecture tour experience stood me in good stead on this occasion.

My actual work at Stanmore was not very interesting and was concerned chiefly with training matters throughout the Command, consisting mostly of paper work and occasional visits to operational stations and Operational Training Units to discuss training problems.

I did endeavour to get a new 'secret weapon' adopted but failed to arouse any interest amongst the experts, which is a pity as I still think that it had great possibilities and it was extremely simple, cheap and easy to make.

While still at Churchstanton I had thought up the idea of carrying twenty-four hand grenades in a special carrier under the belly of the aircraft so that on low-flying attacks on airfields and hutted camps one could open the attack using cannon and machine guns and, when directly over the target, release the grenades. This would not be like an ordinary bombing attack as the grenades would bounce in all directions and I estimated that a considerable amount of damage would be done by both blast and splinters. I think anyone who has seen what one hand grenade can do will agree that twenty-four exploding in fairly close proximity to one another would prove pretty lethal, and when one considers an attack mounted by a whole squadron the damage inflicted would be very considerable.

I had further plans, too, as my scheme included the carrying of thin cased petrol canisters to drop on hutted camps, this followed up by aircraft carrying bundles of incendiaries would brew up the mixture and then, after allowing time for troops to be massed for fire-fighting duties, a third wave carrying grenades could inflict fearful casualties. All this could have been done using the same basic equipment that I had designed, built and tested, but nobody was interested.

During my brief tenure of office at Stanmore I was summoned to Buckingham Palace to receive from His Majesty a Bar to my Distinguished Flying Cross. The routine was the same as before and when my turn came I went forward and the King chatted a bit about my operational career and then said: 'Of course, you got your first DFC in 1940.' 'Yes, sir,' I answered, and then he asked where I was stationed now. 'Headquarters Fighter Command, sir,' I replied. 'Oh,' he said, 'and do you like it there?' What possessed me to say it I will never know but, quite without thinking, I replied, 'No, sir, I don't!' Then, realising that one did not say that sort of thing, I became acutely embarrassed.

By an extraordinary coincidence, When I returned to Stanmore the next day, there was a signal in posting me to the Middle East! In fact, it was pure coincidence as I had applied for such a posting some time before, but it caused a lot of amusement at the time. This was just at the time the North African landings were being prepared under the code name 'Torch'. Speculation ran high amongst the Staff Officers at Command as to where the operation would take place and all sorts of rumours went the rounds. The favourite refrain whenever anyone came out with a new theory was, 'Sand in my shoes, snow on my shoulder' – suggesting that it might be somewhere in the Mediterranean area or possibly the north of Russia – even Norway. Oddly enough it turned out to be a most appropriate ditty considering the weather conditions experienced in North Africa when the operation took place.

It was also at this time that it was announced that Air Chief Marshal Sir Sholto Douglas was to leave Fighter Command and take over command of Middle East Air Forces and Air Marshal Leigh-Mallory was to succeed him at Fighter Command. So, although I was changing Commands, I was to have the same Chief.

While at Stanmore I had become very friendly with Wing Commander Tactics – Barrie Heath, an Auxiliary Air Force Officer. We had both had enough of Stanmore and we had both volunteered at the same time for the Middle East. Neither of us was overly enamoured of the thought of the sea voyage, so we tried to get an aeroplane to ferry us out. This appeared to be a feasible answer to our problems as Alamein was won, the Afrika Korps was in retreat and the North African landings had taken place.

After a lot of to-ing and fro-ing we were instructed to report to Moreton-in-the-Marsh where we would be fixed up. On arrival we found, to our horror, that we were expected to go in separate aircraft as the 'sixth' member of a trainee crew.

On having this explained to us, neither Barrie nor I wanted anything to do with it – particularly when one of the star pupils crashed right in front of us, killing himself and all but one of his crew.

We promptly returned to Stanmore and started pulling more strings in an endeavour to get our own aircraft and crew. This time we were lucky and we picked up a brand new Mark VIII Wellington – the ASV Stickleback – at Harwell where we were provided with a Navigator, Wireless Operator and Rear Gunner, and very good they were too. I was to be Captain of the aircraft and Barrie my Co-pilot.

After completing fuel consumption tests and getting to know our crew, we left Harwell for Portreath in Cornwall where we were held up for a few days by the backlog of aircraft, mostly American, bound for North Africa, they having been held up by bad weather.

Eventually our turn came and, with some misgivings, I taxied out to the runway, final clearance was given and I opened the throttles and away we went – the Captain never having flown a twin at night before and the Co-pilot never having flown a twin at all! Fortunately the rest of the crew were blissfully unaware of all this and were under the impression that with two wing commanders as their pilots they couldn't go wrong – little did they know.

In fact I was pleasantly surprised at how much I could see; it was a great improvement on the Spitfire at night. Once away we carried on under a 400 foot cloudbase and homed on to a beacon on the Scilly Isles. Over the beacon we turned on to course for Finisterre and started to climb, eventually breaking cloud at 6,000 feet where we were treated to a lovely sight, the full moon turning the clouds below us into a carpet of silver. At 8,000 feet I trimmed the aircraft for cruising conditions and engaged the auto-pilot.

It was a pleasant flight and we got some good fixes from French radio stations and also found the ASV radar most useful. As we approached Finisterre the eastern sky began to pale and the cherry-red glow of the engine exhaust ring became less noticeable. At the same time I began to feel most conspicuous as we were soon in full daylight although the sea below us, glimpsed through breaks in the cloud, was still in the dark of night.

This was the most dangerous stage of the flight as it was here that the Ju88s would wait for aircraft being ferried, generally by very inexperienced crews, and the pickings had been good. Consequently I was keeping an extremely wary eye open when, suddenly, to my horror, the rear gunner started firing. I whipped the aircraft into a violent diving, slipping turn at the same time yelling: 'What is it, Gunner – and where in hell is he?'

There was a pause and then an apologetic voice from the gunner: 'I'm sorry, Skipper. I was just warming my guns.'

Another pause as I manoeuvred my heart back out of my mouth and into its proper place and then I let fly with a burst of invective and abuse that I feel has seldom been equalled. I faithfully promised him that if he ever did that again I personally would wrap his perishing guns round his flaming neck – or words to that effect!

Having got over the fright, more or less, I had the Navigator check on the ASV for a blip ahead that should denote Finisterre – sure enough it came up at about thirty miles range. I started a gradual descent and before long we sank down through the cloud and, on breaking out at about 2,000 feet there was Finisterre directly ahead of us, about five miles away.

The cloud cleared completely and we had a most pleasant flight along the Portuguese coast, on to Cape Trafalgar, past Cadiz and thence through the Straits where we kept well clear of the Spanish mainland in case some gunners had itchy fingers. As we passed through we were thrilled by our first sight of the famous Rock.

The wind was westerly so I flew round Gibraltar and made a dummy run along the runway about fifty feet up. Just to the north was a line of barbed wire with machine gunners stationed along it at intervals. Suddenly Barrie, sitting on the right, cried: 'Johnny, keep over to port – those buggers down there are aiming at us!'

There did not seem to be any unpleasant air currents so after another circuit I came in and landed. Having parked the aircraft we got out to stretch our legs and noticed a group of officers standing around talking and laughing and obviously waiting for something to happen. We went over and asked what was going on. 'Oh, you don't want to miss this,' one of them said. 'There are a couple of Fighter Boys bringing in a Wellington and it should be bloody funny!' It was us!

We remained at Gib for several days waiting for suitable weather, but we did not waste time and managed to arrange a tour of the Fortress and to become acquainted with the amenities of the Library – pre-1914 Scotch at eightpence for four fingers! Then I ran into an old friend in the Fleet Air Arm who invited us to a party aboard *Indomitable*, but to beat the curfew we had to kidnap the Town Major and take him with us. We finally left the carrier at about four o'clock in the morning.

Invariably after one has been on such a party, the weather the next day is ideal for flying and so it proved in this case. Even though we were not due to take-off until about eight o'clock in the evening I was still feeling pretty rough. We all got aboard, however, and when I had sorted out the maze of lights I lined up and roared off towards Algeciras on the other side of the Bay. Despite the heavy load the machine was airborne by the time we reached the road into Spain that crosses the runway.

Then followed a long slow climb to 10,000 feet where I trimmed the aircraft and engaged the auto-pilot. Barrie then climbed into the pilot's seat and I went down into the nose turret to get some rest; I told Barrie to yell at me through the intercom if anything seemed wrong.

I don't know how long I had been dozing when I heard Barrie's voice yelling: 'Johnny, come quickly – I'm flying it myself!'

I leapt up and dashed to the cockpit, hoiked Barrie out of the seat and took over. Apparently he had been getting bored as the aeroplane droned on through the night and, finding a small handle that did not seemed to be attached to anything, he idly turned it – only it happened to be the auto-pilot pitch control. It was not long before he noticed that the speed was falling off and, in looking around to see what was going on, he inadvertently knocked off the master switch and the aircraft was virtually out of control.

Having got everything back to normal and the aircraft re-trimmed, I let Barrie back into the seat but with strict instructions not to touch anything; in fact, he was to sit on his hands!

After about another hour I took over from Barrie as we were approaching Tunisia. As we got over Sfax the search-lights came on and vaguely searched for us, but we chucked some beer bottles out through the flare chute and the lights went out, no doubt because the bottles would sound just like bombs. We droned on over the Gulf of Sirte and before long dawn crept up over the horizon. In another hour we let down through cloud and there right in front of us was our landfall – Tocra!

From here I was able to map-read my way to Benghazi and then out to the airfield, Benina – the area had not long been in our hands and I did get a shock when, after landing, I parked the Wellington, switched off and looked out of the window straight at a Stuka. For one awful second I thought that the Germans must have retaken the place, but then I saw the roundel on the wing and all was well – it was, in fact, 601 Squadron's 'Beer wagon'.

The Sector Commander, Dudley Honor, came out to meet us and gave us breakfast, then he kindly saw us to the aircraft and we set off on the last leg of our journey to Cairo. On the way to Egypt we saw an enormous amount of wreckage littering the desert although rising sand obscured quite a lot. Conditions improved as we arrived over Egypt and the Pyramids were clearly visible for many miles.

Finally we landed at LG 224, or Cairo West as it was to become, handed over the aircraft, said goodbye to our crew and made our way into the city preparing to start our Middle East tour and wondering just what it would bring.

9

The Middle East

Although Cairo was terribly overcrowded, Barrie and I managed to get accommodation in the famous Shepheard's Hotel and we spent the first few days taking in the sights while our fate was being decided at Headquarters. Within the week I was posted to take over No. 17 Sector from Dudley Honor and a day or two later I was back at Benghazi.

Conditions were very rough both in the town and on the airfield, as they had received a terrific battering. There were over 120 wrecked Axis aircraft lying around the perimeter of the airfield alone, not to mention those scattered over the surrounding countryside. There was no electric light in the quarters, drinking water was kept in jerry-cans and the rations were bloody. I think it is the discomfort and lack of decent food and water that is the real hell of war; the fighting part is relatively enjoyable, but it makes up only a small percentage of the whole.

Dudley stayed on a few days to introduce me to my new unit which was a bit scattered. The Operations Room was very impressive, being housed in an Italian air-raid shelter, although a bit of a come-down after Fighter Command. Still the Controllers managed to cope most efficiently even though they often looked up from their ops board to meet the baleful stare of a lizard.

On the second evening Dudley took me up to visit the 'low-looking' radar station on the top of the escarpment. Whilst we were there some blips appeared on the screen indicating an attacking force approaching Benghazi, so we settled down to watch the fun. At first there was nothing to be seen, but suddenly the whole port erupted and the streams of tracer seemed to form an impenetrable wall of fire; the Germans however pressed home their attack and one did succeed in dropping his torpedo effectively. The others seemed to be put off by the barrage and we saw one explode right over the centre of the harbour. It was a magnificent sight but I would not have liked being called upon to fly through such a hail of shells.

A night or two later we had another attack when the sky was completely obscured by cloud, but the full moon gave so much light over the top of the cloud that we were able to scramble nearly all the Beaufighters and they were actually able to dog-fight with the enemy it was so bright.

The Eighth Army was preparing for its assault on Tripoli and so business was fairly brisk for the first few weeks that I had the sector, although I was not fortunate in meeting anything myself till some time later.

I had inherited an 'illegitimate' Hurricane from Dudley Honor with which I had had a certain amount of minor serviceability trouble. One evening I took off on an air test and was gratified to find everything working properly. I had only been airborne for about ten minutes when my Senior Controller, Peter Forsythe, called me on the R/T and gave me a vector to intercept an unidentified aircraft some distance to the north-east of Tocra.

I was about twenty miles out to sea when he called again and said that the plot had faded, but I continued to fly on the same vector on the off-chance of making contact. When I was some thirty miles out I decided that I was wasting my time so turned back towards Tocra, flying at 3,000 feet. I was still about twenty miles out to sea and almost due north of Tolmeita when something caught my eye and there, low on the water and approaching me, was a Ju88. Apparently the crew had not seen me as the machine continued steadily on course towards me and I was able to half-roll and attack from dead astern. The German flew steadily on as I approached to within 50 yards still unobserved. I took careful aim and pressed the gun button. Both cannons hammered out their message and flashes appeared on the point of aim, pieces flew off and black smoke poured out of the starboard engine and then – the guns stopped! Nothing I could do would make them fire and I was forced to watch helplessly as the 88, after one or two turns in a feeble attempt at evasion, set off in the general direction of Crete with smoke still pouring from the damaged engine. What happened to the German in the end I do not know as I had, perforce, to return to base, but when I last saw him he was low on the water, only about 500 feet up, and he had an awfully long way to go. I have often wondered if he ever got home; I rather doubt it, but all I could claim was a 'Damaged'.

Not unnaturally I was furious at the stoppage and created hell when I got back to Benina, particularly as I found that my guns had been loaded with ammunition that had been left lying about the airfield in odd boxes. It was all gritty with sand and rust and had probably been left there on one of our previous expeditions to Benghazi. At any rate, it effectively stopped my guns and so prevented me making sure of the German machine which had been an absolute sitter.

Unfortunately, a Combat Report was submitted on my behalf by the Intelligence Officer and as a result the existence of my 'gash' aircraft became known to certain gentry in Cairo, the war being now far enough away for them to take an interest in such things. So, in the end – and much to my disgust – I lost my private machine.

The Eighth Army drove on to capture Tripoli and at the same time the sector parted company with the Desert Air Force and came under the control of Air Headquarters Egypt through No. 212 Group which had its Headquarters at Benina and controlled not only No. 17 Sector but also No. 16 at Cyrene and No. 15 at Bu Amud some miles south of Tobruk.

Shortly after this I moved my Sector HQ from Benina to an ex-Police post on the coast road at a tiny village called Driana about forty miles east-north-east of Benghazi. This was very much better as we had very much more room, were only a few hundred yards from the sea and away from the direct influence and interference of the Group. Unfortunately it was nearly fifteen miles from the new airfield to which the Squadrons had been moved called Bersis and situated near the Tocra Pass.

Another drawback was that we had to revert to tents and I have never liked living under canvas; I acquired a small wooden hut and fitted it out with a comfortable bed, liberated from the Hospital in Benghazi, also a bath, washbasin and wardrobe from some of the bombed out buildings in the town. My scheme turned out to be a mistake as the hut was alive with bed-bugs and sand fleas. I had to wash out the hut with petrol every couple of weeks but the 'beasties' always came back after a few days.

The airfield at Benina became more of a staging post than a base for operational aircraft and the Group communication aircraft were housed there in the one remaining hangar that still gave some protection from the elements. There were quantities of ammunition, bombs and various explosives scattered all over the airfield boundaries and, behind the hangar mentioned, were two 1,000lb bombs rolled up against the wall. Nobody seemed to pay much attention to such things and there they stayed, though they were to play their part in the weeks to come.

There were three Squadrons based at Bersis, No. 89 Night Fighter with Beaufighters, No. 33 with Hurricanes and No. 7 South African Air Force also with Hurricanes, although they did have an extra aircraft – a Messerschmitt 109F they had captured.

I was lucky enough to fly the machine and found it very pleasant but extremely blind, particularly downwards, and this probably explains why, during the Battle of Britain in particular, the German pilots did not attack even when we were only a few hundred feet below them, this happened on numerous occasions and they obviously did not know we were there.

After familiarising myself with the 109 I returned to the airfield and flew low over the dispersal so that some photographs could be taken. I passed over the tents and looked back to see if I had been close enough and was horrified to see a well known silhouette on the sand behind me. Like a flash I whipped the machine into a wild skidding turn – only to realise as I did so that I was trying to evade myself!

By now the Germans and Italians had been driven out of Africa and activity died away almost completely except for high-flying reconnaissance Ju88s and Ju86Ps. The Americans had been busy preparing several of the airfields in the vicinity of Benghazi and it was not long before a number of Liberator Squadrons were moved in. It was this force that seemed to be of most interest to the Germans.

Shortly after the Americans settled in I received a request to visit their headquarters and when I arrived I was informed that they were planning a massive attack on the oilfields at Ploesti in Romania. One of their worries was the possibility of their encountering balloons. They had heard of my experiences and were anxious to know what they could do to protect their aircraft. I was, unfortunately, unable to help much as they had neither the time, facilities nor equipment to fit armoured leading edges and cutters, so all I could say was that they could only hope that their propellers hit the cables as they would be the only protection they would have. Small comfort but all I could give.

A few days later I watched them roaring off, nearly 200 of them, on their way to the oilfields. The story of the raid has been told many times and I do not propose to repeat it here, but I feel that it is only fair to take issue with some accounts that state that 'aside from a desultory shell fired from time to time' no action was taken by anybody when high-flying reconnaissance machines flew over the Liberator bases. In fact, fighters were scrambled after every one of these aircraft and a number of interceptions were made but, of course, miles and miles away from the Benghazi area and well out of sight of watchers on the ground in that area.

The majority of the American crews were very inexperienced and after the attack on Ploesti the force became rather dispersed and Liberators landed on all sorts of different airfields in the Middle East; it was several days before they all returned.

The Hurricanes with which the Day Fighter Squadrons were equipped were virtually useless when it came to dealing with the high-flying German machines and interceptions were continually being missed. Eventually three Spitfires were allotted to each squadron and these aircraft we stripped of all the equipment that could be spared in an endeavour to increase their ceiling and improve their chances of catching the 'shufti-kites' as they were nick-named. Even so we were never successful in bringing down any of these aircraft, although several of us managed to have a fleeting shot at them.

On one occasion, after a long chase, I managed to coax my Spitfire up to an indicated 41,500 feet but was still about 1,000 feet below and slightly behind a Ju86P. While the Spit appeared to have reached its absolute ceiling, the German aircraft was still slowly climbing away so, in desperation, I pulled up the nose of my aircraft and fired a burst hoping that a lucky shot might bring down the enemy machine.

I do not know what became of the Junkers but, as I fired, my machine shuddered, stalled and flicked into a spin from which I was unable to recover until we had reached 20,000 feet. Although this sort of thing was repeated by various pilots without strikes being seen we must have been hitting these exasperating machines as at one time, according to an intelligence report, all the Ju86Ps based on Crete were unserviceable with bullet-perforated cabins.

As the build up for the invasion of Sicily progressed we were called upon to provide air cover for the convoys from dawn to dusk as they passed through 17 Sector's area. In spite of the numbers of these convoys only one was attacked in our area but, regrettably, two ships were sunk with heavy loss of life, one being a troopship which turned over after being torpedoed and over 1,000 men were drowned.

The approach of the attacking force went undetected as it followed a large formation of American Liberators returning from a raid. This was more likely by accident than by design as they could not have known of the Americans' plans. It was well timed, just as dusk was approaching and the enemy were not seen until they had launched their attack. The ships were so close to the coast that the tracer shells could easily be seen from the shore and a very heavy barrage it was. In addition to the aircraft already over the convoy, several others were scrambled and a few of the enemy aircraft were brought down.

The Liberator raids continued with increasing effectiveness against targets in Italy and eventually the Italians decided to retaliate. One very blustery night we heard two aircraft fly over but, as they sounded like Dakotas, we paid little attention to them. Had the wind not been so high as to necessitate the lashing of the aerial of the low-looking radar we would, of course, have known from the direction these aircraft approached that they were enemy machines but, in fact, we had no plots on them at all.

The following morning a stranger stumbled on to one of the heavy anti-aircraft positions not far from Benghazi where he came up against real Cockney shrewdness. At first he tried to pass himself off as a Major in the Free French forces, but after he had given this explanation one of the gunners asked: 'Then wot yer got yer face blacked for, mate?'

He was taken into custody and interrogated, it was not long before he broke down and admitted that he was an Italian and that two plane loads of paratroops had been dropped the previous night, their mission being to sabotage the Liberators. Although he had managed to gather his own group together – they were in fact waiting for him to return – he had not made contact with those dropped from the other aeroplane.

Now that the location of the first group was known they were quickly rounded up and caused no trouble. The second lot were eventually located in a wadi and, to everyone's surprise, they at first showed fight, but suddenly gave up and waved a white flag. It turned out that they had mistaken our Ghurka and Sudanese troops for Libyan Levies and they were almost pathetic in their pleas not to be handed over to the Senoussi. I can understand their anxiety as the treatment they would have received would have been very rough indeed; the Senoussi had not forgotten the behaviour of the Italians under the Butcher of Libya – Graziani.

Two of the members of this second group could not be found and no one seemed to have any idea of what had happened to them. Considering the weather conditions in which the drops were made I was amazed that there were no casualties amongst those taken, but it seemed likely that the missing two had met with an accident and were probably dead.

A wide search was carried out, but the days went by without a sign of the missing pair. During all this time we kept a close guard on the aircraft on airfields within a radius of fifty miles of Benghazi. After nearly three weeks the AOC came to the conclusion, quite reasonably, that the danger was past and he instructed us all to remove the guards. I don't know why, but something made me suspicious and I left the guards on the aircraft at Bersis just in case.

In the middle of the night the people at Benina, including the AOC, were awakened by a series of explosions – the two missing Italians were not dead, but had somehow managed to avoid detection although they must have been close at hand all the time. Now they had succeeded in planting sticky-bombs on five aircraft and on the two bombs behind the AOC's hangar – when these exploded the whole rear wall collapsed inwards and on to the AOC's communication fleet of aircraft and wrecked them.

In the confusion the saboteurs got clean away. How they managed it we never knew, but it is probable that they rendezvoused with a submarine that took them back to Italy. However they managed it, there is no doubt that it was a first class effort and deserving of the highest praise.

At the end of July I heard that I was shortly to return to Cairo and take over as Wing Commander Training from Max Aitken, who was being promoted and appointed to command the Group just outside Alexandria. Although I had had a lot of fun and found both my job and the country interesting I was not all that sorry to leave Benghazi particularly as we were suffering a plague of locusts, the heat was frantic and the water foul – you could smell the chlorine over a hundred yards away when tea was being made.

Transportation for oneself was not very difficult to arrange but it was not so easy if you had any amount of kit unless you were willing to send it separately. I had been around long enough to learn that it is a great mistake ever to be separated from your kit and I was, therefore, forced to find ways and means of transporting myself and my kit together. Eventually I arranged with the CO of the local Maintenance Unit at Berka Main to ferry a Beaufort back to the Delta. Local facilities were limited and aircraft requiring extensive inspection and refurbishing were sent back to the main bases in the Delta if the aircraft were flying at all.

I had never been in a Beaufort before, thought I had heard some lurid tales about them. However I felt that with my Beaufighter experience I should not have any trouble as long as I treated it gently and took no chances. I loaded my kit, said my goodbyes, climbed in and started up. Everything seemed to be in order so l taxied out and started to take-off. Halfway down the runway the constant speed units went crazy and the engine speeds were all over the shop. The aircraft veered first one way and then another. I had to juggle madly with the propeller controls in an effort to retain some control of the situation as I was too far along the runway to stop. At the same time I started to bounce the aircraft off the ground; I had two reasons for this, one was to get sufficiently clear of the ground to retract the undercarriage and so reduce drag and give me more control, the other was to avoid going straight through a Spitfire which, for some obscure reason, had been parked right in line with the runway!

The sweat was literally pouring off me, but I managed to get clear and staggered out across Benghazi harbour, turning gently to avoid hitting the cathedral. Eventually I succeeded in coaxing the beast up to 500 feet by which time I was a good five miles out to sea. At last I got things settled down, turned slowly eastward and made my way along the coast.

Very gradually I began to gain altitude and by the time I had reached Appolonia I had crawled up to 4,500 feet, but I could not persuade the aircraft to go any higher. Everything seemed to be working reasonably well and I began to breathe more easily until halfway between Tobruk and Bardia when the propeller controls went crazy again and the aircraft started to waltz about the sky.

By this time I had had enough of the brute so I turned back and headed for El Adem. On my approach the rate of descent rose alarmingly as soon as I lowered the undercarriage and flaps and I had to open both throttles wide. Despite the fact that my speed was 120 knots, the aircraft just would not stay in the air and it was only the cushion of air close to the ground that enabled me to make the end of the runway. I taxied in to the hangar, switched off and reported to Flying Control, where the duty officer calmly said: 'I'm glad you made the runway, otherwise you would have landed in a minefield!' – happy thought.

I was thoroughly fed up with the Beaufort and wanted no further part of it so I telephoned 89 Squadron, now at Bu Amud, and they very kindly sent an aeroplane to collect me and my kit. The next morning they loaned me a Beaufighter and I went on to Heliopolis. As for the Beaufort, it may still be at El Adem for all I know or care!

When I reported to my new headquarters which now rejoiced in the name of Air Headquarters, Air Defences Eastern Mediterranean, Max had already left and I had fallen heir to his Hurricane based at Heliopolis. It was a very nice hack and after flying it I had the letters MA painted out and JK substituted – I was staking my claim before anyone got ideas of making a take-over bid, even though the machine was quite legitimate.

In my new capacity of Command Training Inspector, one of my first tasks was to acquaint myself with the various units under the control of our headquarters. I knew most of those based to the west of the Delta, so I planned a round of visits to units in Palestine and Cyprus and I lost no time in setting out on my tour.

I found Palestine and the Lebanon quite fascinating and the surroundings, temperature and general way of life a pleasant change from Cairo not to mention the desert and Benghazi. Cyprus was also very nice, but the tempo of life in Nicosia I found to be rather too much like that of Cairo, although on a smaller scale. Some of the Hungarian cabaret girls were most attractive and some of the stories about them were very amusing – unfortunately, most will not bear retelling here. One, I think, can be told as it illustrates the attitude to life and world affairs that most of them seemed to have. One of our officers was dancing with a particularly good-looking girl who asked why he had the top button of his tunic undone. He explained that this was because he was a fighter pilot. She said: 'Oh, I like fightair pilotts – my brudder he is fightair pilott.'

Here was too good an opening to miss so our young hopeful asked what squadron the brother was in, to which she airily replied: 'I don't know the numbair, but he flies the Messerschmitt 109 on the Russian Front!'

My trip, I must hasten to add, was not restricted to a tour of the late spots and I managed to visit quite a number of units including the Group at Haifa. Whilst there I took the opportunity of visiting Acre across the bay where I was astonished at the strength of the defences erected so many hundreds of years ago by the Crusaders. Although I was not able to visit as many places as I would have liked owing to the scarcity of ground transport, I did manage to have a good look from the air at such fabled places as Tyre, Sidon, the Sea of Galilee, Jerusalem and the Dead Sea, not to mention a number of the smaller places that have figured prominently in the turbulent history of the Near East from Biblical times until our own. Altogether I thoroughly enjoyed my tour and I was loath to return to Cairo.

Early in September I was taking my new assistant around the headquarters to introduce him to the other members of the Staff when the Air Officer in charge of Administration said to me: 'Oh, yes, you're off to Palestine, aren't you?'

I thought he had made a mistake and explained that this was a replacement for my assistant, not me, to which he replied: 'I know, but you are going to Palestine. Better go and see the Group Captain Operations – he'll tell you all about it.'

More than a little mystified I went along to the Group Captain's office and asked what it was all about. He became very mysterious, locked the door, drew the curtains back from in front of a map of the Eastern Mediterranean and said: 'We are invading Cos tonight and you are to go to Palestine and supervise the initial airborne assault and the subsequent build up of forces and supplies by air. You are, in fact, the AOC's personal representative and you are to act in his name.'

Up until that moment I had never heard of Cos and when I saw where it was and heard what was planned, I was horrified; I could scarcely believe my ears. Here we were starting off on an operation by placing ourselves in the position of a beleaguered garrison; it was worse than Tobruk and I said so. It was then explained to me that originally the plan had been to go into Rhodes simultaneously with the surrender of Italy but, instead of the much larger force of Italians taking control and imprisoning the German forces on the island, the reverse had taken place. Consequently the plan had to be changed and this was the result. We were now to take the island of Cos with Paratroopers from Ramat David in Palestine. Once the island was secured, a Fighter Squadron, No. 7 SAAF, and three Dakotas would fly in from Cyprus, the latter carrying supplies of spares, ammunition and rations.

The whole thing seemed crazy to me and I asked to see the AOC, Air Vice-Marshal Saul, but he was away and would not be back until late in the afternoon. Still wondering if I was having a bad dream I collected my things and arranged for my Hurricane to be made ready for me.

Eventually the AVM arrived and briefed me as far as he could, but really this amounted to little more than confirmation of what I had already been told by the Group Captain Operations. Apparently I was to be responsible, after the dispatch of the Paratroops, for the loading and dispatch of the transport aircraft in accordance with instructions he would issue from time to time through the Headquarters Staff in Cairo. As an assistant I was to have one Equipment Officer, Flying Officer Thomas.

Finally I got away and dashed out to Heliopolis and took off for Ramat David over 300 miles away. By the time I got as far as Gaza the sun was setting and it was already quite dark on the ground. I had no idea what radio facilities Ramat David had nor was I at all certain of its exact position so I decided to land at Gaza and obtain road transport for the rest of the journey which resulted in my arriving at my destination at midnight. Here I was welcomed with: 'Thank Gawd you've arrived – what in hell's going on?' And I had been expecting them to tell me!

The Paratroops had left some considerable time before I put in an appearance and all we could do at this stage was to wait and hope that all went well. As it turned out it was a perfect drop and although there were nearly 200 men involved there wasn't even a sprained ankle amongst them.

The full story of the abortive Dodecanese Campaign is really worth a book by itself, but I intend to dwell only on those aspects with which I was personally concerned. My chief responsibility was to ensure that the aircraft got away on time and that they were carrying the loads called for by the AOC through Air Headquarters. If it had been as simple at that, life would have been very much easier. Unfortunately, the loads called for equipment that had to be obtained from Maintenance Units miles away from Ramat David and I had not even been provided with a bicycle for ground transport. I had to commandeer two Jeeps that were scheduled to be flown to the island so that poor Thomas could dash about the countryside and collect equipment and I could get around the airfield.

The overall planning seemed to have been even worse than I had at first imagined. For example, a squadron of the RAF Regiment were sent to Cos to provide anti-aircraft defence for the airfield with 20mm Hispano guns; when the squadron arrived at the airfield they turned out to have been trained as infantry and they did not make the acquaintance of their new weapons until they both met at Ramat David. Still, I suppose they could not complain too much as they were given handbooks and instruction manuals – and they had a four-hour flight during which they could read up on how to work their guns!

In fact, they put up a magnificent showing against the low-flying German and Italian aircraft that strafed the airfield unmercifully once our presence was known to them but unfortunately they also suffered severe casualties.

The whole operation as far as I was concerned lasted only about two weeks, by which time the Germans had mounted an offensive that put an end to our hopes of securing a base in the Dodecanese from which to thrust at the 'soft underbelly of the Axis'. During this time, however, although we did not have the exclusive use of the transport aircraft and never had more than seventeen machines available on any one day, sometimes only four, we did manage to fly in nearly 900 men and 523,000lb of assorted equipment ranging from anti-aircraft guns, petrol, and ammunition to sand-bags and camouflage nets. In all it was quite an achievement considering the difficulties under which we had to work, not the least of which was the continual interference from Air Headquarters.

Only on one occasion was I able to visit the island and I went over in one of the Dakotas transporting two Jeeps. By this time the enemy were well aware of our presence and had put the airfield out of action; we were forced to operate at night and to use a small newly constructed strip just outside the town.

The flight took us from Ramat David to Paphos in Cyprus and then north-west to Kasselrosso and along the Turkish coast keeping low so that the German radar on Rhodes would be unable to pick us out from among the permanent echoes produced by the mountains.

We crossed over the narrow isthmus separating the Mediterranean from the Gulf of Cos – in so doing of course we were overflying neutral territory – and then flew low over the gulf and landed on the 1,200 yards makeshift strip. Here we found that some overly enthusiastic crew had taken the ramps needed for unloading the Jeeps back to Palestine. Reluctantly we had to go around and rouse a number of soldiers who were sleeping in nearby ditches. I felt desperately sorry for them but they all came along, if not cheerfully, without a word of complaint, and together we managed to manhandle the Jeeps and lift them bodily out of the aircraft and set them safely on the ground. We then set off on the long flight back to Palestine.

My Hurricane had been flown up from Gaza for me and it was being looked after by the Station Flight – one of whose members, an Australian, had busied himself with painting my score of victories on the side of the cockpit in the form of black crosses. One day I snatched a brief half-hour and went out to fly the aircraft, but when I got to it I found two Assyrian Levies mounting guard over it and they would not let me near it. Every time I approached I was menaced by a bayonet.

I found the Aussie and asked what the hell went on. He explained that the Assyrians thought that this was the aeroplane that had brought down the Germans and they were guarding it. I asked who had told them to do such a fool thing and was told: 'Nobody – they are off duty; it's their own idea!'

Luckily the Aussie could speak enough of their lingo to explain the situation, upon which they were all smiles and gave me a terrific present arms. They were a fine body of men, these Levies, and they took their duties very seriously. One had to be ready to stop at once if driving round the airfield at night and they challenged you; if you did not stop they would not hesitate to open fire.

One of the most exasperating features of the whole operation was the constant changing of instructions from Cairo resulting in our having to change the loads in the aircraft sometimes several times in a day. This all meant extra work, delay and very frayed tempers which became even more frayed by the difficulty in making telephonic contact with Cairo, our calls having to go through nine different exchanges – with most of the operators speaking German! Maybe they were German-Jewish refugees, but one couldn't be sure.

On one occasion there came a panic to send to the island a supply of Mae Wests, 'K'-Type dinghies, helmets and oxygen masks. These we obtained from an MU some eighty miles away, but when the equipment arrived we found that the oxygen masks and microphones were obsolete, the oxygen tubes would not fit the aircraft, the earphones would not fit the helmets and, although 'K'-Type (Fighter) dinghies had been sent, the spare CO_2 bottles that came with them were for 'H'-Type (Bomber) dinghies! Then there was more trouble over repacking a wireless set so that it could be dropped – the airstrips on the island now being all out of action. Although we started preparing this one aircraft at three o'clock in the afternoon the aircraft was still not ready to go at one o'clock the next morning. This was the deadline; to have left later would have meant being caught over the island in daylight so I cancelled the flight. But what a row that caused, all over one wireless set.

Shortly after this episode the Germans attacked by sea and air and although our forces put up a very gallant defence it was a hopeless situation. After a few days' fighting it was all over and we were out of the Dodecanese.

I returned to Cairo feeling very jaded indeed as we had been working at high pressure at all times of the day and night and then, to crown it, a few days later I went down with jaundice. Fortunately it was the 'Benghazi' type and I recovered very quickly.

Towards the end of the year another operation aimed at driving into the Balkans through Turkey got under way. The RAF element was designated No. 217 Group under Air Commodore Guy Carter whom I had first met at Sealand; I was to have command of one of the Wings, No. 234, scheduled to cover the main thrust from Izmir into Greece.

All seemed set and organized on a much more logical basis than before; I was looking forward to getting back into action when the Turks, probably influenced by the Dodecanese fiasco, decided at the last moment not to fight.

The new AOC-in-C, Air Marshal Sir Keith Park, sent for me and was most sympathetic. He expressed his sorrow that he could not offer me an operational appointment in his Command as he did not have any suitable. However, he did offer to do what he could to get me a wing either in Burma or with the Second Tactical Air Force then building up in England preparatory to the assault on Hitler's Fortress Europe.

Having been chased out of France, I promptly jumped at the chance of getting a bit of my own back and opted for the second choice. By the middle of March I was on my way back to the United Kingdom via Tripoli and Gibraltar.

My choice turned out to be a mistake as, after making my number with 'P' Staff at Second Tactical Air Force and being assured that there was a place for me, I was recalled to the Air Ministry. Here it was pointed out to me that, as I held a Permanent Commission, I would have to obtain a Flying Instructor's category. I argued the point and stressed that I did not think that I was the type and, anyway, I had come back from the Middle East to get into the show that was building up. It was pointed out to me, however, that the Air Force was, in fact, paying me for the job it wanted me to do and not for what I wanted to do.

10

Britain and Germany

Altogether I was to spend just over a year in Training Command, most of which time I spent trying to get out of it. In this I was not alone; I found a lot of highly decorated, operationally experienced regular officers who had suffered the same fate as I had and we all resented it. We all saw the Air Ministry's argument but, selfishly I suppose, we felt that it should happen to somebody else.

No doubt our attitude contributed to the general atmosphere that was so noticeable in the Command where many had been stuck for years despite their efforts to get on to operations and were, I think, rather jealous and resentful of us who had escaped it until now. Also, of course, there were the other types who had been only too glad to stay put and so keep well clear of the 'flying glass' – these too resented us, though for a different reason, and were always on the defensive. Altogether I considered it an unpleasant interlude in a career that had otherwise been interesting and exciting. It was not the Training Command I had known before the war nor that which I got to know later on, so I suppose it was just an unfortunate period for all of us.

There is no doubt that I learned a lot and corrected a number of bad flying habits that everyone develops, but sometimes I found the syllabus of training to border on the ridiculous. On one occasion my instructor told me that he was going to teach me front gun air-firing techniques. I thought he was joking and laughed at the idea of anyone trying to teach front gun firing in an Oxford, especially when the only sights available were locally made adaptations of the old fashioned 'ring and bead' sight that was pretty old hat by the end of 1918.

One aspect of the training that I found extremely interesting was the Standard Beam Approach System. This was well taught and the instructors were quite amazing in their ability to fly in incredibly bad weather conditions. I found it fascinating and surprised myself by being able to get down in far worse conditions than I would have believed possible.

Strangely enough, despite my having been relegated to Training Command, I very nearly took part in the Invasion of Normandy by accident. I was on a night cross-country exercise and suddenly found myself among a number of tugs and gliders. I got a nasty shock and could not at first think what all these strange shapes could be, but I turned and flew with them, slowly climbing out of their formation. I had no idea, of course, that it was the real thing and not just another of the many exercises.

After two and a half months at Upavon I was signed off as a qualified instructor on twin-engined aircraft and posted to command a satellite station of the Advanced Flying Unit at South Cerney near Cirencester. It was a pleasant little station that I took over and life on the whole was quiet and agreeable if a little dull.

The general standard of the pilots going through the course had deteriorated and, the war going the way it was, there seemed little likelihood of their ever seeing action; the whole exercise seemed pointless and this had a demoralising effect on pupils and instructors alike. In the autumn I was sent on a course at the Senior Officers' Advanced Training School at Cranwell which I found quite interesting. While there I received word that, on completion of the course, I was to take over another satellite at Charmy Down just outside Bath. The reason being, apparently, that the RAF's first jet squadron was based on Colerne next door to Charmy and it was felt that I, as an ex-fighter pilot, would find it easier to maintain good relations with our neighbours than someone who was not on the fighter wavelength. Whether this was so or not I don't know as no trouble arose in any case.

Not long after taking over my new command I was on leave in London where I ran into an old friend, Chris Paul, who was with No. 2 Group under the redoubtable Basil Embry. In the course of conversation Chris asked me if I would like to take over a Night Interdiction Mosquito Wing. When I said that I most certainly would, he promised to speak to the AOC about it. He thought that it could be fixed easily and he also suggested that I go and see the AOC.

The Group Captain commanding the whole AFU gave me permission to visit the AOC of No. 2 Group when I explained that there was a chance for me to get back on operations. This was a great concession in Training Command so, as he had not specifically asked, I did not volunteer the information that the Group was in Belgium in case it embarrassed him. Two days later I set off for Moelsbroek outside Brussels to see Air Vice-Marshal Embry. It was an interesting trip and I was amazed at the amount of bomb damage that was visible from the air particularly around the V-1 sites. One had to be a little careful, though, as there were still a lot of German troops cut off and isolated but only too ready to open fire on any unwary aeroplane; quite a number of machines had been lost in this way, particularly around Dunkirk.

I was given a nice welcome by the AOC who even loaned me his caravan to sleep in. As we were standing outside talking, the Germans sent a welcome too in the form of a V-1 that flew right over our heads and then dived into the ground about a mile further on. That night I could hear the guns muttering away off to the east and the next morning I was privileged in being allowed to attend the AOC's briefing of his crews. The battle for Wesel was just about to begin. After the briefing I had a long chat with the Air Vice-Marshal and he promised to do all he could to get me out of Training Command and into his Group. In the afternoon I made my departure in a happy frame of mind and confident that I would soon be back in a nice healthy operational atmosphere. Despite Air Marshal Embry's efforts on my behalf, I was doomed to disappointment and fated to see out the war in Training Command, at least as far as the European War was concerned. I must say that VE night in Bath was quite an experience and I never thought that the people would let themselves go as they did – it was great fun.

Not long after the war had ended I was ordered to report to Transport Command Headquarters. At last I was out of Training Command and, although it was not exactly what I wanted, I rather looked forward to flying larger aircraft and getting about the world in relative comfort. Again I was to he disappointed as the 'Union' considered that no fighter pilot could be converted on to four-engined aircraft without a long drawn out period of training and it wasn't worth the effort. I tried to settle for Dakotas as I had already flown them, but no – I would have far too much to learn. The best I could get was command of a Staging Post and so I had to resign myself to my fate which turned out to be that of CO of the Staging Post at Athens – which really wasn't too hard to take.

The new AOC of No. 216 Group, Air Vice-Marshal Darvall, under whom I would now serve, was on the point of leaving England to take up his new appointment and he kindly offered to take me out with him in his own aircraft. In this I was doubly lucky as, in addition to travelling in VIP style, I enjoyed the leisurely trip with its stops at Naples and Athens spending a day or two at each, then a very pleasant flight from Athens over the Greek Islands and on to Heliopolis. I liked the look of Athens and decided that I was going to enjoy my tour of duty.

Alas, it was not to be – three days after arriving in Egypt a signal arrived to say that I had been selected for the Staff College course and I was to return to England. The Staff College, however, was being moved from its old location at Gerrards Cross to Bracknell and this created delays and the starting date of the course kept on being put back. To fill in time I was sent on a course at the School of Air Transport at Netheravon – this over I was still at a loose end so I asked 'P' Staff at Command if I could be attached to their Tactical Development Unit at Netheravon; they seemed rather surprised to find that it was one of their units but, glad to get rid of me, they readily agreed to my suggestion and back I went to Netheravon.

This unit was commanded by another ex-Farnborough Test Pilot, Tam Morrison, who had much the same ideas about flying that I had; consequently I found myself at the controls of a Dakota right away. A few days later I asked Tam if I could fly the four-engined aircraft and said I would like to start with the York. He dug into his desk drawer, pulled out the *Pilot's Notes* for the aircraft and said: 'OK. Grab yourself an engineer and bog off!'

Such was my conversion on to 'fours'.

I only remained with this unit for a month, but during that time I managed to fly eight different types of aircraft, six of them new to me and four of them four-engined!

At the end of August the course started at Staff College and found myself sharing a room with Bill Coles (who later became Air Marshal Sir William Coles) who had been on the staff of the school at

Netheravon. A most likeable person, he had had a remarkable career and wore the ribbons of the DSO, DFC★, AFC and the American DFC, all of which he earned on transport operations.

We got on very well together and because of our totally different experiences in the Service were able to help one another a lot with the involved exercises that were set by the College's Directing Staff which made the work easier for both of us.

This, the first post-war course, was perhaps the most extraordinary of any before or since. Out of the 120 students about 60 were Group Captains whilst the rest were nearly all very senior Wing Commanders. Also there were a number of officers from the Dominions, the Army and Navy and USAF. The majority of the students had held positions of considerable importance during the war and were not used to being talked down to as certain of the outside lecturers were inclined to do. As a rule they regretted this; during question time they could be subjected to some very pointed enquiries and if their answers were not, right they were corrected immediately. By and large they had a very rough time.

On one occasion the Director of Navigation from the Air Ministry was delivering a lecture and it was not long before it became evident that he just did not like fighter pilots and in his opinion, they were a pretty brainless lot. As quite lot of us were fighter pilots we did not take too kindly to this but we bided our time and waited for the question period to roll around – it fell to me to open fire first.

With the greatest respect, I pointed out that it was all very well for him and his staff to criticise the fighter boy but it would have been much better for all concerned if they had tried to understand the fighter's problem and to help with carefully considered advice. I went on to say that, as far as I could remember, none of his staff of experts ever got down to evolving some simple 'rule of thumb' method of navigation that would help the fighter boy especially when, after a fight, he found himself alone over enemy territory. Instead, however, it was left to the likes of us to evolve our own simple systems for getting home.

He reacted as I had hoped he would and sarcastically asked: 'And, pray, what was this wonderful system? We would all be interested to hear.'

I looked straight at him for a moment or two and then said, 'Well, sir, I'll tell you. I used to brief my pilots on operational sorties that, if they became separated, lost and were down on the deck, they were to put the number of their squadron on their compass and fly on that!'

This brought the house down and I thought our lecturer was going to have an apoplectic fit he was so angry. He did not realise that I was, in fact, telling the literal truth: I was referring to the Polish Wing where all the Squadron numbers were between 302 and 315 and, operating over the Pas de Calais as we were, you were bound to hit the south-east of England if you flew a compass course between those numbers.

The course extended into 1946 and although on the whole we had enjoyed it we were not at all sorry that it was coming to an end. We were now asked if we had any particular preferences as regards postings and here I took a calculated risk and gambled on the premise that whatever you apply for you are bound to get something else. The one place I did not want to go to was the Air Ministry – so I applied for it. The gamble came off and I was posted to Germany as Wing Commander, Operations Plans, at Air Headquarters, British Air Forces of Occupation at Bad Eilsen a small Spa about two miles from Buckeburg and not all that far from Minden.

The Spa at Bad Eilsen was a delightful place situated in an attractive valley with a pretty little stream running through the grounds of the several hotels there. Sometimes the smell of this stream is not so attractive, but the waters I am told, are health-giving. Some of the hotels we used as offices and others for accommodation. We lived very comfortably indeed as, unlike the Army, we took over and used all the furniture, linen, carpets, pictures, table lamps and everything else that went towards providing comfort. This was true not only of the living accommodation but also the offices – we just moved in and made use of whatever was there that we needed. The Army, on the other hand – or so I am told – took out all the German property and replaced it with Government Issue trestle tables and iron bedsteads. I couldn't understand this approach and we lived far better except as far as food was concerned and here we were all in the same boat – it was bloody!

It was rather a depressing time to take up my new appointment as it meant being associated with the running down of the Royal Air

Force which up to now had been a fighting machine of such power and efficiency as had never been seen before. Fortunately my duties necessitated my travelling about a lot and this took my mind off the depressing aspects of the rundown.

This travelling gave me an opportunity of visiting all sorts of places that until now had been nothing but a name to me. In a very short time I became familiar with practically the whole of the British Zone and some fantastic sights were to be seen – the Autobahn out of Hamburg lined for mile after mile after mile with rows of vehicles parked side by side, staff cars, lorries, armoured cars, tanks and Lord knows what else! The towns shattered and blasted like Hanover which, to look down upon, seemed for all the world like hundreds of match-boxes standing on end in heaps of rubble. Along the roads one came across a abandoned guns, shattered tanks and wooden crosses with coal-scuttle helmets hanging from them, loco-motives, their boilers riddled and their train of goods wagons shot full of holes, fit only for scrap – only there was nothing to take it all to the scrap yards.

In addition to travelling about the Zone I also paid visits to Paris, Brussels, Copenhagen and Berlin. In the last city, like everyone else I paid a visit to Hitler's shattered Chancellery and the Bunker where he died. I was accompanied by two other officers, but while I was busy taking photographs we became separated. I did not realise I was alone until I noticed two Russian soldiers coming towards me and eyeing my camera. As they got closer their intentions became obvi-ous so I pulled my automatic out of my pocket and, looking them straight in the eye, deliberately pumped a shell into the chamber and brought the gun to bear on the midriff of the nearest one. They took the hint and stopped; after a brief consultation, during which they didn't take their eyes off the gun, they hurried away.

I was quite relieved as although I would not have hesitated to shoot them had they tried anything I was not certain of the official attitude towards such incidents. From what I learned later I don't think anyone would have cared much, including the Russian authorities.

I made a point of speaking to as many German people as pos-sible in an endeavour to find out what they were really like. At first they appeared to be very much like ourselves; they looked like us, lived very much the same way, the language had a strong affinity to

English and it seemed strange that we should have been fighting one another with such bitterness. The longer I was in Germany, however, the more apparent it became that they had an entirely different outlook on life and quite a different scale of values. One could almost say that, in many ways, they were child-like – romantic, chivalrous, generous and cruel.

It was very noticeable when speaking to different individuals that they were always polite but reserved and invariably they got around to asking how many times I had bombed them. Once I explained that I was a fighter pilot their attitude changed and they became almost friendly – at the same time they had developed a healthy respect for the RAF bombers and attributed to them a fantastic degree of accuracy.

In Lubeck, for instance, I was being shown over the Rathaus by the *Burgomeister*. It is a beautiful old building dating back to the fourteenth century and fortunately had escaped major damage. The old man was obviously very proud of it and its contents, but as we made our way around he suddenly grasped my arm and pointed out of the window at a scene of utter devastation in which only one house still stood. In his broken English he said: 'In the war is here coming many Englisher bombers and many, many bombs are here fallen. After all is *Kaput* except this one house and, before the war, this house was the house of the Englisher consul! Dear God, but the English bomber fliers are unbelievably accurate!'

About the middle of 1946, it appeared likely that Tito might make a bid to take over Trieste in which event the depleted British forces in Italy would be called upon to resist him. It was decided to send a Fighter/Bomber Wing from BAFO to Northern Italy to reinforce the remnants of the Desert Air Force.

It fell to me to write the Operational Plan for this reinforcement and to some others to produce the Administrative Instructions so a party of us set off by air to visit the potential battleground. Our route took us via Frankfurt and Vienna to Klagenfurt in Austria where we stayed the night, going on to Udine the next morning.

Based at Udine we toured the area and the various airfields that could be made available to us. It was not long before we had a pretty clear picture of the sort of problems we were likely to be faced with should it become necessary to provide the reinforcement Wing.

Having completed our mission we were making ready to return to Germany when the AOC of Desert Air Force, who turned out to be Air Vice-Marshal Darvall who had so kindly taken me out to Egypt just over a year before, insisted that we spend a weekend in Venice – it sounded good to us so we leapt at the suggestion.

We all had a wonderful time and stayed at the Danielli Hotel where the AOC's launch collected us each morning and took us to the Lido to swim. We were also lucky in that our visit coincided with the annual Regatta of the Gondolas. It was a most interesting and colourful sight and I wouldn't have missed it for anything – altogether I took a very good view of Venice and much regret that I have never had the opportunity to return.

Our holiday over, we started back to Buckeburg but the clouds were building up so much over the Alps that it was impossible for us to return the way we had come. However, return we must, orders already having arrived from Air Headquarters to that effect. To make sure we fully understood the impossibility of getting over the mountains, the clouds themselves took a hand and we suffered a downpour the like of which I have never experienced before or since.

This demonstration convinced us so we re-routed ourselves via Pisa, where we refuelled and had a look at the Leaning Tower, then went on to Istres, not so far from Marseilles and then on to Paris where we stayed the night. The next day we took the opportunity of calling on the squadrons at Wahn just outside Cologne. After this we flew on to Buckeburg so completing a very enjoyable and interesting round trip.

In point of fact, the need to move the wing to Italy never arose, but some interesting problems came to light. Although there was no difficulty in getting the aircraft to Italy the problem of getting stores and equipment was quite another matter. One difficulty was that a lot of the heavier equipment, when loaded on railway wagons, would not go through the tunnels. Another was that the Communists were so active in France that it was not safe to route trains carrying stores and equipment for use against Tito through France as they would almost certainly be sabotaged.

Eventually we came to the conclusion that we might well have to move a large quantity of freight back to Antwerp and ship it to Italy from there – not a very satisfactory answer and I, for one, was very glad that Tito decided against embarking upon his little adventure.

Not long after this I had another interesting flight from Berlin to Copenhagen. I was cleared for a direct flight and did not have to use the corridor through the Russian Zone. I flew at about 1,000 feet and it was quite uncanny to fly for mile after mile with an almost total lack of movement or sign of life on the ground. The whole way from Berlin to the coast I saw only one farm cart and two staff cars moving along the roads.

I did see a large country house which appeared to be a military headquarters of some sort judging by the number of army type vehicles that were parked around it. Even here there was no movement, no sign of life, and it was really quite eerie. I was very glad to cross the coast and out to sea, away from it all. I was even more pleased when I saw Copenhagen in the distance. As usual it was a thoroughly enjoyable visit – it is a strange place and I have never been able to put my finger on just what it is that makes this city so different from others but it certainly has something.

Back in Bad Eilsen three of us decided to go to the Officers' Club in Buckeburg one evening, but on the way we called in at a civilian officers' club run by the Control Commission. There were only a few people there, most of them in CCG uniform, but one medium sized chap dressed in ordinary civilian clothes came over to us and started a conversation. When it transpired that all three of us were fighter pilots he was very thrilled and insisted on buying us drinks.

We had quite an amusing time with him and several others who joined in, but he kept asking us what the weather was going to be like the next day, Sunday, as he had to get back to England; he had, he explained, 'a date with Mr Heath on Wednesday'. Alternatively he kept inviting us to come and have a drink with him in his pub when we got back to England.

After he had extended this invitation about ten times I said to him: 'Look, we would be only too pleased to come and drink your pub dry, but we have no idea where it is, nor do we know who you are, but if you'll write your name and address here,' handing him my pocket diary, 'we will call on you one day!'

'Yes, o'course,' he said, writing away and then handed the diary back to me. I glanced at it and the penny dropped with a fearful suddenness. The signature was that of the Public Hangman – hence

his date with my ex-Squadron mate, Mr Neville Heath, the following Wednesday.

Towards the end of the year I was selected to succeed Bob Wright
as Personal Staff Officer to Sir Sholto Douglas, who had followed
'Monty' as Commander-in-Chief and Military Governor of the
British Zone of Occupied Germany. This meant that I would have
to leave Bad Eilsen and move to the official Residence, Schloss
Ostenwalde, not very far from Osnabruck. The C-in-C's Headquarters
and offices were in Lubbecke some twenty miles from the Schloss
while there was another Residence in the British Sector of Berlin
as well as more offices.

To go into details of my duties as PSO would mean a fairly
detailed description of the organization of the Control Commission
in Germany, which has been more than adequately covered in Lord
Douglas's own book. Suffice to say that I was required to accompany
the 'Chief', as we called him, on all his journeys, see to it that the
office was run properly through his Personal Assistant and Secretary
and that the Household was similarly run efficiently through the two
ADCs – one a Naval Lieutenant and the other an Army Captain.

To ensure that there was a reasonable balance among the Staff
the appointments were filled by members of all three Services and,
in addition to those already mentioned, there was also a Military
Assistant with the rank of Lieutenant Colonel.

Meetings of the four-power Control Council were held at regular
intervals in Berlin and I always accompanied the Chief on these trips
and attended the meetings making sure that he had his 'briefs' ready
to hand during the discussions with the Commanders-in-Chief of
the other three Zones.

On these trips to Berlin the Chief and his staff used the delightful residence at Kladow, right on the banks of the Havel and
directly opposite the island upon which some 3,000 SS troops and
Hitlerjugend had held out for four days after the rest of Berlin
had fallen. Eventually the Russians had effected a landing and the
Germans were wiped out to a man. One day I went over to the island
on an exploring trip and came across a field gun and, beside it, an SS
helmet. I picked it up and saw that there was a dent, obviously made
by a bullet, just above the part that would cover the right forehead

– but the dent had been made from the inside of the helmet. I feel sure that the unfortunate owner of the helmet had been wounded and as he lay on the ground a Russian put a pistol behind his left ear and pulled the trigger – I knew this sort of thing had gone on and here was evidence of it.

On the whole the Control Council meetings were, subject-wise, pretty dull but I found an interest in the way the Russians behaved. It was very obvious that their C-in-C, Marshal Sokolovsky, was only authorised to negotiate with the other Commanders-in-Chief up to a certain point, after which the matter had to be referred to Moscow. It was very evident, too, when he had reached this limit and there was absolutely no point in trying to continue the discussion; all that could be done was to proceed with the next item on the agenda.

I noticed too that they were very sensitive and always on the lookout for the veiled innuendo. On one occasion when Sokolovsky had been particularly irritating and lapsing into the Russian habit of speaking in proverbs, Sir Sholto made the remark that, in his opinion, the Marshal was drawing a red herring across the trail. This broke up the meeting as the interpreters were unable to explain to Sokolovsky the meaning of this saying and it was funny to watch the consternation caused: 'What is a herring? Why should it be red? How does this affect the Soviet Union?'

Another interesting aspect of my appointment was the opportunity it gave to meet a great many prominent people, perhaps the most outstanding being ex-President Hoover. He was most charming and very pro-British; when he spoke of the days of 1940, there were tears in his eyes as he expressed his admiration for the British during the days when we stood alone – and this was no political speech, it was sentiment genuinely felt and expressed to me personally over lunch.

During the time I held this appointment I became involved in a variety of situations, some comic, some semi-tragic and others grim, but I do not feel that they have any real place in this narrative. It was a strange life and one in which one's scale of values could very easily become completely distorted. This was particularly noticeable amongst the more junior members of the staffs of the various dignitaries concerned with the running of Germany. These ADCs and their civilian counterparts were generally known as members of the

'Flunkeys' Union' and it was amusing, if a little irritating, to watch them each assume the mantle of his or her master.

When Sir Sholto handed over to his successor, General Sir Brian Robertson, there was an official farewell arranged in Berlin. During the ceremonies I was approached by several of the flunkeys, who told me that they had heard that Sir Sholto's Military Assistant had been accepted by Robertson as his MA, but what, they wanted to know, was happening to me, as they had heard that there was no place for me on the General's staff?

I was able to assure their eager little ears that it was quite true and that I had, in fact, been given a new appointment back in England – that of Chief Test Pilot at Farnborough. They looked rather shocked and one said: 'Oh, I say, what frightfully bad luck!'

11

Chief Test Pilot

Living conditions at Farnborough were a decided come-down after the luxury of Germany. Admittedly the food at Bad Eilsen had been pretty poor but the Mess was very comfortable indeed whilst the Schloss at Ostenwalde and the Berlin Residence were quite palatial. It is not to be wondered at then that when I found myself accommodated in a room about ten feet by twelve and given one bucket of coal a week to heat it I was more than a little fed up.

The Mess was very old fashioned and anything but warm while the food was ghastly. It was neatly summed up, with unconscious humour, by Charles, our Austrian waiter, a tiny man who had been seventy-three for years. It was his custom to come in to the bar in the evening to enquire as to whether or not any of us would be dining. This particular evening he came in and said to me: 'Are you dining to-night, sair?'

So I said: 'I don't know, Charles; is it edible?' – to which he replied: 'No, sair, it ess feesh.' – and how right he was!

The RAE and the airfield had grown almost out of all recognition and where I had flown from a small grass airfield there were now great long concrete runways and in place of the old wooden Watch Office there was an enormous new Control Tower. There were no squadrons and what was left of the RAF Station was in the process of folding up. In what had been the School of Photography the Empire Test Pilots' School was now ensconced while alongside it were the new brick buildings of the RAF Institute of Aviation Medicine, a far cry from the rough wooden huts it originally occupied.

The Experimental Section had been renamed the Experimental Flying Department but it retained its old organization in general although it was much larger and was now comprised of seven flights whereas pre-war there had been only four. In addition there was a

Meteorological Flight which was more in the nature of a lodger unit. But things were not by any means all strange – my new CO was Silyn Roberts another pre-war Test Pilot whilst his Secretary was the same Miss Betty Grinsted who had been so helpful to me when I was Adjutant, and to whom everyone still referred if they wanted information. She was a walking encyclopaedia as far as the RAE was concerned and if she did not know the answer to a query she invariably knew who would know. Then there was Gil Harris now graduated from the Watch Office to the post of Senior Air Traffic Controller and 'King' of the new tower.

I was also pleased to find that one of the Flight Commanders was Squadron Leader Dickie Martin whom I had known for many years and he had, in fact, been in my Sector in the desert during the war. He was an exceptionally fine fighter pilot and turned out to be an even better test pilot; the flight he commanded was the Structures and Mechanical Engineering Flight and among the various aircraft he had was a Sikorsky R4 Helicopter called a 'Hoverfly' by the RAF.

Never having been in a Helicopter I decided that I must learn to fly one and I chased up one of the four civilian test pilots, 'Denny' Dennis who was the expert on 'whirly birds', and asked to be checked out on the R4. Here my theory of 'Fly one – fly any' came unstuck – helicopters are not like any other heavier-than-air machine; nowadays they are becoming more simplified, but this little thing really gave you a work-out. It was the first helicopter bought by the Service and really was underpowered – it was only possible to 'hover' on the bubble of air formed beneath the rotor and this was only effective a few feet off the ground. Everything vibrated madly and this, coupled with the continual alteration of the position of the pitch control and the throttle setting when trying to hover, made it all very hard work – after half an hour of it you felt like a wet dish-cloth.

Despite the hard work I found it all very interesting and enjoyable but even now, having flown quite a number of different helicopters and put in a fair amount of flying time in them, I can't say that I was ever quite as much in control of the situation as I would have liked. At times they can exasperate one almost beyond endurance. I remember a young Naval officer arriving in an R4 to visit Dickie's flight; he approached in the approved manner and, on arriving over the spot on which he intended to land, pulled up the nose to check the forward movement before putting it down. Unfortunately he was not quite quick enough in levelling off and the machine slid backwards off its bubble of air hitting the tail on the ground which first shattered the tail rotor and then slammed the machine forward on to its nose. Out jumped the pilot and kicked the wreckage hard – I knew just how he felt!

I spent the first few weeks at Farnborough getting to know my way around and familiarising myself with the various projects and aircraft. So far I had never managed to fly a jet so I was very pleased that I was now in a position to fly several different jets more or less whenever I liked. The first one I flew was a Vampire which struck me as being remarkably small for an operational aeroplane and, in the cockpit, I felt as though I was sitting on the ground.

Having mastered the start-up procedure and 'learned the taps' I taxied out, lined up on the long runway, applied the brakes fully and opened the throttle until I had nearly full power and the nose strut was well compressed, then I released the brakes and opened the engine fully. We fairly shot away and, being in the nose and so close to the ground, the runway came rushing at me at tremendous speed. I began to wonder what I had let myself in for and momentarily I thought of closing the throttle and having a think about it but it was too late – we were already in the air!

I whipped up the undercarriage and the little aeroplane climbed away beautifully; I rapidly overcame the initial shock and was amazed at the smoothness and lack of vibration. The aircraft handled very nicely and reminded me very much of a Spitfire but perhaps the most impressive thing was the visibility from the cockpit – there was no great Merlin engine or propeller to get in the way.

After spending the best part of an hour getting used to the machine I returned to the airfield and prepared for my first landing. Just as I was joining circuit, one of the Naval pilots got caught by the South Gate Gremlin and his Sea Fury dropped out of his hands and crashed on the approach end of the main runway. I passed over the top of the crashed Fury and rounded out to land, but the little Vampire just kept flying and we floated along the runway about five feet up until I forced it on to the ground. As soon as I raised the nose to reduce speed, back into the air we went. Again I forced it on to the ground and this time applied full brake which had the desired effect; when I turned off the runway and stopped. I had a look round the cockpit to see if there was anything that I had forgotten and there was – I had been so interested in the Fury on my approach that I had forgotten to lower the flaps...

During these first few weeks I managed to get in several new types including the B17 Flying Fortress, Sea Hornet, Hastings and a funny little German single-seater called a Zaun Koenig – Wren in English – which the designer claimed could be flown by anyone after only half-an-hour's instruction on the ground irrespective of whether or not they had ever flown before. He may have been right, but it wasn't our task to find out.

I was very fortunate also in having the opportunity of flying the world's first turbo-prop aeroplane, a Meteor fitted with two Trent propeller-turbine engines. The propellers were of small diameter to give adequate ground clearance but had five blades so that when in fine pitch they produced quite a considerable amount of drag.

The take-off was a great improvement on the pure jet, as was the initial climb, and altogether the machine impressed me very much although it gave me a bit of a shock when I tried its single-engined handling qualities. From level cruising flight conditions I suddenly closed the port throttle, the propellers tried to maintain revolutions and went fully fine, this produced the drag already referred to and the next thing I knew the aeroplane and I were smartly upside down. I realised what had happened and rapidly opened the throttle and rolled the aircraft right way up again. On landing and shutting down I got another shock as the mechanics casually put their hands on the propeller spinners as they were still turning so helping them to slow down. I rather felt that such familiarity might lead to them picking on a piston-engined machine one day which would not be so funny.

One of the major projects with which the Experimental Flying Department was concerned was the Flexible Deck, the scheme being to land an aircraft on its belly – without undercarriage – using a rubber deck and an arrester wire. One of the most important advantages of such a scheme was that it could make it possible to do away with the undercarriage altogether which, on fighter aircraft, would be a saving of 15% in weight. Also it would permit of much smaller ships being used as carriers and the equipment could be made air transportable so that 'airfields' could be established in all sorts of otherwise inaccessible spots.

The deck itself consisted of a thick, reinforced rubber sheet laid over a number of transverse air hoses about five deep. The installation at Farnborough consisted of this 200-foot long deck, an arrester wire at the approach end supported on poles to keep the wire at a height of some two and a half feet from the surface of the deck and then further towards the direction of approach came a steel deck and a 'round-down'.

A number of dummy tests had been carried out using old gliders but the actual live test programme was for the initial landings to be made by Lieutenant Commander Brown who commanded the Aerodynamic and Naval Aircraft Flight. He had a great deal of experience in deck landings and it was logical that he should do the first landings. Next was one of Brown's pilots Flight Lieutenant 'Jumbo' Genders who had done a deck landing course some years before and who, incidentally, was one of the very few pilots to shoot down one of the high-flying Ju86Ps in the Middle East. The third pilot was to be me; as I had never had anything to do with deck landings, it was considered that if I could manage to land-on successfully then anybody could!

The approach path to the deck was rather like an obstacle race and took the aircraft over buildings, trees, the main road, laboratories and past hangars, old catapults and down into a dip before crossing a short stretch of open ground and on to the deck.

Brown had been practising the approach for quite a long time even before I arrived at Farnborough but eventually the day came when everything was ready for the first actual landing. On his approach Brown was unfortunate in getting into a most unenviable position where he could only maintain height by using full power which, in the attitude of the aircraft, was insufficient to enable him to climb away. At the same time he could not lower the nose to gain speed as the machine would have sunk on to the ground. He was, therefore, committed and had to continue towards the deck with the arrester hook actually dragging along the ground until finally the tail booms of the aircraft – the Vampire was of twin-boomed construction – struck the round-down. This jammed the controls and knocked the nose down. The Vampire dived over the arrester wire, plunged into the deck, bounced, came down again at the end of the deck bounced once more and crashed into the ground beyond the deck. The fuselage split round the cockpit and the aircraft was written off but Brown, remarkably was unhurt although rather badly shaken which was understandable.

This put back the programme somewhat, but we continued to carry out the practices and to analyse the films of the dummy runs until all was ready for a second live attempt. This time all went well and Brown landed on successfully although to lookers-on it looked most hair-raising.

Jumbo was next, and he was successful and then it was my turn. By this time I had completed 128 dummy runs over the deck on 32 of which I had the arrester hook down but so arranged that it could not pick up the wire. One could, however, feel it hit the wire and it was satisfying to have this reassurance as to one's accuracy in flying to these narrow limits. It did not take me very long to master the technique of the approach and I was soon quite confident in my ability to pick up the wire, although when the time came for the actual landing I must admit to being a little dubious about the whole thing. I first of all made a couple of dummy approaches and then lowered the hook and commenced my approach for the actual landing. Everything went well and I settled into a nice steady approach, gradually losing height and speed as I passed all the familiar landmarks on the way in. As I got closer the deck looked smaller and smaller and not nearly big enough to take the Vampire, but I was now committed. The airspeed dropped slowly until it registered a steady 105 mph and then I crossed the round-down, felt a slight tremor through the aircraft as the hook hit the wire, followed by a sensation as though the machine was on a length of elastic. I realised that I had caught the wire properly so I quickly closed the throttle and almost immediately the aircraft thumped on to the deck. Although I was snapped forward against my harness rather sharply, the landing was not at all uncomfortable.

On this first landing I had managed to pull off a copy-book approach and pick up the wire, but on my second landing I was slightly low and the belly of the aeroplane brushed the wire. This time everything happened at terrific speed, one instant I was flying and the next I had been snatched out of the air and flung violently on to the deck. I had no time to close the throttle and as I was flung forward my hand also went forward and opened the throttle wide; the engine seemed to scream in agony. I immediately slammed the throttle shut, but it all seemed to take rather a long time and I was sure that I must have burnt a hole in the deck surface. When I climbed out I was surprised to discover that not only had I not damaged the deck but I had apparently moved so fast that none of the on-lookers realised that I had opened the throttle.

Work continued on the project and a deck was installed on HMS *Warrior* for trials at sea. Plans progressed for the three of us to land-on. Then the Admiralty suddenly decided that their regulations forbade anyone landing on their carriers who had not qualified at a deck-landing school. I, therefore, had to take myself off to Scotland and undergo training, thereby defeating the object of the exercise.

For one reason or another I had to wait until mid-October before I could start my course at Milltown, a satellite of Lossiemouth near Elgin. The accommodation was unbelievably frightful; the station had belonged to the RAF but, being no longer required, was abandoned and everything had fallen into decay. Then the Navy took it over, much to the disgust of the unfortunates who found themselves stationed there. I stuck it for nearly a week and then moved into a hotel.

The initial part of the training consisted of learning the meanings of the signals given by the batsman so thoroughly that one automatically reacted to them. Then came the airfield dummy deck landings, or 'Addles' as they were called, and usually there were three aircraft in the circuit at once just following the signals of the batsman, landing, then immediately opening up and going round again. In ten days I made no less than fifty-five of these dummy deck landings, as many as seven in a twenty-minute flight.

Eventually the carrier HMS *Illustrious* arrived in the Moray Firth and the time had come for the actual landings. The aircraft were all flown aboard by the instructors while we pupils were taken by bus through Inverness to, I think, Invergordon where we went aboard a destroyer which took us out to *Illustrious*.

The following morning we were given a final briefing and allotted our turns to fly. I was to be first away with one of the Naval officers following, the aircraft operating in pairs. We climbed into our aircraft, carried out the required drill and then came the order to start up. I pressed the starter button, there was a chup as the cartridge fired and my engine was running. Not so with the other aircraft; the pilot fired cartridge after cartridge but with no success and, eventually he had so overdoped the engine that there was no hope of starting it until it had had a chance to dry out.

I was cleared to go and taxied forward, ran up on the brakes then, on the signal being given, I was away and found the whole thing very much more simple than I had imagined. I gained height and started to circle the ship while the other aircraft was pushed for'ard against a 30-knot wind to be taken below on the for'ard lift, all of which took some time and each time I circled the ship it got smaller and smaller until, when I got the signal from the bridge to make my first landing, it had assumed the proportions of a matchstick!

On my first landing I caught No. 3 wire and came to a sudden halt with the cockpit canopy slamming shut so violently it practically took my ears off. My instructor, Lieutenant Russell, immediately leaped on to the wing and tore me off a real strip for landing with the canopy shut and pointed out the dangers involved had I gone over the side. I explained that it had been open when I started and had only shut on landing – then I discovered that I had not locked it properly through being used to a different Mark of the same type of aircraft. Quite a simple mistake and easy to make, but one which could easily have had fatal consequences – in fact, Russell himself was to die in a similar accident years later when his Scimitar plunged into the sea after the arrester gear failed.

I completed my series of landings without mishap and so qualified as being 'proficient in deck landings'. Then, having acquired this rather unnecessary distinction, I returned to Farnborough ready for the next phase. In spite of all this preparation and several trips to sea in *Warrior* I never, in fact, had the opportunity of landing aboard and gradually I lost interest, particularly as the original purpose of my taking part in the trials had been defeated by red-tape.

One of my trips in *Warrior* I remember only too well as the weather deteriorated very rapidly once we were clear of Portsmouth and out into the Channel and it was soon evident that we could not hope to fly. The Captain therefore put back to Portsmouth only to find that the seas were such that he could not get into the harbour. This necessitated sending for the Admiral's barge – as the Admiral was aboard – but the seas were too much for it and so a tug had to come to the rescue fighting its way out and finally managing to come alongside.

I watched all the proceedings with interest, particularly as a rope ladder had been slung over the side to dangle a few feet from the deck of the tug. I was not so intrigued when an officer came up to me and said: 'Righto, sir, you're first!'

I looked at him aghast and said: 'What, me climb down that?'

'Yes – that's right,' he replied. 'Over you go!'

I could not very well refuse with all these dark blue perishers look-ing on and grinning, so over the side I went, hating every second of it. Slowly I made my way down, taking care to keep looking upwards to prevent any onset of vertigo. I was about three-quarters of the way down when someone shouted, 'Hold it, sir. Hang on!' – just as if I wasn't – my fingerprints are probably still on the rungs. Anyway, I stopped, glanced down and the tug had gone! There was nothing below me but the pounding sea, which had made it impossible for the tug to keep station. It was now manoeuvring itself back into position. I waited until it bumped the side of *Warrior* and then I just let go and arrived in a heap on the deck – I haven't been to sea in a carrier since.

While I had been waiting to go on my course with the Navy there had been a lot of other activity at Farnborough, the most important being the preparations for the Exhibition and Flying Display of the Society of British Aircraft Constructors which was to be held at Farnborough for the first time in September of 1948. It created a whole host of fresh problems and interfered with our test programmes.

As Chief Test Pilot I was automatically on the Flying Control Committee along with the CO, the Senior Air Traffic Controller and several of the more senior and experienced civilian test pilots such as 'Mutt' Summers, Gordon Slade and Bill Pegg. I was to be a member of this committee for the first two displays and had a great deal to do with the organization and preparations for the third, though I had been posted by the time it took place.

The original displays bear little resemblance to the vast and highly organized show that it is today and the famous 'caravans' as they are still called, although more closely resembling expensive restaurants were, in fact, real caravans and originally numbered about four! The display was a huge success and it has since, of course, become a major national event.

Silyn Roberts was posted to Germany and in his place came Allen Wheeler, one of the very few officers, if not the only one, to command the Experimental Flying Department twice. In addition to a host of varying interests he was a trustee of the Shuttleworth Trust that maintains a number of vintage aircraft in flying condition.

In May of 1949, the Royal Aeronautical Society held its annual Garden Party at White Waltham near Maidenhead and part of the attendant flying programme was the appearance of some of these old aircraft. Jeffrey Quill, of Spitfire fame, was to fly the Bleriot IX of 1909, Dickie Martin the Blackburn Monoplane of 1912, while I was given the 1911 Deperdussin Monoplane powered with a 25hp Y-shaped Anzani engine.

The engine started easily and ran beautifully and the aircraft came off the ground very quickly, but I found that the wing-warping control, whereby lateral control was achieved by twisting the whole wing, left quite a lot to be desired! It was great fun, but unfortunately the fact that we were only permitted to make a straight hop gave rise to a lot of binding from the old-timers who wrote rude letters to the press about the pitiful display put up with the aircraft with which they, in their day, performed great feats or daring.

While not in any way wishing to decry the magnificent achievements of these early flyers, I fear that their memories were, in some cases a little faulty; on this very day, I remember one of them telling me how he used to fly the Bleriot and Deperdussin in a gale, yet in the next breath he told me that he had developed the smoking habit through flying. When I asked how, he explained that they used to go out in the morning, light a cigarette and watch the smoke – if it blew away at more than a certain angle they didn't fly; some gale!

As a change of scene it was only a few days after flying the Deperdussin that I first flew the de Havilland 108 Swallow, the tailless research aircraft. It is the only aircraft of this configuration that I have ever flown and I must admit that I would not go out of my way to fly another. Although under normal conditions of flight it did not present any difficulties, under certain conditions it could become extremely dangerous. The popular comment on it at the time was that there was nothing wrong with it that a damned good tail wouldn't correct.

During the SBAC Display just mentioned I managed to fly in several of the aircraft including the Cierva Air Horse, an enormous three-rotor helicopter powered with a de-rated Merlin engine. It was a very strange looking craft and when the throttles were closed on landing great sheets of flame would belch forth from the exhausts in the roof, a frightening sight. Not many months later the front rotor of this machine failed and it crashed killing both pilots, Alan Marsh and 'Jeep' Cable, two of the most experienced rotary wing pilots in the world. Later in the month I was invited to attend the Battle of Britain display at North Weald and to be interviewed for BBC Television along with Douglas Bader and Bob Doe, the interviewer being Richard Dimbleby. It was the usual drill, the three of us lined up alongside a Hurricane and the question was put: 'Which aircraft won the Battle of Britain, the Spitfire or the Hurricane?' One said it was the Spitfire and the other said it was the Hurricane, while I said, 'Both!' – for which I was gently chided by Douglas in his newspaper column. After the interview we were all standing chatting when a small boy appeared and walked straight past Bob Doe, right past me, past Douglas and up to Richard Dimbleby and said: 'Kin I 'ave yer autograph, sir?' Remarkably, a photograph was taken of this incident unbeknownst to us, and it appears in the book about Douglas Bader, Reach for the Sky; it is appropriately captioned 'Sic Transit Gloria!'

In addition to the SBAC Display which was becoming a regular feature at Farnborough we were faced in 1950 with having to have the Royal Air Force Pageant held on the airfield about two months earlier than the Display. For months we had an ever-growing RAF Unit on our doorstep and by spring the place was decidedly overcrowded. I was not looking forward to any further disruption of our test programme, so when Sandy Johnston, another old fighter friend who was handling officers' postings in the Air Ministry, rang up and asked if I would like to go to the States I leaped at the opportunity. He explained that one of the officers who had been on exchange to the All-Weather Flying Division USAF had recently been killed in an accident and they were looking for a replacement. Despite the unpleasantness of stepping into a 'dead man's shoes' I was very keen to go.

During this second tour of duty at Farnborough, a time which coincided with what was the most dangerous period of its history, we had suffered a number of casualties as had the Empire Test Pilots' School. Our first loss, which we could ill-afford, was that of Squadron Leader Wittome who, having miraculously survived a very nasty crash in a Meteor, lost his life in a Spitfire very shortly afterwards. Aside from our thus losing a very nice person we also lost an outstanding test pilot who had come top of the course at the ETPS.

Second to Wittome only by a hairbreadth at ETPS was Squadron Leader Stewart Muller-Rowland, the youngest of three brothers all of whom had distinguished themselves during the war. When Brown was posted back to Naval duties Muller-Rowland succeeded him as Flight Commander and an extremely efficient one he was too.

At this period the Delta configuration was undergoing investigation and development and two designs were in being. One, the Avro 707, had made a number of flights but no test programme had been started; on its first flight at Farnborough piloted by the firm's test pilot, Red Essler, it crashed some miles from the airfield killing the pilot. The second design was being built by Boulton and Paul to RAE specifications and the initial flight trials were to be conducted by the RAE test pilots, which meant that I should make the first flight.

Wind tunnel stability tests had been anything but encouraging and, in view of this and my slight experience of the 108, I was not, perhaps, as enthusiastic as I might have been. On the other hand, Muller-Rowland was just itching to pet his hands on it, but still it was my responsibility.

We discussed this at length one day and, although we could both see and appreciate the other's point of view, it was obvious that he would be very disappointed if he did not make the first flight. I made it clear that I did not in any way wish to steal his thunder, but it was a risky thing and I felt that it was my duty to make the first flight.

He quite saw my argument but said: 'I understand, but I do not think that you should automatically take on every risky job just because you are Chief Test Pilot although, in fact, this thing I am flying this afternoon is far more dangerous than the Delta.'

We were obviously not getting anywhere so I said: 'OK, we'll have another talk about it nearer the time and maybe we can thrash out something suitable to both of us.' Twenty minutes later he was dead.

I watched him take off in the Swallow and climb away to the north-east. It seemed no time at all before I had a telephone call telling me that the aircraft had been seen coming out of cloud in pieces and that the pilot's body had been found in the wreckage. This loss was a frightful blow and it affected everybody, even those who had not even known him personally, while to me, with the memory of our last conversation, it came as a bitter blow.

The post of Flight Commander thus left vacant had to be filled by someone upon whom we knew we could rely and whom we knew had the requisite experience and ability. 'Jumbo' Genders had been posted away a few months previously and, in the normal course of events, would not have been allowed to come back to experimental flying until he had completed at least one tour on normal RAF duties. In view of the unusual situation, however, I did manage to have an exception made and Jumbo returned to us and took over the Aerodynamics Flight.

Three 108s were built in all, the first was basically a Vampire with a special swept wing and fixed slats, but was not capable of any great speed. The other two were very much cleaned up and John Derry had become the first Briton to exceed the speed of sound in a British aircraft whilst flying the same machine in which Stewart Muller-Rowland was later to be killed. Previously Geoffrey de Havilland himself had been killed in the other high-speed model when it disintegrated over the Thames Estuary.

Within a month of taking over the Flight, Jumbo went off in the remaining 'slow' 108 to carry out some stalling tests. The next I heard was that the machine had crashed some ten miles from the airfield. Jumbo had baled out but was too low for his parachute to save him. Progress must go on and research continue to enable it to do so, but I have often felt that the price we pay is too high and in the loss of these three quite outstanding young men I feel it was much too high.

Not all the accidents that occurred were fatal by any manner of means and some of them were highly amusing, although expensive.

One I will never forget occurred during the arrester trials of a Westland Wyvern piloted by one of our Naval officers Lieutenant Jock Elliott.

One of the runways at Farnborough is fitted with an arrester gear and aircraft scheduled for the Navy are proof-tested here before actually landing on a carrier. Different entry speeds are obtained by starting the run into the wires from greater distances up the runway and on this occasion the speed was to be fairly high. Jock positioned the aeroplane, ran up on the brakes and then released them and shot off down the runway, his hook picked up a wire and the arrester gear 'bottomed' – the cable pulled straight out and then stopped dead!

The aircraft parted at the transport joint just aft of the cockpit and Jock found himself gazing skywards through the propeller blades as he and the front end of the aircraft careered along the runway to come to rest on the golf course. Meanwhile the whole rear end quivered momentarily against the stretched cable and was then shot backwards like a stone from a catapult to come to rest at the other end of the runway. Jock was quite unhurt although a little startled.

There were numerous other instances of similar extraordinary accidents but space precludes their inclusion here.

Shortly before the Royal Air Force Pageant was held I handed over to my successor, Wing Commander Tommy Calnan, a very experienced photographic reconnaissance pilot. I handed over with mixed feelings, as I would very much liked to have stayed on, but I would almost certainly have been posted within the next six months to a year and I was looking forward to my tour in the States.

After the handing over formalities were completed we retired to the Mess and as I drove out of the gate for the last time as Chief Test Pilot I met the Delta coming in!

12

Exchange Officer

My wife Betty and I – for I had married soon after the war – crossed the Atlantic very comfortably in the RMS *Mauretania* to New York then went on to Washington to complete various formalities before taking the train to Dayton, Ohio. On arrival at our destination we were met by 'Tich' Whiteley and Jock MacIlwain, two other exchange officers, and their wives. They very kindly took us in hand and explained the general organization as regards the RAF element, there being sixteen officers altogether. After this they took us off to the apartment that had been organized for us on a temporary basis. Later on we rented a nice little bungalow which was more spacious and was also nearer to the base.

On the second day Jock gave me a lift out to the base or Wright-Patterson Air Force Base, to give it its full title, where my new unit, the All-Weather Flying Division was located. Situated a few miles out of Dayton the base was quite staggering in size; some ten miles in length it incorporated two airfields both larger than Farnborough. Over 20,000 private cars went in and out of it daily and although predominantly civilian manned, there were 1,500 more officers on the base than there had been in the entire Royal Air Force when I was first commissioned.

Such an enormous organization had to have an enormous paper empire and a complicated procedure for admission; it took several days to be Processed, Orientated and Indoctrinated.

While going through the appropriate motions required by this procedure a series of intermittent explosions started somewhere on or near the airfield, or so it sounded. I put it down to blasting or old ammunition being disposed of but the Korean War was only a few days old and the upset caused by the bangs amongst the staff in this large room in the Headquarters was quite astonishing. One would have thought that the Russians were knocking on the door, although Dayton then was well beyond the range of the bombers of any potential enemy.

At this time nobody had, apparently, considered that an aeroplane in exceeding the speed of sound would make a bang. There were, of course, very few aeroplanes capable of exceeding Mach One and the only one in service was the North American Sabre. For some time past ranchers in the vicinity of Edwards Air Force Base, the Research Station in the Mojave Desert, had been reporting explosions for which there seemed to be no explanation. Then it was noticed that the times of these reported explosions coincided with the diving tests of the F86 Sabre so some trials were carried out and it was definitely established that the aeroplanes were causing the bangs – or 'sonic boom' as it is now called.

The pundits, as so often happens, refused to accept this and so a number of them had been invited to Dayton to hear for themselves. Major Dick Johnston, then holder of the world's speed record, climbed to height over Wright Field in an F86 and aimed a number of dives at the 'Doubting Thomases' so producing the bangs that satisfied the pundits and scared the secretarial staff.

The All-Weather Flying Division to which I had been assigned was located on the larger of the two airfields – Patterson. It had established a great reputation for itself through an intensive research programme investigating the problems associated with flying through thunderstorms. The results of this programme constituted a most valuable contribution to flying techniques, de-bunked a lot of old theories and produced a vast amount of information from which techniques could be evolved for the penetration of thunderstorms, or other conditions producing severe turbulence, by various types of aircraft.

From this research work had grown a special Branch of the Division called Phase 5 Test Branch and I was placed in charge of it. Without going into great detail I should explain that all new aircraft going into service with the USAF have to undergo certain routine tests before being accepted. These tests are divided into 'Phases' and the 'Fifth Phase' was that wherein the aircraft and its equipment are tested as to their suitability for all-weather operations. After completion of the tests reports were written recommending the best handling techniques for the particular aeroplane.

This was only a part of the Division, the head of which was Colonel Jack Taylor, and the other sections of it were concerned with a variety of test programmes involving investigation into the use of various pieces of equipment and instrumentation designed to facilitate all-weather operations. This included automatic landing systems, automatic air traffic control systems and cockpit lighting to mention but a few.

I had not been at Wright-Pat for long before there came an opportunity to visit the research centre at Langley Field and I flew over in a B45 four jet bomber accompanied by my Branch Aeronautical Engineer, Mr Binckley, and Captain Kesterson, one of my pilots. We were all very impressed with the visit and thoroughly enjoyed it but, on the second day, we suddenly realised that we had not signed the Visitors' Book at Reception.

We went to Reception and duly put the necessary details in the book provided by a charming assistant receptionist who, as we were about to depart, asked, as a routine, 'You are all American citizens?' She looked quite shaken when I said, 'No, I'm not.' So she asked me what I was and I replied that my entry in the book should tell her – I had written *RAF*. It was my turn to be taken aback as she then asked: 'What does RAF stand for?' I should have had more sense and realised that, at this time in particular, Americans had little or no sense of humour when it came to the subject of Communism, McCarthy being very much in the ascendancy just then. Very stupidly I replied to her question by saying: 'Surely you know? – RAF means Russian Air Force!'

That did it – I thought the whole place would burst asunder, questions fairly hurled themselves at me, where did I come from, how did I get there, how long had I been there, what had I seen? She rushed off and returned with her boss and I began to recall tales of Torquemada, but at long last I was permitted to go. I felt very sorry though as it raised a ridiculous storm and my two American companions got a further telling off after we had returned to Dayton.

The Americans were becoming very interested in the British Flight Refuelling Company's 'probe and drogue' system of in-flight refuelling and representatives of the Company were at Wright-Patterson for trials of the system using B29s. I ran into Pat Hornidge, the

Company test pilot whom I had known in England and so was able to fly on the tests. Although I had watched a demonstration of this in a Meteor, which was fitted with a probe in the nose, I had never personally tried it. In the B29 the probe was fixed above the cabin so that the pilot was not lined up with it and consequently it was quite difficult to judge the approach. In addition the aircraft created quite a bow-wave and this affected the drogue, a conical metal contraption which was meant to provide an easy aiming mark and to guide the probe into the socket at the end of the refuelling hose. Quite often, just as contact was about to be made the bow-wave pushed the drogue away from the probe and sent it battering around the windshield of our B29: I expected the glass to shatter at any moment – in fact, it didn't even crack.

Having acquired a small private aircraft I got to know a number of the American private owners around Dayton and it was extremely interesting to see how the average person regarded an aeroplane. With 93,000 civil machines within the Continental United States, most of them privately owned, the aeroplane has almost acquired the status of the family car.

One man I met who was well on into middle-age but with less than thirty hours flying experience thought nothing of taking his wife with him in a small 65hp two-seater monoplane all the way to San Francisco and back. To do this he had to fly over miles of featureless prairie, cross mountain ranges going up to 10,000 feet and vast stretches of desert. To navigate he relied upon his compass, maps and a twenty dollar radio receiver on which he could pick up the Radio/Range. He did not, however, have any transmitter and so could not call for assistance and, just for good measure, a good deal of the flight was at night!

At my request Jack Taylor kindly arranged for me to go through a course at the USAF Instrument Examiners' School in Florida. I took my wife, Betty, and drove down with our young son Stuart bouncing around in the back seat, but he didn't seem to mind too much. Our accommodation which was provided for us on the base was really most comfortable and was right on the shore of the Gulf of Mexico. The service too was excellent and it soon became clear that we had been given the nicest quarter on the base. It was only later that I discovered that I had been described as a Wing Commander and the local authorities had assumed that I was commanding a wing in the USAF and was, therefore, of General Officer rank.

On the course I ran into the trouble that has caused the loss of too many pilots and their passengers. I was doing what is called a range let-down under the hood from 30,000 feet; as I got lower and lower on my approach to the airfield I waited for my instructor in the front seat, who could see out, to either take over or tell me to overshoot. Nothing happened, so when I got down to 300 feet I opened up and started to climb away. At this point he asked what I was playing at, so I told him that I was not prepared to land the beast, a jet, under the hood. He then quietly informed me that I still had 10,000 feet to go! It was a classic case of misreading the three needle altimeter by 10,000 feet.

Fortunately, I had misread it the safe way. Only a few weeks later after my return to Dayton one of my more experienced Officers, Captain Hank Raschke, was carrying out a series of trials with the Northrop Scorpion or F89, and flying under the hood. It was a two-seater aircraft, but an automatic recorder had been installed in the rear seat so an observer could not be carried. To provide a lookout a 'chase plane' always flew alongside the test machine to warn the pilot of the approach of aircraft or other hazards. In this instance Hank had done a number of let-downs from 20,000 and 30,000 feet breaking off each time he reached his minimum altitude. This time, we think he must have misread his altimeter as, having made his let-down, he continued on down below the break-off height despite frantic warning calls from the pilot of the chase-plane and eventually he flew straight into the ground and was killed.

The whole organization at Wright-Patterson including Flight Test Division, the various laboratories and other test and research cells came under the overall control of Wright Air Development Center commanded by, at this time, Major General Dent. In 1951, he decided that he would take a number of officers to the SBAC Display at Farnborough. Because of my association with Farnborough he included me in the number he selected to accompany him. Others in the party included General Al Boyd who was commanding Edwards Air Force Base and Major 'Chuck' Yeager, the first man to exceed the speed of sound.

Altogether there were sixteen of us and we all climbed into a

Douglas C54, and took off for England. Our route took us via Pittsburgh where we stayed about half an hour and then on to Goose Bay in Labrador where we refuelled. The next leg took us over the southern tip of Greenland where we had a magnificent view of the most gigantic ice-bergs. After an eight hour flight we landed at Keflavik in Iceland. Here we stayed most of the day and had a look round the capital before leaving for Paris where we landed some seven hours after leaving Iceland.

I left the party here and went on to England to make such preparations as were required. The others paid a visit to Wiesbaden and Brussels before returning to Paris to get ready for London.

After a few days in London and taking in the display at Farnborough we started on our return trip to Dayton – first stop Madrid. Here we were accommodated in the Hotel Velasquez which was quite palatial. The food was excellent and the wine superb and in the city everything was ridiculously cheap, even taxis to the late spots – until you wanted to leave and then the price became about ten times what it had been on the way to the night club.

One evening three of us went out to one of the more popular clubs, the other two being ex-bomber pilots. One of them had wanted to be a naughty boy while he was on the trip but so far he hadn't had the nerve – this was his last chance. Looking around he spotted a very decorative blonde and, turning to me said: 'You know, John, I reckon I could pick her up!' As it was obvious that was why she was there I said that I thought he could, too. He gave her the 'high sign' and in a flash she was there.

He was the only one of the three of us who could speak Spanish so he had it made all along the line as the saying goes. At one point during the floor show one girl was doing a very wriggly suggestive dance and the other non-Spanish speaking member of the party said: 'Hey, John, how would you like to fly that?'

I watched the gyrations and said: 'No, there is too much aeroelastic distortion for any self-respecting fighter-boy to take that on!'

At this our little Spanish friend wanted to know what I had said, but it was beyond the capability of our temporary Don Juan to explain. After some confused exchanges I got a piece of paper and drew a Spitfire with its guns firing and a B17 dropping bombs. This I handed to her and, pointing to myself indicated the Spitfire and then the others I related to the B17. 'Ah, si, senor,' she cried grasping the pencil and sketching madly; then she handed the paper back with a triumphant smile – she had drawn a bed!

We spent a week in Madrid and when I went to pay my bill I fully expected something that would resemble the National Debt but, to my amazement, I was only charged for a cake of soap, shoe-polishing and a cable I had sent to Betty. I queried this and asked about the meals, the room and the wine, but the staff did not seem to understand what I was getting at. Eventually one of the few who could speak English explained – we had all been the guests of the Spanish Air Force.

Regretfully we had to take our leave and took off on the return flight to Dayton. We landed at the Azores to refuel and then went on to Boston, but about halfway number two engine started to cough and belch forth sheets of flame. I was most unhappy, but Al Boyd who was at the controls shut down the engine and ten minutes later restarted it; from then on it ran beautifully. I don't know what was wrong with it, but it took us back to Dayton quite happily. On arrival Al Boyd and Chuck Yeager promptly climbed into another aeroplane and took off for Edwards another 2,000 miles on. Although neither of them looked it they both had the constitution of an ox!

Shortly after our return the Flight Test Division absorbed the All-Weather Flying Division which, in effect, became a fourth 'Branch' under the older division and ranked with the 'Fighter', 'Bomber' and 'Cargo, Training and Miscellaneous' Branches. I was now moved over to Wright Field as Assistant to the Chief of Flight Test Division, a post I found very much more to my liking as I was able to flying with all four branches and so increase and broaden my experience as well as flying a lot of new types of aircraft.

One of the projects in which the division was interested involved a lot of tests with ski-equipped aircraft and a detachment was sent to Kenora on the Lake of the Woods in Ontario – a place I had known since I was six. For some reason nobody seemed to think about making use of my experience in flying on ski-planes and, not being all that keen on the really low temperatures, I did not draw it to anyone's attention. As Winnipeg was to be the supply base for the detachment I did manage to take one of the test-support aircraft up to my home town on one occasion. I was somewhat taken aback to hear that when I had first called the tower on approaching Winnipeg, one controller turned to another and said: 'Hey, what's this Limey voice doing coming out of a Yankee aeroplane?'

The British idea of the flexible deck had begun to arouse interest in America and I was approached by the project officers charged with investigating the possibilities of adopting the idea. One of the schemes involved the use of an F86 and the other a B45, the former being the more practical as the B45 was not stressed to stand up to the vertical G-loads that would be imposed on it on landing. As far as controllability was concerned it was really delightfully easy to fly it to the fine limits required and I made a number of dummy runs on a 'deck' marked out on the airfield. I recommended that the bomber concept be abandoned and this was, in fact, done.

As my tour of duty was nearing its close I took leave and took Betty and young Stuart on a trip to California to see my father and stepmother. Our car was ideally suited to long trips such as this and we thoroughly enjoyed the experience. Our route took us through vast tracts of prairie, desert and mountainous country. Places we visited bore such fascinating and well known names as Wichita, Tucumcari, Las Vegas, Santa Fe, Albuquerque, Flagstaff and Palm Springs. We saw the Painted Desert, the Grand Can-yon, Meteor Crater, the Mojave Desert, which was just bursting forth into bloom, Boulder Dam and many other fabulous places like the Indian Pueblos at the Ranches of Taos and the Cliff Dwellers' home and beautiful Oak Creek Canyon in Arizona.

Like all tourists we took dozens and dozens of coloured photographs with which we still bore unfortunate guests. One I failed to get, however, which I have always regretted – in Flagstaff I noticed a large sign which read: *See the Grand Canyon from the Air – Fly by Grand Canyon Air-ways*! Directly under the sign was parked a long 'Queen Mary' transporter loaded with the wreckage of a Dakota upon which one could just make out the words – *Grand Canyon Airways*!

We spent three weeks with my father and stepmother in Carmel, California, a delightful little place with a wonderful beach only a few hundred yards from my father's home. After this we stayed a few days with friends in Los Angeles and then made our way back to Dayton, taking much the same route as that by which we had come out to the West Coast.

On my return I was pleased to learn that I had been promoted to Group Captain but this caused some consternation as many of the Americans thought that I had been demoted, a Wing being a larger formation than a Group in their Air Force.

I had hoped to be able to ship my little aeroplane back to England but it was all too complicated and expensive, so I regretfully had to sell it. Fortunately, we were spared the frightful job of packing our goods and chattels, most of which we had acquired during our stay in America. The USAF came to our rescue and took over the whole thing and we were left with just the things we would need on the trip.

During my tour with the USAF a lot of publicity was being given to Flying Saucers or in Service parlance 'Unidentified Flying Objects'. The Air Force had investigated a great many of the reports of the sighting of the saucers and I was privileged in being permitted to read a summary of the reports, the investigations and the findings. Although a rather larger number than I would have imagined remained unexplained, for most of the cases a perfectly ordinary answer had been found. One day, however, I noticed people on the base getting quite excited and many were pointing upwards so I approached one group and asked what was happening. I was told there were dozens of saucers directly overhead. Sceptically I looked up and, to my intense surprise, I saw them too – little silver discs very high up glinting brightly in the sun and moving across the sky at a terrific speed. Fascinated I watched them and made a mental note never to disbelieve anything ever again and then my eyes focused on one of them – they were dandelion seeds about fifteen feet up.

My time with the USAF was of immense value to me and it broadened my experience greatly, introducing me to quite a different approach to problems similar to those experienced in the RAF which stimulated one's thinking quite considerably. During my year in charge of Phase 5 Testing we dealt with no less than fourteen aircraft upon all of which reports were written and published. In addition tests on two others were well advanced when I moved over to Flight Test Division.

My final effort was the writing of a long report upon my tour in which I made various recommendations which I thought would help both the RAF and the USAF to obtain greater benefit from such exchange postings. I also gave an outline of my own experiences during the two years with particular reference to flying techniques that I felt could well be adopted by the RAF. It had always struck me as strange that I have never been questioned officially on my time with the USAF nor, as far as I can make out, have any other officers who have been on exchange, which seems very odd.

Finally the day of departure arrived and, with mixed feelings, we set off for New York. We were sorry to leave, but looked forward to getting back to England and finding out what fate, in the shape of the Air Ministry, had in store for us. For most of the journey to New York we drove along the fabulous Pennsylvania Turnpike, a highway having six lanes of traffic in each direction and about a thousand miles long. At times the road carrying the west-bound traffic was far enough away to be out of sight.

After a few days in New York we went aboard the Queen Elizabeth for our trip back to England and, being now a Group Captain, we travelled 'First', and very plush it was too. We were met at Southampton by Betty's parents and, after a little trouble getting our twenty-two crates of luggage through the Customs, we all drove off to the home of Betty's parents in Virginia Water.

The following day I telephoned the Air Ministry and was told – to my pleasure and surprise – that I was to take over command of RAF Station Odiham, a Fighter Station, only a few miles from Farnborough – we were back on very familiar ground!

13

Final Fling

I officially assumed command of RAF Station, Odiham late in August 1952, after having reported to the Commander-in-Chief, Sir Basil Embry, at Fighter Command Headquarters where I learned that I had been earmarked for the appointment since the previous April. Very shortly after this I met my new AOC, Air Vice-Marshal the Earl of Bandon, whom I knew well by repute but had not met before. Like several others of about the same vintage, he was one of the 'personalities' of the Service and was known throughout the Air Force.

There were two fighter squadrons at Odiham. Nos 54 and 247, both equipped with Meteor 8s. The Wing Commander Flying was another Battle of Britain pilot whom I had known for many years, Dennis Crowley-Milling, and the same applied to Pete O'Brian, the Wing Commander Administration – another Canadian who also had just completed a two year tour of duty with the USAF.

Almost immediately I ran into a bit of difficulty and that was over the question of parades. In the normal course of events this would present no difficulty to a new Station Commander but I had last been on a parade early in 1937, and then as a Pilot Officer relegated to the rearmost rank. Just to add to my problem was the fact that the drill had been changed and the men no longer 'formed fours', they operated in three ranks instead. I hadn't the faintest idea of how they got into that formation and I came to the conclusion that the best thing to do would be to put them into fours and then dismiss the rear rank!

Fortunately for normal parades the CO had little or nothing to do, so all went well – but I had quite a lot of reading to do to catch up with the new routines.

Odiham, being a modern station and perhaps because it had the unique distinction of being the only RAF Station to have been officially opened by a General in the *Luftwaffe* – General Milch in 1938 – has always been a favourite for special occasions. The fact that it is easy to get to may also have some bearing on this but, in any case, it has had its fair share of official visits and visitors. It was only a few weeks after my arrival that I was told that we were to have a Royal visitor in the person of King Feisal II of Iraq.

The impending visit caused quite a lot of extra work, but everything seemed to drop into place and all went well on the day. The King was most interested in everything and was very easy to talk to and it was obvious that he had a considerable knowledge of aircraft. The C-in-C, Sir Basil Embry, and Lord De Lisle and Dudley, the Air Minister, also attended and I acted as host at lunch which was also a success.

The next important piece of news I received was that Odiham had been chosen as the station at which would take place the Royal Review of the Royal Air Force by Her Majesty Queen Elizabeth. This was only the second time that the Royal Air Force would be so honoured, the first occasion having been in 1935, when King George V reviewed the then tiny Air Force at Mildenhall and Duxford.

In all we had about six months to make all the preparations and some three months of this period had gone by when I received a call from the AOC saying that he wanted to see me the following morning at Group Headquarters. He sounded rather mysterious and would not give me an inkling as to what it was all about so I assumed that it must be something about security arrangements to ensure Her Majesty's safety.

I was quite unprepared for the shock and disappointment of the following day when the AOC informed me that 'it had been decided', by whom I never discovered, that I was too junior to be allowed the responsibility. It had further been decided that the most senior Group Captain should take over from me, especially as 'there would be a Gong going for it' and this should, of course, go to the senior officer.

This was a line of reasoning quite outside my understanding and I said so, but it made no difference. I tried to draw a parallel with wartime situations where the seniority of a person had little or nothing to do with either the tasks assigned to him or the rewards accorded him. Though sympathetic to my arguments, the AOC remained adamant that I must hand over to the officer commanding Tangmere for the period of the review. I was to take over that station until after the Review when I would return to Odiham. Against this, however, I rebelled and pleaded that if I was to exchange posts then it was to be permanent and this was agreed. A few days later, and very reluctantly, I handed over to my successor.

While in the States and wondering what the future held on our return to England, Betty had once asked what posting I would choose if I had a free choice and I said: 'Tangmere – but there isn't a hope of getting it as there are too many people on the spot who are after it.' Now here I was with the very appointment I would have chosen, but what a hell of a way to get it! I was thoroughly upset and this incident weighed very heavily when the time came for me to consider whether to stay in the Service or not.

While all this was going on, I was asked to accompany some other Battle of Britain pilots on a trip to Washington to attend the Premiere of a film called, *Angels One-Five*. I was in no mood for this but the film people were very insistent and Betty was very persuasive so eventually I agreed to go.

My fellow travellers turned out to be Mike Crossley, Arthur Donaldson, Bob Tuck and Don Kingaby. We were flown from London to Paris by Air France and then taken over by the USAF and flown to Washington via the Azores.

The 'let-down' at the Azores I didn't like at all; it was at night, heavy and overcast. Being well acquainted with the instrument flying techniques of the USAF, I didn't like the way the aeroplane was being handled. I gave a large sigh of relief once we were safely down. The rest of the journey was straightforward and we arrived in Washington on schedule where we were introduced to all the interested people.

We spent a week in Washington during which we attended numerous parties, were interviewed on television, made radio broadcasts and finally made personal appearances at the Premiere. Most of these activities were organized by the Washington Branch of the Royal Air Force Association.

There were quite a number of amusing incidents during this very hectic week but the funniest of all was the final act at the Premiere. The USAF did their best to help and, amongst other things, they provided a Colour Guard to stand at one side of the stage whilst the RAF provided one for the other side.

To start the ceremonies three USAF officers who had served in the RAF were introduced by a representative of the American equivalent of the RAF Association. He did this remarkably well, as most Americans do, saying: 'Ladies and Gentlemen, I would like to introduce to you a young man who has shot down so many enemy aeroplanes, shot up so many enemy trains, set fire to so many enemy ships' – and so on and so on. Then, after a pause, he would announce the name of the hero with a flourish.

Having introduced all three American officers he next announced that he would now hand over to his British colleague who would introduce the British aces. Our representative could not match this expertise at all; after all he had only been pressganged into the job that morning, but he did say something about 'never in the field of human conflict…' He then said that it gave him great pleasure to introduce the first of the British Fighter Pilots. This was my cue and I strode out on to the stage and halted beside him. He said: 'Ladies and Gentlemen, Group Captain —!' A dreadful pause and then he turned to me and asked: '*What* is your name?'

It was all I could do to keep a straight face, particularly as I could see the horrified expressions on the faces of the organizers sitting amongst the audience.

We attended one final party that night and set off for Europe the next day, not overjoyed to find that we had the same pilot as on the way out. Everything went well, however, and after a relatively short stop at the Azores we took off on the flight to Paris by which time it was dark. Some hours later I was dozing when I came wide awake with a jerk and saw that number two engine was out. By this time it was daylight and we were roughly halfway to Paris; despite this and the fact that the whole Continent of Europe stretched in front of us our Captain decided to go back to the Azores – Gawd knows why!

On arriving back at the Azores we found that he had radioed that he was returning on three engines and asked for a relief aeroplane to be sent out from Boston. A few hours after we had landed this relief aeroplane arrived, on three engines and with a full load of passengers. There just wasn't room enough for people and we spent all that day wandering about and had difficulty finding anywhere to sit let alone sleep.

Late that night a rather dilapidated C54 arrived from Lisbon and there was a terrific rush to get it refuelled and turned around. There was also a terrific rush on the part of the passengers to get aboard. I elbowed my way through and found a corporal making out a list so I called to him. In answer I got a snarled: 'Jest a minute, I'm tendin' tuh th' Major!'

So I said: 'Corporal, do you know what a Four Star General is?' 'Yeh, I do,' he replied.

Pointing to the four rings on my sleeve, I said: 'Right, Corporal, one per star.'

'Yes, sir,' he said — and we were aboard!

The old C 54 did its stuff and delivered us safely in Paris, but being a day late we had some difficulty in getting back to London though eventually we made it.

Despite this rather amusing interlude I was still in a pretty foul mood when I arrived at Tangmere to take up residence. Like most of the other stations its organization was disrupted by the Review arrangements and I found the Odiham Wing based at Tangmere while the station's own squadrons, Nos 1 and 29, were based elsewhere. Because of its geographical position, Tangmere was selected as the airfield for the debriefing of the formation leaders after each practice fly-past. This meant that whenever there was such a practice we were flooded out with all sorts of aircraft, most of them needing some form of servicing.

Later in the year the Hawker Company decided to make an attempt upon the world's speed record using a special Hunter fitted with an afterburner. The pilot was to be Neville Duke, an ex-92 Squadron member whom I knew well and who was one of the war's leading aces. Tangmere was considered to be the most suitable base from which to make the attempt and permission to use it was granted by the Air Ministry.

It was hoped that everything could be done secretly and an announcement made only after a new record had been established. In my view it was a pious hope and I was proved right — as a result of his experiencing undercarriage trouble Neville had to return to Dunsfold and the secret was out; the next day we were inundated with press reporters and cameramen – eighty-five in all – and they stayed with us for a week. We could not possibly accommodate or feed them in our normal premises, the situation being in no way improved by our having over 200 Allied officers descend upon us for an escape exercise.

All we could do was to turn the Gym into a dormitory and produce a bar at which tea, coffee, milk, soft drinks, beer and spirits could be had at any time along with a variety of snacks. The staff were all voluntary and were paid through the Hawker Company's Advertising Agents.

With so many people about I felt it necessary to issue them each with a list of instructions as to where things were, places they could go to and places they could not, plus a map of the station showing relevant buildings and installations. This proved well worth while and despite the criticisms so often levelled at representatives of the press, I had nothing but the fullest co-operation from them for which I was truly grateful.

And finally the successful attempt on the record made all the extra work and worry worth while.

Directly opposite the entrance to the station and next to the COs residence was Tangmere Cottage which was used as a Mess by our wartime spies and agents as they waited their turn to go over and on their return to this country. The house now belonged to Ronnie Clifford Brown an ex-fighter boy with whom I had been stationed both at Northolt and Kenley – it was a happy coincidence and through Ronnie and his charming wife we met a great many pleasant and interesting people.

There was also plenty of activity on the station itself which added to the interest. One event was the presentation of the Squadron Colours to No. 1 Squadron by Air Vice-Marshal Longcroft, this being the first Standard ever to be presented. About eighteen months later the station was honoured in being officially presented with its crest.

In addition to being a fighter station, Tangmere was also a Master Diversion airfield and had its own Customs Officer. Consequently we had a great many visitors arriving either on their way abroad or returning; in fact, the numbers totalled over 2,000 aircraft per year.

His Royal Highness, the Duke of Edinburgh, became quite a frequent visitor to Tangmere as it was so convenient for both

Goodwood and Cowdray. Being keen on flying, he used to fly on every possible occasion whenever he and the Queen were staying at Goodwood with the Duke and Duchess of Richmond or at Arundel with the Duke and Duchess of Norfolk for Goodwood Week. He was always most considerate and went out of his way to avoid causing us any extra trouble or work.

It was from Tangmere that His Royal Highness departed on his way to Canada to open the Olympic Games. At the time the Queen and he were staying at Arundel and through the Prince's Equerry I had a hint that Her Majesty might possibly come to see him off. Later I received more definite news from Commander Parker, the Duke's Private secretary, who was to accompany him.

The Royal Canadian Air Force provided a special aircraft which was positioned at Tangmere and to my pleasant surprise I found aboard it Ernie McNab who was to act as Special Equerry to Prince Philip during his trip to Canada. The last time I had seen Ernie was in Winnipeg when I was saying goodbye to my mother and was on my way back to England during the war.

The Queen did arrive and I was duly presented to her. After inspecting the accommodation provided for the Duke in the aircraft she left the machine and waited in her car – it was a very wet and blustery day – until the aircraft took off. During this waiting period I took the opportunity of inviting her to the Officers' Mess and she graciously accepted. I went on ahead to ensure that all was ready to welcome her; she duly arrived and I was able to present Betty and my three Wing Commanders and their wives. We then went into the Ladies' Room that we had redecorated especially for her visit, although we had been by no means certain that she would come until the last moment.

After sipping a glass of sherry and chatting very informally, she prepared to depart with the Duke and Duchess of Norfolk. She thanked me very graciously as we made our way to the door and then – I remembered. In a rush I said: 'Ma'am, I'm most frightfully sorry, but I've forgotten…' I got no further as she laughed and said: 'I know – the Book' and then she came back and signed it.

The next day Betty and I went to Goodwood and were making our way towards the paddock and studying our race cards when, on looking up, we found ourselves face to face with Her Majesty. She was smiling and gave us a friendly 'Good afternoon!' as though she had known us all her life.

Each year the squadrons were involved in the Air Exercises and they thoroughly enjoyed the intensity of the activity although I am afraid that some of our more adjacent civilian neighbours were not so enthusiastic. I could appreciate their point of view and understand their annoyance at being startled and deafened by the sudden and frightful din made by our fighters scrambling on an interception, but there was nothing I personally could do about it. I did all I could to explain why it was necessary and, for the most part, people accepted it.

Although there were only two squadrons on the station when I arrived, a third was formed not very long afterwards giving us a two-squadron Day Fighter Wing equipped with Meteor 8s and a Night/All-Weather Squadron with Meteor NF11s. I was singularly fortunate in having excellent Squadron Commanders upon whom I could rely implicitly. No. 29 was commanded by Peter Horsley who handed over, on being appointed Equerry to Prince Philip, to Teddy Sismore who had a very distinguished war record as did Freddie Lister who took over No. 1 Squadron, whilst the new Squadron, No. 34, was commanded by Alistair Wilson, an ex-pupil of mine at Heston in 1941 who had also distinguished himself in combat. Finally another old friend and colleague, Pete Simpson, arrived as Wing Commander Flying. Altogether it was a very happy station and, without fear or favour, I can say it was extremely efficient.

An instance of how highly trained the units were occurred on the occasion of one of the Comet disasters. It was a Sunday and the squadrons were not flying. Except for a small working party both the aircrews and groundcrews were at home in their quarters and all was quiet. Suddenly I got a call from London Airport saying that a Comet was missing and a plot on the London Airport radar had faded at a position just off the French coast: it was possible that this was the missing Comet. Could I send off some aircraft to search the area? I said I would try and started the ball rolling by ringing Teddy Sismore who, fortunately, was at home. There were no aircraft out but the small working party belonged to his squadron and within twenty minutes the first aircraft was airborne and in less than half an hour three more had followed it and two others were standing by! It was a magnificent piece of work but, unfortunately, to no avail as the Comet had, in fact, crashed off Italy.

However I was very, very pleased to see how efficiently the machine worked in a real emergency – it was most satisfying.

Very close to Tangmere was the Royal Naval Air Station at Ford and the traffic pattern of the two airfields was really too close for comfort, particularly as both airfields were operating fighters. Various near misses were reported and the importance of always keeping an extra sharp lookout was stressed time and again to the pilots, but this was not easy at the speeds at which the aircraft were travelling. Eventually, of course, it happened and one of 34 Squadron's pilots met a Naval Vampire head-on just near Arundel. The resultant explosion was heard at Thorney Island over fifteen miles away and mercifully neither pilot ever knew what happened.

Only a day or two later I was flying low over the sea parallel to the coast and approaching the Ford circuit. Although I could not see any aircraft I decided to be sure of keeping clear and so pulled up into a steep climbing turn to port. I had got to about 7,000 feet and just to the north-east of Ford when a Sea Fury shot past under my nose a bare hundred yards away. He must have been hidden under my starboard engine nacelle and I must have been under his port wing and I do not think the other pilot saw me at all – it was a very nasty feeling.

Although we all liked the old Meteor it really was getting a bit long in the tooth and we looked forward to re-equipping with Hunters which would at least make it possible to catch the Canberras – which was more than could be expected of the Meteors. It was with great joy that we heard that both Nos 1 and 34 were shortly to be re-equipped. Poor old 29, however, had to soldier on with their NFIIs as the Javelin was not yet available. The conversion on to Hunters was completed very quickly and easily and everyone was delighted with the aircraft. It was, I found, one of the most pleasant aircraft I have ever flown, real fingertip control and most docile.

During my last year at Tangmere Prince Philip used the airfield a lot while he was gaining experience in helicopters and I was given a chance to fly his machine, an S55 – a far cry from the little Hoverfly at Farnborough and I quite liked it.

News that my tour at Tangmere was coming to an end arrived in the form of a letter from Tich Whiteley, one of the officers who had met Betty and I at Dayton. He wrote to say that he had been informed by Air Ministry that he was to be my successor. This struck me as very odd as he was in Singapore and it seemed to me that, if they could tell him, they could have told me at the same time. I telephoned the AOC, Air Vice-Marshal Patch, who had succeeded the Earl of Bandon, and he confirmed that I was to be posted later in the year. He added the ghastly news that I was to become Staff Officer in charge of Administration at Headquarters No. 12 Group at Newton near Nottingham.

It was unpleasant news, but there was nothing I could do about it. Apparently the Careers Branch decided that I required administrative experience in an administrative appointment before I could be considered eligible for promotion.

One Saturday morning when Prince Philip arrived to fly his helicopter I told him that I would shortly be on my way and invited him to my house for a pre-lunch drink. He graciously accepted and duly appeared after his quota of flying along with his Naval Officer Instructor. He made himself at home and fairly made my father-in-law's day by asking him if he was on leave. This really flattered the Colonel as he had been retired for many a long day. When His Royal Highness climbed into his car to take his leave, my small boy, Stuart, then six years old suddenly piped up, 'I know what that is, it's a Jag!' The Duke laughed and said: 'Actually, son, it's a Lagonda; I couldn't afford a Jag!' Then with a smile and a wave he was away.

Very shortly before leaving Tangmere Gordon Slade and Peter Twiss of Fairey's came to see me to ask for my help in arranging certain facilities for an attempt upon the world speed record – I was almost becoming an expert at this! However, knowing so many of the local dignitaries and officials by this time I was able to smooth the way considerably but, unfortunately, I had departed to take up my new duties before the successful attempt was made and Peter Twiss became the first man to establish a world speed record of over 1,000mph – at the same time I am proud to have had some hand in helping to make it possible.

Very regretfully I handed over 'my' Station to Tich Whiteley at the end of October and departed for 12 Group where I reported to my new AOC, Air Vice-Marshal 'Paddy' Crisham, whom I knew well and who introduced me to my new duties. Although it was not the appointment that I would ever have chosen for myself I found that, as time went on, I began to become quite interested in the various administrative problems with which I was faced in this appointment.

About the time of my move I received a tentative offer from a firm in the aviation instrument industry and I began to review my future. The question was, should I stay on in the Service or should I retire prematurely and try to carve myself a niche in the civilian world?

There were many factors to be considered not the least of which were the problems associated with educating our two children – either they were to suffer through continual moves, upsetting their educational routine, or we should have to face the financial burden of sending them both to boarding school, which had the additional disadvantage of depriving us of the pleasure of their company. Obviously a static base was to be preferred.

Also, although it would give me great personal satisfaction to go on to the rank of Air Vice-Marshal or further, and there was every indication that this was on the cards, I was not at all certain that all that went with the sort of appointments these ranks carried was quite what I wanted – in war, yes, but in peace, I was not at all sure.

Finally I decided to accept the offer from industry and in the late autumn I submitted a request to be permitted to transfer to the Retired List. This was granted and on 1 December 1956, I said goodbye to the Service that had been my life for nearly twenty-two years.

My career and experiences had been, I think, unique; I had survived uninjured, flown over 200 different types of aircraft without damaging a single machine except on purpose, I had destroyed my quota of enemy aircraft and, in short, had had the best of the Air Force; of this I am convinced.

In conclusion, I hope I have succeeded in giving the reader some idea of the sort of people my generation of Air Force officers were and the sort of work they were sometimes called upon to do in addition to their combat flying. With regard to the Battle of Britain itself, around which this book has been written, I think one can say without fear of contradiction that it already ranks with the classic battles of history and, looking back upon it one realises more and more how enormous was the mental and physical strain endured by the youngsters who fought the battle. The effect of this strain is, in many cases, only now becoming evident and in the years gone by there have been many casualties attributable to what we went through in those critical days when the fate of the world as we knew it hung in the balance.

Personally I am very proud to have been honoured and decorated by both his late Majesty King George VI and the President of Poland, the late General Sikorski, for my efforts during the battle but I am even more proud of the simple fact that I am – One of the Few!

THE HISTORY PRESS

The Defence and Fall of Singapore
1940-42

BRIAN FARRELL

'A multi-pronged attack on those who made the defence of Malaya and Singapore their duty... [an] exhaustive account of the clash between Japanese and British Empire forces' *BBC History Magazine*

'An original and provocative new history of the battle' *Hew Strachan*

£13.99   0 7524 3768 2

Zulu!
The Battle for Rorke's Drift 1879

EDMUND YORKE

'A clear, detailed exposition... a very good read' *Journal of the Royal United Service Institute for Defence Studies*

£12.99   0 7524 3502 7

Paras
The Birth of British Airborne Forces from Churchill's Raiders to 1st Parachute Brigade

WILLIAM F. BUCKINGHAM

£17.99   0 7524 3530 2

Voices from the Trenches
Life & Death on the Western Front

ANDY SIMPSON AND TOM DONOVAN

'A vivid picture of life on the Western Front... compelling reading' *The Daily Telegraph*

'Offers the reader a wealth of fine writing by soldiers of the Great War whose slim volumes were published so long ago or under such obscure imprints that they have all but disappeared from sight like paintings lost under the grime of ages' *Malcolm Brown*

£12.99   0 7524 3905 7

Loos 1915

NICK LLOYD

'A revealing new account based on meticulous documentary research... I warmly commend this book to all who are interested in history and the Great War' *Corelli Barnett*

'Should finally consign Alan Clarke's farrago, *The Donkeys*, to the waste paper basket' *Hew Strachan*

£25   0 7524 3937 5

The Last Nazis
SS Werewolf Guerilla Resistance in Europe 1944-47

PERRY BIDDISCOMBE

'Detailed, meticulously researched and highly readable... a must for all interested in the end of the Second World War' *Military Illustrated*

£12.99   0 7524 2342 8

Omaha Beach A Flawed Victory

ADRIAN LEWIS

'A damning book' *BBC History Magazine*

£12.99   0 7524 2975 2

The English Civil War
A Historical Companion

MARTYN BENNETT

'Martyn Bennett knows more about the nuts and bolts of the English Civil War than anybody else alive' *Ronald Hutton*

'A most useful and entertaining book – giving us all precise detail about the events, the places, the people and the things that we half-know about the civil war and many more things that we did not know at all' *John Morrill*

£25   0 7524 3186 2

If you are interested in purchasing other books published by The History Press, or in case you have difficulty finding any The History Press books in your local bookshop, you can also place orders directly through our website

www.thehistorypress.co.uk

THE HISTORY PRESS

R.J.Mitchell
Schooldays to Spitfire
GORDON MITCHELL
'[A] readable and poignant story'
The Sunday Telegraph

£12.99   0 7524 3727 5

Forgotten Soldiers of the First World War
Lost Voices from the Middle Eastern Front
DAVID WOODWARD
'A brilliant new book of hitherto unheard
voices from a haunting theatre of the First
World War' *Malcolm Brown*

£12.99   978 07524 4307 2

1690 Battle of the Boyne
PÁDRAIG LENIHAN
'An almost impeccably impartial account of
the most controversial military engagement in
British history' *The Daily Mail*

£12.99   0 7524 3304 0

Hell at the Front
Combat Voices from the First World War
TOM DONOVAN
'Fifty powerful personal accounts, each vividly
portraying the brutalising reality of the Great
War... a remarkable book' *Max Arthur*

£12.99   0 7524 3940 5

Amiens 1918
JAMES MCWILLIAMS & R. JAMES STEEL
'A masterly portrayal of this pivotal battle'
Soldier: The Magazine of the British Army

£25   0 7524 2860 8

Before Stalingrad
Hitler's Invasion of Russia 1941
DAVID GLANTZ
'Another fine addition to Hew Strachan's
excellent *Battles and Campaigns* series'
BBC History Magazine

£9.99   0 7524 2692 3

The SS
A History 1919-45
ROBERT LEWIS KOEHL
'Reveals the role of the SS in the mass murder
of the Jews, homosexuals and gypsies and its
organisation of death squads throughout occupied
Europe' *The Sunday Telegraph*

£9.99   0 7524 2559 5

Arnhem 1944
WILLIAM BUCKINGHAM
'Reveals the real reason why the daring attack
failed' *The Daily Express*

£10.99   0 7524 3187 0

If you are interested in purchasing other books published by The History Press, or in case you have difficulty finding
any The History Press books in your local bookshop, you can also place orders directly through our website
www.thehistorypress.co.uk

THE HISTORY PRESS

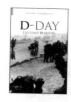

The Wars of the Roses
The Soldiers' Experience
ANTHONY GOODMAN
'Sheds light on the lot of the common soldier as never before' *Alison Weir*
'A meticulous work'
The Times Literary Supplement

£12.99   0 7524 3731 3

D-Day
The First 72 Hours
WILLIAM F. BUCKINGHAM
'A compelling narrative' *The Observer*
A *BBC History Magazine* Book of the Year 2004

£9.99   0 7524 2842 2

English Battlefields
500 Battlefields that Shaped English History
MICHAEL RAYNER
'A painstaking survey of English battlefields... a first-rate book' *Richard Holmes*
'A fascinating and, for all its factual tone, an atmospheric volume' *The Sunday Telegraph*

£18.99   978 07524 4307 2

Trafalgar Captain Durham of the Defiance: The Man who refused to Miss Trafalgar
HILARY RUBINSTEIN
'A sparkling biography of Nelson's luckiest captain' *Andrew Lambert*

£17.99   0 7524 3435 7

Battle of the Atlantic
MARC MILNER
'The most comprehensive short survey of the U-boat battles' *Sir John Keegan*
'Some events are fortunate in their historian, none more so than the Battle of the Atlantic. Marc Milner is *the* historian of the Atlantic Campaign... a compelling narrative' *Andrew Lambert*

£12.99   0 7524 3332 6

Okinawa 1945 The Stalingrad of the Pacific
GEORGE FEIFER
'A great book... Feifer's account of the three sides and their experiences far surpasses most books about war' *Stephen Ambrose*

£17.99   0 7524 3324 5

Gallipoli 1915
TIM TRAVERS
'The most important new history of Gallipoli for forty years... groundbreaking' *Hew Strachan*
'A book of the highest importance to all who would seek to understand the tragedy of the Gallipoli campaign' *The Journal of Military History*

£13.99   0 7524 2972 8

Tommy Goes To War
MALCOLM BROWN
'A remarkably vivid and frank account of the British soldier in the trenches' *Max Arthur*
'The fury, fear, mud, blood, boredom and bravery that made up life on the Western Front are vividly presented and illustrated' *The Sunday Telegraph*

£12.99   0 7524 2980 9

If you are interested in purchasing other books published by The History Press, or in case you have difficulty finding any The History Press books in your local bookshop, you can also place orders directly through our website

www.thehistorypress.co.uk

THE HISTORY PRESS

Private 12768 Memoir of a Tommy
JOHN JACKSON

'Unique... a beautifully written, strikingly
honest account of a young man's experience of
combat' *Saul David*

'At last we have John Jackson's intensely
personal and heartfelt little book to remind us
there was a view of the Great War other than
Wilfred Owen's' *The Daily Mail*

£9.99   0 7524 3531 0

The German Offensives of 1918
MARTIN KITCHEN

'A lucid, powerfully driven narrative' *Malcolm Brown*
'Comprehensive and authoritative... first class'
Holger H. Herwig

£13.99   0 7524 3527 2

Verdun 1916
MALCOLM BROWN

'A haunting book which gets closer than any
other to that wasteland marked by death'
Richard Holmes

£9.99   0 7524 2599 4

The Forgotten Front
The East African Campaign 1914–1918
ROSS ANDERSON

'Excellent... fills a yawning gap in the
historical record'
The Times Literary Supplement
'Compelling and authoritative'
Hew Strachan

£12.99   978 07524 4126 9

Agincourt
A New History
ANNE CURRY

'A highly distinguished and convincing account'
Christopher Hibbert
'A *tour de force*' *Alison Weir*
'*The* book on the battle' *Richard Holmes*
A *BBC History Magazine* Book of the Year 2005

£12.99   0 7524 3813 1

The Welsh Wars of Independence
DAVID MOORE

'Beautifully written, subtle and remarkably
perceptive' *John Davies*

£12.99   978 07524 4128 3

Bosworth 1485 Psychology of a Battle
MICHAEL K. JONES

'Most exciting... a remarkable tale' *The Guardian*
'Insightful and rich study of the Battle of
Bosworth... no longer need Richard play the
villain' *The Times Literary Supplement*

£12.99   0 7524 2594 3

The Battle of Hastings 1066
M.K. LAWSON

'Blows away many fundamental assumptions
about the battle of Hastings... an exciting and
indispensable read' *David Bates*
A *BBC History Magazine* Book of the Year 2003

£12.99   978 07524 4177 1